WITHDRAWN

A Reason to Live

The true story of one woman's love,
courage and determination to
survive

by

Billy Hills & Dale Hudson

A Reason To Live:
ISBN 0-9708424-0-6

Interior design and typesetting by Kathy Bloodworth, Custom Typography.

Published by Front Street Publishing, Corp., Myrtle Beach, South Carolina.

Printed and bound in the United States of America.

To Our

Mothers

Authors' Note

This is a true crime story detailing the 1979 crime spree of two notorious outlaws from West Virginia. The information for the story was derived from interviews, detectives' notes, newspaper articles, and transcripts of court proceedings. Consistent with other contemporary books in the true crime genre, the story told here contains descriptions of the careless and wanton activity of criminals. In these pages are suggestions of possible motives for the described criminal behavior and a dissection of the criminal personality.

Readers should note, however, that the similarity of this story to traditional true crime stories ends there. The primary focus of this book is the seldom-told story of what it means to be a survivor of crime in modern society. What happens to ordinary citizens who suddenly and inexplicably find themselves at the mercy of brutal criminals who have no morals? How do everyday people pull together in the face of overwhelming tragedy to regain a sense of normalcy in their lives?

In the *note* for our first book, *An Hour To Kill: Love, Murder and Justice in a Small Southern Town*, we indicated that the story was "not a simple recitation of the facts of the case." That statement applies to this book as well. Once again, we have told the events of a series of heinous crimes in story form in order to keep the reader actively engaged. We have made every effort to keep all information consistent with fact. Dialogue was used only when a conversation was known to have taken place and content and meaning of the conversation were known. Quotes were maintained in exact form wherever possible, and transcript dialogue was edited for clarification purposes only.

In accordance with an agreement made prior to the beginning of work on this book, Wanda Summers read and approved the entire manuscript prior to publication.

"You know, ladies and gentlemen, the trouble with our country is not in Washington. It's in the unbuttoned minds of a few misfits like Ronald Woomer who deserve nothing more than what they have decreed for everybody else in society. On February 22, 1979, Ronald Woomer declared war on all of us. Ladies and gentlemen, rid our society of this prophet of terror. **"**

—Assistant Solicitor Carroll Don Padgett,
closing remarks in the sentencing
phase trial of Ronald "Rusty" Woomer.

Prologue

A man can only take so much, Jimmy thought bitterly.

He quickened the pace of his shuffling feet on the shiny linoleum. The scent of disinfectant filled his lungs. The phone number he had been challenged to produce was firmly clenched in his fist.

"Mr. Summers," the psychiatrist had droned just minutes before, "I'm not saying I don't believe your story." The middle-aged bespectacled woman paused midway through the session. From one side of the gray metal desk she stared at her patient and added, "But you've got to admit, it has some remarkable elements."

Jimmy was unsure how to respond and simply looked around the small room. Devoid of personal objects, the office had the feel of a makeshift space that was used only on occasion by transient visitors.

Looking first at her watch, the psychiatrist then glanced reflexively at Jimmy's hand and winced at the missing fingers. Jimmy told her that while working as a stevedore years earlier his hand had gotten caught in a pulley as a cable sped through. The accident happened in an instant. He felt a sting and could only watch as his gloved fingers rolled to the ground.

The psychiatrist speculated about the likelihood of self-mutilation. But that was not what bothered her most about the story Jimmy told her. The newest bit of information he gave her finally opened the door to an intervention. What Jimmy said about his wife couldn't be true.

"It's time for me to meet your wife," the psychiatrist said and slid the phone across the desk. "I want you to call her right now."

To Jimmy, these were the most sensible words he had heard in days, maybe even weeks. He stared at the phone.

Though he knew he was in a hospital, he wasn't sure why. He was vaguely aware of collapsing at work and an ambulance ride. But his memory fell apart after that. There had been something about blood clots in his lungs, but he couldn't recall any details about the first hospital or the transferal process to where he was now. He heard someone say he was on the tenth floor, and he did remember thinking it odd that no one at this hospital had taken his temperature or blood pressure. And where was all of the fancy equipment? When he was finally allowed to get out of bed to explore his surroundings, Jimmy was unable to find his clothes and had to settle for a pair of drab green pajamas. The medications he was given made his movements seem erratic and all else seem dreamlike. What was he doing in a psychiatric facility?

"So, you should go ahead," the psychiatrist prompted. "Call your wife. Tell her I want to meet her. I think then we may be able to move ahead, when we see together that she is all right."

"What do you mean, 'all right'?"

"That her face isn't missing."

Jimmy's eyes looked from the doctor to the phone. *Why can't I remember my number?* he thought.

The psychiatrist looked at Jimmy's chart as she waited for his response. He wasn't the most communicative patient, and he had refused to participate in tests that involved projective stimuli.

"I'm not here to act stupid," he had said, "and I'm not going to play any damned silly games." What little he divulged had sounded to the psychiatrist as textbook fantasy material.

She read from her notes.

"I practically raised myself," Jimmy had told her earlier, "except for the brief period when I lived with a man and a woman who took me to their home one Sunday after a church service. I had a wonderful family then with a dog and a pony and new clothes for school. I even talked to Santa Claus on the phone."

The reportedly ideal childhood had ended abruptly when Jimmy's father reappeared and, without explanation, whisked Jimmy away and back to the mean streets of another world. Jimmy said he had never seen or heard from the mysterious couple again.

"I'll have to go get the number," Jimmy said. He rose awkwardly from his chair.

The psychiatrist nodded her head but continued to study the notes. "That would be good," she said calmly. "I'll wait here."

Jimmy turned and looked from one end of the hallway to the other before stepping out into the foot traffic. While Jimmy had begun to feel better shortly after arriving at the facility, he had looked forward to being able to leave his room during the day to escape his strange roommate and avoid being cornered when someone wandered in unexpectedly. But outside his room he found unpredictable people, some of whom paced from one end of the hall to the other and said bizarre things out loud. As of late, he had begun to spend most of his time alone in the recreation room, watching television or shooting pool.

Moving quickly down the hall, Jimmy entered his room and found the phone number in the desk adjacent to his bed. As he turned, a particularly unkempt man, with long hair and a bushy beard, stepped through the doorway and smiled. John was one of the few persons with whom Jimmy had reasonable conversations, and John was the first person to give Jimmy a clue that he was in a mental hospital.

"Why do you think they keep the doors locked?" John had asked Jimmy.

John confided that his own commitment was due to numerous drug experiences involving emergency room visits. But when Jimmy witnessed John's frantic flitting around the ward, he suspected there was more to it than that.

When the two men first met, John had focused on Jimmy's St. Christopher medal and immediately adopted the irritating habit of grabbing and attempting to kiss Jimmy's hand. The missing fingers on Jimmy's left hand only seemed to add to the intrigue. Jimmy later learned that John had shot himself in the chest with a shotgun in an attempt to kill roaches he imagined were crawling on his body. John had showed Jimmy the scars on his chest from the gunshot wound.

As usual, John's eyes, staring brightly from beneath his shaggy mane, were out of focus. Jimmy recognized that John's menacing appearance didn't help when decisions were made concerning John's commitment.

Jimmy hid his hands behind his back and stepped around the large man. "Not now, John," he said. "I'm getting out of here."

"What?" John asked, as if someone, somewhere in the unit didn't say that every day.

"I can't do whatever this is anymore," Jimmy said.

"What?" John repeated. Jimmy left his room and hurried down the hall.

As he returned to the desolate office, the psychiatrist stopped writing, put down her pen, and sat back. Standing at the edge of the desk, Jimmy turned the phone to face him. His fingers felt clumsy on the rotor as he dialed.

"Wanda," he said when his wife answered the phone, "you have to come get me. I can't stay here anymore."

Turning to the psychiatrist, Jimmy asked, "I can leave here, can't I?"

"Yes, Mr. Summers, you've been free to leave here the entire time. You were placed here because of a psychosis, but –"

Psychosis? Jimmy thought. *That's the first I've heard of that.*

Ignoring the psychiatrist, Jimmy said into the receiver, "And please bring me some clothes."

"Mr. Summers, you're not ready to leave here, yet. But I believe you'll be closer when your wife can join us and we can discuss why you seem to believe part of her face is missing."

"I guess you don't believe anything I've told you, do you?" Jimmy said angrily, his voice rising as he put down the phone.

"It's not that I don't believe you –"

"You know," Jimmy continued loudly, "I'm in here with these loony-tunes, and I don't know why."

Jimmy glared across the desk. The psychiatrist looked back, warily.

"Now you're telling me that you don't believe anything I've told you about what's happened in my life. If that's true, then why have you been asking me these things? Why in the hell am I in here?"

"I believe you've had something happen in your life that has hurt you and caused you to be angry, yes I do. But until we get to the –"

"Angry? You don't know what anger is, lady."

"Well, I can tell you certainly appear to be angry now."

"I'll tell you what anger is," Jimmy said acidly. "I'm so goddamned angry right now I could pinch your head off."

Quickly rising from her chair, the doctor slid from behind the desk and walked briskly out of the office. Still flustered, Jimmy remained standing as two orderlies in white uniforms entered and stood by the door.

Jimmy understood from experience that the job of these serious-looking men was to control situations before and when they got out of hand. On the first day Jimmy arrived on the ward, he had watched as a woman was dragged, screaming and kicking, down the hall. When the melee passed where Jimmy sat in a wheelchair, the woman discontinued her resistance long enough to look at Jimmy and smile. He continued to hear her screams as the orderlies dragged the woman down the hall and the trio disappeared into a room where the door was slammed shut.

"I'm OK," Jimmy reassured the orderlies. "I'm just going to my room to wait on my wife."

●   ❖   ●

It had been two years since her accident and in that time she had not driven alone. Wanda Summers took a deep breath and turned the key in the ignition of the new Pontiac. Jimmy had been gone forty-five days and those had been days of pure hell for Wanda. Through her sleepless nights and countless surgeries, Jimmy had been more than a comforting husband, more than a man willing to get out of bed night after night to help with medications for pain and depression. Jimmy had become her lifeline. Since Jimmy's call that morning, Wanda had agonized over what she knew she would do. She would go and get her husband and bring him home.

Two hours after leaving home, Wanda finally arrived at the hospital. She hurried across the parking lot and into the lobby. The woman seated at the front desk phoned the tenth floor and asked for the psychiatrist whose name Wanda had been given. Wanda tried to ignore the receptionist's embarrassed attempts not to stare.

When summoned, Jimmy walked from his room down the hall and reentered the office of the psychiatrist.

"How are you feeling now?" the doctor asked cautiously.

"If my wife is here, I'm all right."

"Your wife is here. She's on her way up."

"Good," Jimmy said. "I need to go home."

"Do you want to tell me anything before she arrives?"

"Like what?"

"Mr. Summers, I want to help you. You could experience pain when she walks in. You're not going to be able to hide behind delusions of fantasy-families or faceless persons. You're going to have to talk about –"

"You still don't get it, do you?" Jimmy shook his head.

"Get what? Why you're so angry?"

"I'm angry because you're not helping me," Jimmy said. "I'm not crazy. That can't be it." Jimmy took a deep breath. "You know," he continued, "things may not make sense at home, but it's still a damn sight better than here."

Hearing footsteps approach and stop just outside the door, the psychiatrist rose and said, "OK, we'll do this your way, Mr. Summers."

On seeing his wife for the first time in over a week, Jimmy rushed to embrace Wanda.

On seeing Wanda for the first time, the psychiatrist simply said, "Oh, my God."

1

"**I**t's just like I told you," Fred Whitehead said excitedly over the phone. "The old man carries it around in the trunk of his car and then stores it in his closet." The young coin dealer was speaking earnestly to John Fisher of Huntington, West Virginia, of a plan to steal a valuable coin collection.

"And the coins are in his closet? At his house?" Fisher asked incredulously.

"Yeah," Whitehead said, and laughed. "Can you believe it? I just know this can work out."

Several months earlier Fred Thomas Whitehead acquired the only coin shop in the Myrtle Beach, South Carolina, area and began establishing a good reputation with local collectors. Sensing that incredible opportunity was headed his way, Whitehead had studied tradable commodities and quickly expanded his growing word-of-mouth business to include collectible stamps. Putting his people-skills to work, the affable thirty-year-old cultivated the image of an energetic young entrepreneur, eager to learn from more experienced collectors. He spent hours talking shop with customers he had lured to his small store with better-than-fair pricing. No one suspected the clean-cut, well-mannered coin dealer had spent two years in a Florida prison for auto theft. Nor did anyone know that since arriving in Myrtle Beach three years earlier Whitehead had narrowly escaped another jail term. As punishment for multiple counts of housebreaking and larceny, he had simply paid a fine.

The plan Whitehead hatched with Fisher began when Whitehead attended a coin show in Charleston, South Carolina. He registered at the show as a business owner, and had been given credentials and allowed to roam freely among the valuable displays of both professional and amateur collectors from the southeastern portion of the country. The scheming ex-con moved easily among the older pros, asking the right questions and listening patiently to stories of great trades and fantastic bargains.

Whitehead returned again and again to the table of one particular collector, a retired civil engineer from a nearby small community. Though the older gentleman's collection was not as extensive as some at the show, the tidy display belonging to John Turner matched the impeccable appearance of its owner and was impressive for its overall quality. Whitehead learned through casual conversation that following heart surgery Turner was not able to attend shows as he once had. His attendance now was more symbolic and reserved for shows close to home. The real thrill for Turner, Whitehead learned, was visiting with long-time friends and swapping stories of his beloved coins. In fact, Turner said, the coins he had with him were simply representatives of the best of his collection. Turner further confided that his coins had become so heavy for him he no longer kept them at the bank. They were kept in a large storage case in his closet. His daily ritual of sorting and cataloguing the heavy coins was now usually accomplished from a wheelchair and required the assistance of his wife.

The information gleaned from Turner was exactly what Whitehead had been looking for. Whitehead told Fisher that personal collectors were marks for robbery because their valuable collections were often shown in places such as malls and hotels where security was relatively lax. At the end of the shows, dealers often packed up their collections and simply loaded the valuable merchandise in vans or station wagons for transport.

Whitehead explained to Fisher that following a robbery a collection could be broken up and sold with little risk of being traced back to the seller. Fisher was immediately interested in the plan. Whitehead needed Fisher to supply the out-of-town "talent" for the robbery part of the scheme, and Fisher was eager to help.

"All right," Fisher said, satisfied that Whitehead had done his homework. "I'll send Gene down to take care of it."

"Good," Whitehead replied. "Just as long as you think Gene's OK."

"What do you mean 'OK'?" Fisher asked. "You met Gene."

"I mean he's not gonna run off and do the job without us, is he?" Whitehead intended the robbery to be the first of many, if things went well.

"No, Gene wouldn't do that," Fisher assured him. "Besides, what would he do with the coins? He needs us. You let me worry about Gene. I'll impress on him again that this could be a good thing." Fisher and Eugene Skaar had met with Whitehead in Myrtle Beach a couple of weeks earlier. Though Fisher had stayed with Whitehead at his house, Skaar had only been invited over for dinner one evening.

"All right, then," Whitehead said. "I'm still not sure I trust him, but I'll expect to see him soon."

Fisher hung up and then immediately called Skaar.

"Gene, I got a job for you. And this could be the big one we talked about." Fisher had been looking for a no-nonsense guy when he met the former convict and was impressed that Skaar had once killed two persons during a robbery in Minnesota. The men's previous business transactions had mostly been trades of stolen goods for money.

The stocky, balding forty-one-year-old listened with interest. "What is it?" Skaar said.

"My man at the beach, Whitehead, has found someone. An old man has some coins that I want you to go steal," Fisher said.

"Are they old coins?" Skaar asked.

"What do you care? It's a coin collection, a valuable one."

"How valuable?" Skaar asked.

"Ten thousand to you, when the job's done."

Skaar smiled. "I'm listening," he said.

"Someone Whitehead met at a coin show keeps a valuable collection in his home. It just sits in his closet. Apparently, it's not even in a safe."

Skaar continued to listen. *Ten thousand dollars,* he thought. *That could help me disappear for a while.* Just days earlier, a deputy sheriff had tried to pull Skaar over when he was found driving a stolen car for which there was an APB. Skaar shot at the officer with a .30-.30 rifle. A three-county manhunt had ensued when Skaar abandoned the car and fled into the woods, but the manhunt was called off when the police became convinced Skaar had escaped into Ohio.

"And you want me to do what?" Skaar asked.

"All you have to do is go pick the coins up," Fisher said.

"Just like that?" Skaar asked.

"He's an old man. How much trouble could he be? You're a tough guy, aren't you? You just keep from getting yourself shot long enough to get the coins to Whitehead. He'll do the rest."

"The old man has a gun?"

"I imagine so. Wouldn't you? Hell, you do, and you don't have anything to protect," Fisher said. The men laughed. Skaar routinely carried a silenced pistol in a coat pocket he'd had sewn inside a leather jacket.

"Sounds too easy," Skaar said.

"Does, doesn't it?" Fisher replied. "But you know how these things go. If this job works, Whitehead says there're lots more. That coin shop could turn out to be a real gold mine."

Skaar thought about it and then said, again, "Still sounds too easy."

"Well, Gene, I thought you wanted to get out of town. Maybe you'd just rather hang around Huntington selling groceries," Fisher said, and laughed. Fisher knew that after Skaar's oil company job fell apart, Skaar had tried running a grocery store and ended up with a load of groceries that he had been selling out of his home.

Skaar ignored the remark. "I'm gonna take Rusty with me," Skaar said, referring to Rusty Woomer, a good-looking twenty-four-year-old who had helped him build a porch on his house. A friendship had developed between the men as they worked, when Skaar found that Rusty had also done time. Skaar thought Rusty was stupid, but he also noticed that women didn't seem to mind that. In fact, a girlfriend of Rusty's knew that he had served time and was on parole for a rape conviction. Skaar found that he enjoyed the attention he received from females by simply being with Rusty.

"Yeah, take the boy with you if you want," Fisher said. He had met Rusty. "But you're responsible for him."

"He'll be all right."

"Look Gene, I ain't telling you how to run your business. But Rusty don't have to know how much you're getting, if you know what I mean."

Skaar smiled again. "I do."

Skaar knew Rusty wanted to get out of town as badly as he did. Within the last month, Woomer had failed to show for a court appearance for passing a forged check, and he had eight warrants filed against him for burglary charges.

When Skaar hung up, he immediately dialed the home of Rusty's latest girlfriend. He knew Rusty had been sleeping there. The disinterested young man was watching television. "Hey, man," Skaar said. "Pack your swimming trunks. We're going to Myrtle Beach."

"Oh, yeah?" Rusty said. "I ain't never been there."

"You're gonna like it. We're gonna rob an old man and make us some easy money."

Rusty continued to look at the screen; his emotionless face was highlighted by a vacant stare produced by two weeks of amphetamine consumption. "Cool. I'd like to get out of town," he said slowly. "Only thing is, see, I ain't got no money or no clothes."

"We can take care of that," Skaar said. "Meet me at my house later on, and I'll give you the details." For what Skaar had in mind, he was willing to supply Woomer with money, clothes, drugs — whatever it took.

Woomer went to Skaar's house and ended up staying until the men left for Myrtle Beach two weeks later. Woomer left for the beach with one hundred and fifty dollars and an assortment of drugs in his pocket. He still wore the same dirty clothes.

It is unclear whether Fisher and Whitehead knew or cared that their partners in crime were leaving West Virginia as fugitives from the law. Woomer and Skaar left Huntington on February 20, 1979, convinced that they were about to make the easiest money of their lives.

2

"**D**on't you want to wait until closer to Sunday?" Jimmy asked.

"Well," Wanda teased, "the weather has cleared some." Traci's sixth birthday was still four days away. Wanda had suggested they go ahead and pick up one of her presents. "We could at least go look again," Wanda added, smiling.

The weather was still a drizzly and cold reminder of the snowstorm that had all but paralyzed the southeastern portion of the country the weekend before. The temperature had steadily risen through the week to well above freezing, but patches of ice and snow still lingered under eves and in shadowy nooks.

"I thought you wanted the puppy to be a surprise," Jimmy said.

"Puppies," Wanda corrected. "And I do. I just can't wait. Traci is going to be so surprised." It had been all Wanda could do to keep the secret as long as she had. The snowstorm had helped by keeping everyone occupied. But now the snow was practically gone.

"Puppy," Jimmy replied. He looked out the picture window at the snowman, still standing tall, but with a definite lean toward the dirt road running along the front of the yard. "Look, he lost his arm."

"Can't hardly fix it without making it worse," Wanda said, taking a position by her husband. She slipped an arm around his waist.

"You know I can fix anything, honey," Jimmy said softly and pulled her close. He and Wanda stood quietly for a moment. "I could put his eyes and nose back on anyway."

The snowman had been a first-of-its-kind family project for the Summers' family. The freak snowstorm had been unexpected, but Jimmy had been working overtime for months in preparation for an expected February layoff. A couple of days off from work because of bad weather had turned out to be most welcome.

"We could go tomorrow if you want," Jimmy said. "Roads are clear."

"There's two puppies, you know. I hate to split them up."

"Traci will be with us if we go tomorrow," Jimmy said.

"That'd be all right, don't you think?" Wanda asked. "It's just a little early. Besides, with her party and all, it might be better to let her get used to them."

Them. Jimmy masked a smile. "Fine with me."

"We should put the puppies up for the party," Wanda said. "Maybe just bring them out long enough to show the kids."

"That would be good," Jimmy replied. "You're working tomorrow until when? Three?"

Wanda nodded her head. "I'm gonna make another trip into Georgetown before Sunday to get her a special card. I want everything to be perfect."

"We talked about making sausage tomorrow," Jimmy reminded her.

"We still can. I just looked in the cabinet to make sure we have everything we need. Help me remember to get some pepper and sage from work."

"Consider it done."

Jimmy liked the idea of expanding the household to include a pet. He and Wanda wanted another child, and would have another, they had decided, but all in good time. For now, a wife, a child, and a puppy, even two puppies, were just fine for Jimmy.

The pair continued the embrace, lost in their shared memories of the last few days. Jimmy was normally a very busy person, even when he was at home. His remodeling work on the house had slowed, however, because the ice mixed with snow had been very heavy. Wanda had actually enjoyed having him underfoot. Now she hugged his waist as if he were a soldier getting ready to ship out the next day.

Wanda didn't care why or when Jimmy had become a

fix-it guy, someone who could turn bad into good. She only knew that she had found someone who would love her and never leave her.

• ❖ •

Six-year-old Wanda sat on the stoop of the small house and watched the police car roll to a stop in the drive. Something was up and Wanda was getting nervous. Though Wanda thought her mother was so tall and attractive, that day her mother hadn't seemed at all like herself. She appeared old and tired, and she had been crying all morning.

A nurse in a white uniform stood by her car door and reached into her purse as Wanda's Uncle Claude, the deputy sheriff, walked around the car. Wanda turned around at the sound of her mother's crying and she saw her looking through the screen door, holding a handkerchief to her face.

Wanda saw the candy cane in the nurse's hand even before it was extended to her.

"You must be Wanda," the nurse said, smiling. "Here, this is for you."

Wanda took the candy cane and watched as the grown-ups went inside. Though it was the day before Christmas Eve and a little chilly, Wanda's mother had told her to wait outside. Her four younger brothers, including the two babies, were still inside.

When the screen door opened again, Wanda became more confused. Her mother's crying intensified. The nurse and her uncle each carried one of the baby boys and a bag and moved quickly across the porch and down the steps. As the nurse passed where Wanda sat holding the candy cane, she turned, and smiling gently, said, "We'll be back to get you tomorrow, darling."

"What?" Wanda said, becoming alarmed. "Get me? What do you mean?"

The nurse continued toward the car. Wanda rose and felt tears spill down her cheeks. "Momma," she shouted.

Wanda pled and cried that day until her tears dried up and she had a terrible headache. Her mother was equally pitiful. She sobbed and rocked, alternately mumbling to herself and trying to console Wanda and her brothers. Wanda later learned that her mother was desperate to get away from her father and had known that she couldn't care for five small children by herself.

"It'll be for the best, honey, you'll see," she told Wanda.

"You're not going to let them take me, are you, Momma?" Wanda cried.

"The oldest boys will be with you. You're going where there are little animals and lots of things for children to do."

"I want to be with you, Momma. What have I done?"

Wanda and her brothers were taken to a new home the next morning, on Christmas Eve. When they arrived, toys, games, and the warm-hearted embraces of their new family awaited.

Wanda wouldn't see or hear from her real mother or father for over twelve years. She never saw her two youngest brothers again.

3

The plan seemed simple enough. Upon arriving in Myrtle Beach, Skaar and Woomer would get directions from Whitehead and then drive the 130 or so miles to Cottageville, a little town near Charleston, where John Turner lived. After robbing the old man, Skaar and Woomer would take the coins back to Whitehead and get paid. It seemed to the pair to be an easy afternoon's work.

The preparations the ex-cons made for the trip to Myrtle Beach included borrowing a tan Ford Maverick from Gene's son and then loading it with guns and drugs. During the two weeks prior to leaving West Virginia, Woomer and Skaar were involved in two armed robberies. The first robbery was of two West Virginia men and netted firearms and a driver's license in the name of John Wolf. Rusty would later use the license as a false identification. The other robbery occurred when Rusty became angry with his grandmother. She spoke for the family and refused to allow Rusty to visit his sister in the hospital where she was recuperating following heart surgery. Forcing their way into the grandmother's home at gunpoint, Rusty and Gene stole a .32 pistol and holster the old woman kept by her bedside. The men took this pistol, along with Quaaludes, Valium, marijuana, whiskey, and an assortment of other guns, including a sawed-off shotgun, on the trip to the beach. Might as well be prepared for anything, they reasoned.

Following a stopover in Charlotte, North Carolina, for the night, Woomer and Skaar pulled into Myrtle Beach on Wednesday morning, February 21, 1979.

The Komo-Mai Motel in Myrtle Beach was typical of the mom-and-pop motels along the beach in 1979. The small, two-story, L-shaped motel had accommodations for a live-in manager who provided guests, many of whom returned year after year, with a familiar face and smile. As Gene and Rusty checked into the motel, Gene reestablished an acquaintance with the motel manager's wife.

"Hello, again, Mrs. Braddock," Gene said and politely shook hands with the cheerful woman behind the counter.

"Mr. Fisher," she said. "Good to see you again." Skaar had stayed at the motel on two earlier occasions, always signing in as John Fisher. "You going to stay with us again?"

"Yeah, another business trip," Skaar answered. "I brought an associate with me, John Wolf."

Woomer sat in a chair by the window of the office. He nodded at the mention of his alias but said nothing.

"We'll probably be here for several days this time," Skaar added, as he signed the register. "How much for the both of us?"

"Put your money away, John," Mrs. Braddock said. "We trust our good customers. Just pay when you leave."

"That's mighty nice of you."

"Just glad to have the business. My husband will be back later. He'll be sorry he missed you." On previous trips, Skaar had talked fishing with the amiable couple.

"I'm sure we'll see him. Tell him 'hey' for us," Skaar said.

"Sure will," she said and handed Skaar a key. "We're gonna put you in Room 8 this time."

Once in the room, Skaar immediately phoned the Myrtle Beach Coin and Stamp Shop and talked to Whitehead. With nothing to do until the arranged meeting later in the day, Skaar and Woomer went to the store, put some food in the small refrigerator in their room and turned on the television.

"Where's Fisher?" Whitehead said quickly when the two men walked into his shop late that afternoon.

"He ain't here," Skaar said. "Not coming."

Whitehead looked at Woomer.

"This here's Rusty," Skaar said. "Fisher told you about him. Things still look good?"

"Yeah, everything's OK. Did Fisher tell you that the old man has a dog?"

"No."

"Well, he does. Just so you know." Whitehead held out a piece of paper. "Here are the directions. You got a map?"

"We'll find it," Skaar said, slipping the paper in his pocket.

"All right," Whitehead said. "Leave around noon and you should be back by suppertime. Call me the moment you get in and I'll come to you. Don't come back here."

Skaar looked around as he had on his last visit at the displays of coins and stamps. Every square inch of the small store seemed filled. "So, we're all ready?" he said.

"I think so," Whitehead said.

"OK." Skaar appeared to study Whitehead for a moment and then added, "You realize what's happening here, don't you?"

"I do," Whitehead said.

In a phone conversation earlier that afternoon, Skaar informed Whitehead of what he and Woomer had discussed before the Maverick pulled out of West Virginia.

"You realize you're not going to hear from the old man again after this," Skaar told Whitehead, indicating that the plan included killing any witnesses to the robbery.

"That's OK," Whitehead replied.

Young Jimmy Summers wanted a family and knew how to get one. He would introduce his father to his best friend Henry's mother, and they would all live happily ever after. Yes, there were several problems. Jimmy's father worked all of the time, rarely showing up at their little apartment except to sleep. And, there were Henry's brothers and sisters to consider. Oh, and maybe Henry's mother should be told. Nonetheless, the plan seemed solid enough to a couple of ten-year-olds wiling away the hours on the side streets of Charleston, South Carolina. And why shouldn't it work? Jimmy figured having a family simply meant making a commitment and sticking to it.

Jimmy quit school for good when he was in the eighth grade. The day he was threatened at Bonds-Wilson Junior High by an older student wielding a straight razor, Jimmy left school and never returned. The decision to leave wasn't that difficult. Jimmy remembered being the only-child-out at school: the only child in dungarees instead of slacks, the only child who never had lunch money, the only child to still be barefoot when fall weather began to turn cold. School didn't offer him the pleasant experiences he noticed that other children seemed to have. There wasn't anyone at Jimmy's home encouraging him to read and study. What made the most sense to the thirteen-year-old was that he should get out of school, go to work, and start looking out for himself.

Jimmy thought he was in heaven working the job he chose. The three-to-eleven shift at Beacon Lanes Bowling Alley provided him with a meal each evening and a paycheck with his name on it at the end of the week. Best of all, he got to bowl each night after work as much as he wanted.

The world of work was all Jimmy had imagined it would be and more. In his mind, the work was a logical extension of his earliest memories – being paid fifty cents as a five-year-old by Mr. Mims to stay out of the way when his father and the itinerant farm hands came in on the drag lines in the late afternoons as the sun was setting. Lining up for a paycheck at the bowling alley seemed to be directly connected to his memories of standing in line with the field hands on Fridays at the company store to spend his own money and buy his own refreshments. He remembered that a dime bought a soda and a pound of sugar cookies from the jar on the counter.

But then for reasons unknown to Jimmy, his father moved from the country to the city where his life became different. The loud and sometimes scary and lonely city was disconnected for Jimmy from his earlier life and offered little in the way of the predictability he had found so comforting in the country. Gone for Jimmy in the city was any sense of being in control of what happened in his life. That is, until Jimmy quit school. When the job at the bowling alley came along, Jimmy discovered work all over again.

An additional benefit of Jimmy's job at the bowling alley was that it got him off the streets at a time of life when young boys begin to get into adult trouble. Jimmy was at work in the afternoons and evenings learning to be responsible when the pranks of his friends were turning to acts of vandalism. He knew breaking into houses was a far cry from stealing watermelons from the front of the supermarket. Remarkably, he also realized that it wouldn't be possible for him to completely dissociate from the trouble brewing for his friends as long as he remained in Charleston.

"When trouble comes down the street," Jimmy recalled, "you either go with it or get on the other side of the road." Jimmy chose the other side. At fifteen years of age, Jimmy informed his father that he was moving to Pawley's Island to stay with his sister.

Jimmy's brother-in-law worked at the Litchfield Country Club and got Jimmy a job working forty-hour weeks at the golf course.

"I made forty-eight dollars each week," Jimmy remembered, "out of which I put forty dollars in the bank and had eight dollars in my pocket for food and fun."

The eight dollars went mostly for food.

"There wasn't much to do in Pawley's Island in those days, but drink and fight," Jimmy said. His brother-in-law had lost his driver's license, so in exchange for chauffeuring, Jimmy was given a place to sleep. He drove his brother-in-law back and forth to work, and then in the evenings and on weekends, he took him from one bar to the next in nearby towns. "But I had a good job," Jimmy said, nodding his head, "and I liked living in the country again."

In Pawley's Island, Jimmy lived in a shack located close enough to the Waccamaw River to allow him to catch fish and shoot squirrels just outside his door.

"I slept in a bed where I could see the stars over my head," Jimmy said. "When I got off work at the golf course, and I didn't have to take my brother-in-law somewhere, I found something fun to do outside."

It was on one of those fun outings that he met Wanda Altman.

Wanda's family lived just up the river from Jimmy where they owned land and operated a boat landing. For twenty-five cents, a person could get some bait, launch a boat and fish all day.

In 1953, Wanda's father, Reggie, and a brother bought 48 acres of land on both sides of the road near the Litchfield Plantation for $3,000. When the brothers eventually split their investment, Reggie got 40 acres of land on Chappel Creek that led into the Waccamaw River. No stranger to hard work, he cleared his land, began raising livestock, and started farming.

When the opportunity arose several years later, Mr. and Mrs. Altman adopted Wanda, who was then six-years-old, and her two younger brothers. Arriving on Christmas Eve day in 1960, the children settled in to an orderly life and enjoyed the benefits of country living and a large extended family. The family members worked together to take care of the inside and outside chores on the small farm. While Reggie worked at International Paper during the day, his wife, Betty, managed the children and took charge of the household. In turn, the brothers learned to take care of the animals and work in the fields, while Wanda's duties consisted of helping to clean, cook, wash dishes, and do laundry.

"I worked in the garden some," Wanda said, "but I hated that. I learned that if I cooked well, I didn't have to work in the garden. So when I came home from school I went straight into the kitchen."

During the summer, everyone in the family helped Reggie run the tackle and bait shop.

One particularly hot summer day, when Reggie went out to call his sons in to eat, a teenage boy was standing on the landing. Reggie asked his sons as they came in who the boy was.

The brothers explained that they had met Jimmy out squirrel hunting one day in the woods. He lived in a shack down the road, said the brothers. They had seen him around a lot after that. He apparently didn't have a real home.

"What will he do for his dinner?" the concerned father asked.

"Nothing, probably," was the reply. "Sometimes he doesn't eat."

Wanda then watched with disdain as her father had one of the boys go out and invite Jimmy in for a middle-of-the-day dinner. One more mouth to feed, and a boy, at that, meant more work for her.

Jimmy readily accepted the invitation. That afternoon, he entered a world unknown to him.

Jimmy had never before seen the variety and abundance of food that he saw in the Altman household. Betty could make southern dishes and desserts from scratch and baked nearly every day. Jimmy quietly noticed that Wanda had acquired many of her adopted mother's talents in the kitchen. That he found a fly in his sweet tea that first day only made him more interested in Wanda. He caught her smirking at him when he raised his glass for the first sip. Jimmy smiled and drank the tea anyway.

Jimmy was quickly smitten with Wanda and became a frequent visitor to the Altman home. As he sat with the

family around the kitchen table playing board games in the
evenings, he marveled at the family dynamics. Jimmy
understood that he was seeing what he always knew existed.
It was possible for families to have order and respect for one
another within a home.

Despite his lack of formal education, Jimmy eagerly
joined in to play a game that was an Altman family favorite -
Scrabble. A quick learner, he remembered words from game
to game and never seemed to tire of playing. Giddy from the
excitement of just being included, Jimmy often had to be
asked to leave as bedtime approached.

Night after night, Jimmy left the Altman residence and
began the dark walk back to the shack where he lived, a trip
that took him by the All Saints Episcopal Church and a
graveyard. Where the road dipped under the canopy of oaks
near the church, Jimmy began running. Through the hooting
of owls and the shrill, layered sound of cicadas piercing the
night, Jimmy ran until he was breathless, slowing only when
he was well past the graveyard and out of reach of any of its
resident apparitions.

Jimmy had heard all of the ghost stories of the low
country, but nothing could dissuade him from visiting with
Wanda and her family.

Wanda quickly warmed to Jimmy's winsome
personality and his smooth manner of talking. The two soon
secretly became a couple and began to venture out together.
On weekends, Wanda was allowed to go to the movies with
Jimmy as long as her brothers went along. After the movie,
the carload of teens rode by the Whistling Pig, a local
nightspot, and Jimmy gradually began to meet some of the
schoolmates of his new friends. He and Wanda became closer
and closer until they were spending all of their time together.
"I felt very comfortable with Wanda," Jimmy said. "From the
first time I met her I knew I could talk to her. I believed she
cared about me, and it made me feel good just to be around
her."

Several months after Jimmy's arrival at the Altman
household, Wanda's parents became alarmed at her
suggestion that she and Jimmy were getting serious. Mr.
Altman had other ideas for his headstrong daughter and

decided to pay Jimmy a visit.

Reggie was a large man, physically imposing at six feet four inches and over two hundred fifty pounds, and he had fiery red hair. Jimmy's surprise with Reggie's unannounced visit turned to shock when Reggie pulled him out onto the porch of his little shack. Wanda's determined father pulled a small pistol from his pocket and shoved it in Jimmy's stomach.

"Leave my daughter alone," he growled.

Jimmy didn't know that the pistol Reggie brandished wasn't real. The frightened teen clearly got the message that he wasn't to visit the Altman home again, he wasn't to visit Wanda at her work place, and he wasn't to try and contact her in any way.

Jimmy thought about his predicament and finally told Wanda he was leaving town and going to stay with relatives in Hemingway, a neighboring town. That evening Wanda argued with her parents. The following morning she parked her car at school and got on a bus to Hemingway. Jimmy was delighted by Wanda's assertive move but felt that as a couple they couldn't run from circumstances. The next day Jimmy and Wanda returned to Pawley's Island and went directly to Wanda's home.

"I remembered telling my father that I wasn't coming back home without Jimmy," Wanda said. "I had recently turned eighteen, and he knew he would have to accept that."

When Wanda's father asked Jimmy of his intentions toward Wanda, the sixteen-year-old stood resolutely, with shaking knees, and declared that he loved her, he was going to marry her, and he would always take care of her, no matter what.

Jimmy and Wanda left the Altman home together and were jubilant with their actions. Their celebration appeared to be short lived, though. When they got to the bank to get money out of Jimmy's account for a wedding dress and rings, they found that the account no longer existed. The person Jimmy had needed as a co-signer, since he was underage, had taken his money. In addition, when they returned to Jimmy's house the two pigs he had been fattening to sell were gone. Jimmy suddenly had a bride-to-be and no money. The determined couple borrowed twenty dollars from Reggie and Betty for a marriage license, and on March 25, 1972, Jimmy and Wanda were married before a justice-of-the-peace. Because Jimmy was sixteen years old, he had to have someone sign the license for him. Jimmy's father signed the license, but did not attend the wedding. Reggie and Betty did attend.

"My father was like the others," Jimmy said. "He didn't think it would work. 'Easy to get into, hard to get out of,' he told me. Everybody thought our marriage wouldn't last."

Everybody, it seemed, but Jimmy and Wanda.

Jimmy always wanted a family but had been disappointed during his childhood in the efforts of others to provide for him a stable family life. Instead of becoming disillusioned, however, Jimmy made a promise to himself. Once he was old enough and found someone he could love and trust, he would build his own family.

The day after the wedding, Wanda went back to school and Jimmy went back to work, convinced that his dream of a family was about to become a reality.

Seventeen months later, the dream came true with the birth of Jimmy and Wanda's daughter, Traci, the first grandchild for Reggie and Betty. When asked when he first felt he finally had the family he'd always wanted, Jimmy replied, "I knew it when I stood beside Mr. Reggie at the hospital and we looked through the glass together at Traci. When I saw the way he looked at Traci and then at me, I knew I was finally there. I had my family, and I knew I'd never leave 'em. And I damn sure knew that wouldn't nobody take 'em away from me."

5

Thursday, February 22, 1979, was overcast and drizzling but still warmer than it had been. After sleeping in until about 10 a.m., Woomer and Skaar began making preparations for the day's journey. Skaar spent 30 minutes or so talking with the motel manager who delivered and installed a new heating and air unit in Room 8. Woomer lay in bed for the first few minutes of the visit but adjourned to the bathroom to roll joints for the trip.

Skaar told the motel manager that he and Woomer would be going to work that day but would return in the early evening. The manager was under the impression that Skaar had construction interests in the area.

When the men finally loaded the car to leave town, just about noon, Skaar gave Woomer two of the four Quaaludes he'd brought along on the trip. Rusty slugged one down with the half-full fifth of whiskey they'd opened the night before. In an effort to keep from having to stop along the way, they drove to the liquor store around the corner and purchased an additional fifth.

Cottageville was a friendly community of about four hundred residents in 1979. Located just northwest of Charleston, the quiet, close-knit community offered genuine low country living to older farmers and generations of families that worked at the shipyards of the Charleston Naval Base but chose to live in the country. Residents in town knew one another, and many shared seasonal fruits of the large plot gardens they carefully maintained in their yards each evening following work.

Outside of the center of town, Cottageville boasted vast acres of pine trees and farmlands dotted with dogwoods and camellias. Interspersed among the graying skeletons of barns, now stripped of their prized, weathered boards, hid the remnants of rice plantations, some still adorned by oak-lined canopy drives. Sightseers ambling along the miles of country roads could pull over, take a picture and often get back on their way before another car passed by.

Cottageville is the kind of small town where strangers are easily noticed under normal circumstances. If those strangers pull over at the edge of town, get out and spread a map on the hood of their car, they will be noticed by every person who rides by and might even be asked if they're lost by someone friendly enough to pull over to help. Those strangers will also be noticed if they go into the town's only store and ask where a resident lives.

● ❖ ●

Skaar and Woomer were unable to follow the directions they'd been given and finally stopped at the Center Grocery of Cottageville. The proprietor and his wife were at work that afternoon.

"Good afternoon," Skaar said to the woman behind the checkout counter. "Ma'am, do you have a phone book we can see? We need to find a local number."

"Well, I believe we do," Gladys Dandridge said. "It's in the back of the store. I'm sure my husband can help you."

Gladys walked around the counter. "Hubert?" she called. "Can you help these gentlemen? They need to use the phone directory." Turning to Skaar, she said, "I'm sure he'll get it for you. Go right on back."

"Thank you, ma'am," Skaar replied.

"Good afternoon, sir," Skaar said as he reached the back of the store. Hubert Dandridge momentarily stopped stocking the shelves and looked down from the ladder on which he was standing.

"Yes, sir. What can I do for you?"

"We need to see your phone book, if we can," Skaar said. "We need a local number."

"We can help you there," Mr. Dandridge said. He climbed down, reached under a counter and handed Skaar the directory. "Looking for anybody in particular?"

Dandridge asked.

"We're here to visit my uncle," Woomer said, taking the directory. "He lives around here somewhere."

"A lot of country, but not a lot of people," Dandridge said. "I might could direct you."

"Thomas," Woomer improvised, "Jim Thomas is his name." Woomer turned the pages of the thin directory as if he were scanning the columns of names. Several seconds later he said, "I don't see his name here."

"Thomas?" Dandridge repeated the name. "Thomas. There is a Thomas family, moved in a few years ago. Don't know the first name, though."

"I bet that's them," Woomer said quickly.

"They're supposed to live near a man named John Turner," Skaar added. "Is there a school nearby?"

Dandridge hesitated. "Well," he explained, "John Turner lives on the other side of the school from the Thomases'. I don't know if you'd say it's that close. Of course, nothing's far away in Cottageville."

"How 'bout if you just give us directions to Turner's place," Skaar said. "We'd appreciate it. We can get to the Thomases' from there."

"All right," Dandridge said.

The Turners lived several blocks over from the store in a house set back from the road on a large wooded lot. A long circular drive around the house connected to the road in a single lane that was used by both incoming and outgoing cars.

Skaar and Woomer drove over to the right street, but again found that they had to ask for directions. When a twelve-year-old boy on a bicycle turned and pointed three houses over, Skaar eased the Maverick to the mouth of the winding drive and turned in. Half way up the dirt path, though, Skaar had to quickly reverse and back out to allow a car leaving the Turner residence to get by.

Mrs. Turner and her sister were on their way to the hospital to visit a sick friend. Mr. Turner had watched his wife and sister-in-law leave from where he sat in his wheelchair by the front window.

Skaar and Woomer drove two blocks to a school

parking lot, waited a couple of minutes, and then returned to the drive of the Turner's house.

When John Turner got up from his wheelchair to answer a knock on his door, he found himself staring into the barrel of a .32.

"What do you want?" Turner asked the armed men.

"We understand you got some old money," Woomer said.

"What do you mean 'old money'?" Turner asked.

"Old coins."

"They're not old coins. I have some foreign coins," Turner replied, indicating the small collection of coins he had been examining.

After briefly eyeing the coins, Skaar said, "That's not what we came for. Give us the good stuff. Where is it?"

Skaar told Woomer to make the old man sit down and to keep an eye on him. Skaar began to search the house, and eventually found the chest of coins in a closet in the back bedroom, as Whitehead had predicted.

"I found 'em," Skaar hollered, and began to lay the coin books on the bed. In addition, Skaar examined some suits he found in the closet and made a determination that he and Turner were just about the same size.

Skaar left the bedroom. "Go in there," he said to Woomer as he entered the living area, "and start carrying those coins out."

Woomer laughed and headed to the bedroom.

"Where are your guns?" Skaar asked Turner.

"What guns?" Turner replied, his tone surly.

Skaar pointed his weapon at Turner and asked again.

"I have a .357 in my car," Turner said.

"Is it locked up?"

"Yes, I'll have to give you the keys."

As Woomer passed through the living room he discontinued carrying coins and took the keys to Turner's car.

"Go get his gun," Skaar told Woomer. Turning to Turner, he asked, "Where is it?"

"I think it's under the seat," Turner said.

Woomer searched Turner's car but was unable to find

the gun.

"Well, then," Turner said, "it must be in the wheel well, in the trunk."

Woomer made a second trip, and then a third, before throwing the keys on the kitchen floor. "There ain't no gun out there," he said.

"Never mind that," Skaar said. "Finish carrying out those coins. And get those suits I put there on the bed."

"You're not going to take my clothes, are you?" Turner asked indignantly.

"Shut up," Skaar said. "We'll take whatever we want."

When Woomer finished loading the car, he re-entered the living room and stood with Skaar behind the chair in which Turner was seated.

"I'm going out now," Skaar said to Woomer. "Take him in the back bedroom and when you hear the car crank up, shoot him. Then hurry up and come on."

"All right," Woomer said. "Give me your gun."

"What happened to yours?" Skaar asked.

"It's lost somewhere."

Turner stood up before Woomer told him to and slowly began to move in the direction of the bedroom. Turner made it as far as the hallway when Woomer heard the car crank. Holding the .32 approximately a foot from the back of Turner's head, Woomer fired one shot. When he saw Turner falling, he turned and ran out to the car.

"Did you shoot him?" Skaar asked.

"Yeah," Woomer answered.

"Where did you shoot him at?" Skaar asked.

"In the head."

"Good," Skaar said. "That's the way you're supposed to do it. That way can't nobody tell on you."

Woomer and Skaar began the trip back to Myrtle Beach.

● ❖ ●

Approximately an hour later, Mrs. Turner returned to her home. When she saw that her husband wasn't sitting by the front window, as he usually did, she became worried. He had a serious heart condition. Suppose he had another heart attack while she was away?

Something else was strange, too. As she climbed the steps to the porch, Mrs. Turner immediately saw a cigarette butt that someone had crushed in front of the door. She knew it wasn't there when she left, and John Turner didn't smoke.

Mrs. Turner found her husband on the floor in the hallway. Blood covered the back of his head. She quickly discovered that her phone didn't work and ran next door to a neighbor's house to call the doctor.

● ❖ ●

Deputy Sheriff Lonnie Crosby was making his routine rounds and had just pulled up to Dr. J. R. Smith's office; the time was a little after five o'clock. Dr. Smith explained that he had just received a call from Mrs. Turner. Mr. Turner was on the floor at their home, and Mrs. Turner was afraid her husband was dead. When the officer and the doctor arrived at the Turners', Deputy Crosby quickly determined that a robbery and murder had occurred and he secured the Turner property as a crime scene. While Crosby and other local law enforcement officers waited for the crime scene lab provided by the State Law Enforcement Division (SLED) in Columbia to arrive, person-to-person interviews were taken through a quick canvass of the neighborhood.

News travels fast in a small town. Within a couple of hours after the murder, several persons who had seen the strangers in town provided good descriptions of both men and the car. The search was on for two white males. The younger of the two was slim and appeared to be 20 to 25 years of age. He had shoulder-length, blond hair that was parted in the middle. The older man, probably 40 to 45 years of age, had short, dark hair and was heavier than the other man. The car the men drove was a dirty, tan, Ford Maverick, with out-of-state tags, possibly Louisiana.

6

"**Y**'all ready to go?" Jimmy asked. He knew they were. Since finding out about the puppies Traci was as excited as any six-year-old would be. "Who was that on the phone?" he added.

"That was Don," Wanda replied, referring to the night manager at the store where she worked. "The cash register's stuck." Wanda had been home from work less than an hour.

"Good timing, then," Jimmy said. "We'll just do everything at once." Wanda had remembered at work to set aside the pepper and sage needed for the sausage they planned to make, but had forgotten to bring the spices home. "Where's Traci now?" The exuberant little girl had been in and out of the kitchen all day.

Traci came running in. "Are we going now?"

"Yeah, we have to go by the store, too," Jimmy said. "Get your coat, baby girl."

"Oh, boy, oh, boy," Traci said excitedly. "We're going now," she said to her mother.

Wanda laughed. "Yes, Traci, we're going now. Do as your daddy says, and get your coat."

"Can we get the puppies first?" Traci asked, still jumping up and down.

"Yes, honey, but we can't go anywhere until you get your coat."

"She's been like this all day," Jimmy said, smiling. "You missed it." Traci had been told that morning that she was getting puppies for her birthday. "Puppies?" Wanda had asked when Jimmy told Tracy. "You said 'puppies'?"

"Of course," Jimmy answered, and then added, "Hadn't you already made the decision, sweetie?"

Wanda had worked until three o'clock at Jack's Mini-mall, a convenience store five minutes from their house. Business had been brisk early in the day, with people getting out again after the snowstorm, but few customers had been by the store in the afternoon. Wanda and Jimmy had started the sausage when she got home from work but, just as she suspected, they needed more pepper.

"Let's go, y'all," Jimmy prompted. "We got to ride out in the country." Turning to Traci, who still didn't have her coat, he said, "Only the ones who got their coat gets to go."

"My coat," Traci said suddenly, as if surprised. Her large eyes opened expressively. "I'm gonna get my coat."

Jimmy and Wanda stood and listened to her footsteps as she clomped through the house.

"Great day," Wanda said, laughing. "Is she excited or what?"

"Told ya'," Jimmy said, turning to go out the door. "Been like that all day. I'll crank the car."

"Honey," Wanda said.

Jimmy stopped at the door and turned.

Wanda stepped across the kitchen and kissed him. "Thank you," she said.

"What's that for?" he asked.

"You know," she said. "The puppies."

"No need for that. We made that decision together." Jimmy kissed her in return. "Anything for our baby."

"Well, I just wanted you to know I was thinking about you."

Jimmy watched Wanda check her purse and begin to put on her coat. Traci's footsteps grew louder as she headed back toward the kitchen with her coat.

"Honey," Jimmy said.

Wanda turned. Jimmy had never seen her look more radiant than at that moment.

"Anything for you," he said.

7

Skaar noticed the temperature gauge as he turned the bottle up for another swig. He began to slow the car. The second fifth of Canadian Mist had been disappearing rapidly.

"Damn," he said. As the car decelerated, he saw the steam seeping out from under the sides of the hood.

"What is it?" Woomer asked, looking up. Since leaving Cottageville, Woomer had smoked pot nonstop as he rifled through Turner's stolen wallet and examined the coins.

"Car's overheating," Skaar replied. This wasn't a good time for car problems. At least the traffic was light. Highway 17 ran from the north end of Charleston to Georgetown and carried most of the through traffic. Woomer and Skaar were traveling north on 17A, the alternate route that served the small towns that dotted the countryside northwest of Charleston and southeast of Georgetown. They approached the Sampit community.

"Look for a house," Skaar said.

"We gonna stop now?" Woomer asked.

"Gotta get some water, or at least let it cool down."

The sawed off shotgun lay on the seat between the men. The hissing of the radiator blended with the sound of the Maverick's tires on the asphalt and rock surface of the road. Woomer and Skaar looked ahead.

"What about that one?" Woomer asked, as they approached a two-story house set back from the road. "I don't see anybody."

"Looks dark," Skaar said. The Maverick crept to a stop in front of the drive.

"Well, then, what about that one up there?" Woomer asked, noting the lights on a small, one-story brick home just up the road. "That looks like a good one."

• ❖ •

If it had not been drizzling, twenty-seven-year-old
Arnie Richardson would probably have greeted the pair of
outlaws outside of his house. Richardson was a bona fide
outdoorsman and loved nothing more than building a fire
and pitching a tent for a night. Just the afternoon before he
had been clamming and picking oysters at a spot he knew in
Georgetown's Winyah Bay.

Arnie had just gone into the small house he rented with
his family and was adjusting the television antenna to allow
his five-year-old daughter to see "The Brady Bunch." His
wife was at work and their infant daughter was at the
babysitter's. Thirty-five-year-old Earl Dean Wright was also
home that afternoon with Arnie and his daughter. Earl Dean
was Arnie's sister-in-law and she had suffered from Bright's
disease as a child. Unable to work, Earl Dean lived with the
Richardsons and helped with the children. The gentle, quiet
woman spent most of her time reading her Bible and playing
with her Chihuahua.

"Pull around to the back," Woomer said.

Skaar and Woomer eased up the back steps to the
porch. Woomer held the .32. The back door to the house was
open as if someone had just entered.

Hearing a noise, Arnie went into the kitchen. Woomer
and Skaar burst through the doorway before Arnie could do
or say anything.

Arnie was backed into the living room at gunpoint and
forced to sit on a sofa beside his daughter. Earl Dean sat
close by on a spread-covered couch.

"Where's your old money?" Woomer said.

"What?" Richardson asked.

"Old money," Woomer repeated as he gestured with the
.32.

"Don't lie to us," Skaar said. "We know you've got
some money."

"There's no money here," Richardson said.

Skaar took the .32 from Woomer and instructed him to

go out to the car to get the shotgun. Woomer hurried out.

"What about guns?" Skaar asked.

Richardson held his daughter and said, "Guns? Is that what you want? I've got guns that I hunt with in the hall closet."

"Get his wallet," Skaar said when Woomer came back in holding the shotgun, "and check the closets."

Woomer took Richardson's wallet, several guns and a sealed beam flashlight he found in the hall closet out to the car.

When Woomer returned he looked in the bedroom closet and then reentered the living room.

"You know what to do," Skaar said to Woomer.

"What's that?" Woomer asked.

"You know. What we did at the other house."

Skaar hesitated at the door and turned just as Woomer aimed the shotgun toward Richardson and his daughter and fired. The blast struck Richardson in the face and his body was repelled off the back of the couch. His arms had been wrapped tightly around the little girl and he dragged her to the floor with him as he crumpled forward. The instant after the shotgun blast, Arnie lay atop his daughter on the floor. Skaar stepped quickly out the door of the room as Woomer turned and opened fire again. This blast struck Earl Dean in the upper chest and she fell to her side on the couch, but continued to scream. When Woomer fired the shotgun a third time, striking Earl Dean in the face, the room was quiet.

Woomer then walked outside, leaving behind three spent shotgun shells on the floor of the house, and got in the car. He and Skaar rode away in the Maverick without the water they had stopped to get.

Several minutes later, the five-year-old little girl climbed out from underneath her father and ran out of the home into the cool, damp night air.

8

Georgetown County Sheriff Woodrow Carter had just gotten home and pulled his boots off when the call came. *What now?* Carter thought. Even considering that the residents of a small town such as Georgetown typically rely on their police force for everyday occurrences, it had still been a busy week. Because of the snowstorm Carter and his deputies had patrolled for looters, charged batteries, pulled vehicles out of icy ditches and delivered food to persons stranded without electricity and transportation. Tempers had been running hot all week, and it seemed that the half of the local population that still had phone service had called the station to complain about something. When Carter or any of his men left the station to patrol the area, they had been flagged down by those without phones who needed assurance or wished to lodge a complaint. It had been a long week, and it was only Thursday.

Learning of a possible murder, Carter immediately headed to a home in the Sampit community. He arrived at the Richardson's home at about the same time that David Wilson got out of his truck with his shotgun. Wilson, the brother-in-law of Arnie Richardson, explained what he knew to a reporter.

"It was about 6:50 and they had just finished telling the news on television when we heard a knock on the door," Wilson said. "You could tell it was a child's knock. Well, I opened the door and my five-year-old niece was standing there shaking, bloody, and real jittery.

"She said, 'Somebody killed my daddy. They shot him and they shot Earl Dean.' I said to my wife, Janice, 'That young'un is telling the truth.'"

"Did she see all this?" Carter asked.

"Yeah, that's what she told us," Wilson continued. "She said, 'I tried to wake my daddy, but I couldn't.'"

"Is she hurt?" Sheriff Carter asked.

"She doesn't appear to be," Wilson said. "But I believe they meant to kill her, too." In addition to the emotional trauma of watching her family members gunned down, the little girl had suffered a cut on her ear from the shotgun blast.

Following the murders, the little girl got on her bicycle and rode over five miles in the dark and drizzle to the home of her aunt and uncle. After she explained what happened, Wilson called and asked a neighbor of the Richardson's to check on them. Then after calling the sheriff, Wilson got his shotgun and rode over there himself, arriving at the same time as the sheriff.

Inside the home, the sheriff found the bodies of Arnie and Earl Dean, both dead from what appeared to be shotgun blasts to the head. On the floor lay the spent shells.

Sheriff Carter questioned the five-year-old girl and got a good description of the two men responsible and the events that took place inside the home.

"Why they didn't kill the child, I'll never know," Carter said later to a reporter. "When her father's body fell on her, I reckon they thought she was dead. This is one of the worst things I've seen in Georgetown County in my 30 years as sheriff. To kill a man and his sister-in-law savagely, without cause, while a child looked on – I'll be glad when we catch those two men."

9

After a couple of years of fighting in Vietnam and a restless early adulthood, thirty-six-year-old Don Sellers was finally beginning to feel settled. His job as the night manager of a rural convenience store allowed him to make a good, honest living and also to spend time with his wife, Della Louise, who worked as the night cashier. Together they ran the small store in the evenings and had gotten to know all of the local folks who dropped by. Jack's Mini-mall was a quick stop for a loaf of bread or an iced beer from the drink box. Neither Don nor Louise had found it difficult to make the adjustment to living in the little trailer behind the store because they had each other. Their three-year marriage was, by all reckoning, going exceptionally well. Each day the happy couple moved closer to their shared goal of building their own home close to the ocean.

Earlier that winter Don had become alarmed when Louise's weight plummeted to 78 pounds following emergency surgery and a 21-day stay in the hospital. When Louise was released from the hospital, Don promised the doctor to devote himself to her recovery. She needed rest, food, and lots of love and attention. Well, actually, Don would say to friends, he had added the part about love and attention, and then he'd smile. What had continued to amaze Don was how much he enjoyed taking care of his lovely wife. Calling on family and friends when necessary, Don watched as Louise's health improved day by day. She did her part by resting and eating and when her weight reached 96 pounds, just four pounds short of the goal set by her doctor, she went back to work.

At 3 p.m. on Thursday, February 22, after relieving Wanda Summers, who was the day manager, and the boy who helped her, Don set about his task of opening boxes and replenishing shelves. Thursdays were stock days and though Louise didn't normally help restock the store, she had helped this day in an attempt to stay warm. It seemed the only customers braving the raw weather were workmen trying to regain lost wages after the ice and snow had closed the roads.

"I'll get this, honey," Don said, looking around at the boxes. "There's not much here, anyway."

"That's OK," Louise replied. "I'd rather stay busy."

"All right," he said slowly. "Just do what you think is best."

Don eyed his wife carefully for signs of fatigue. That morning they had driven to Murrell's Inlet to get Louise some fresh fish at one of the seafood markets. Because of the weather, Don had at first balked at Louise's suggestion. But she did love fish enough to eat a lot of it, he reasoned, and so he agreed. They both welcomed the chance to get out of the cramped trailer.

The couple worked side by side until about 5:30 when Louise suddenly sat down. "I guess I am tired, Don," she said, breathing deeply. "I'm just not feeling very good."

"Let me feel," Don said as he leaned down to press his lips to her forehead. "Hmm, you could be just a touch warm. I tell ya, there's nothing going on here. Why don't you go lay down for a while."

"I think I will," she replied. "Did you turn the heat off?" Louise normally returned to the trailer at about six o'clock to adjust the heat and begin making preparations for their return after the store closed.

"No," he shook his head. "I thought you might need to rest and I left it on a little. Just bump it up." He watched her walk toward the door of the store and added, "I'll give you a call if I get busy or something and you can run back over."

The February sun had begun to set and the lights inside the store shone brightly into the parking lot. A clothes-dampening mist still hung over the ground and had been turning to fog each evening as darkness came on.

Don finished splitting boxes and sat down just as Louise walked back into the store.

"What is it, honey?" he asked. "Can't rest?"

"No," she said and perched on her stool by the cash register. "I was just thinking. Let's take the weekend off and go up to Concord and see that new grand youngun. Think we can?"

"I don't see why not," he replied. "We're due a couple of days." A loud muffler sound from outside caught Don's attention, and he turned his head to watch a tan-colored car slow down as it passed the front of the store. "We can take Saturday and Sunday," he continued.

The car swung around and into the parking lot. From where Don sat on an upended Coke crate by the hotdog machine, he could see steam pouring out of the front of the older-make vehicle as it pulled up directly in front of the store. "Overheated," he casually observed and turned back to his wife. "I'll make sure we're not needed at the store for anything this weekend."

"Good," Louise said and smiled. "I can't wait to see that little baby. Can you believe I haven't seen her but once?"

The front door to the store suddenly burst open and a thin, blond man stepped inside. Quickly scanning the small room, the man stepped forward and held up a pistol he was carrying by his side, aiming it at Don and Louise.

"Whoa," Don said and began to rise from his seat. He recognized the pistol as a .32 and tried to step in front of Louise. "What's going on, fella?" Don saw Louise smiling and knew that she did not comprehend the situation.

"I want some money," the man yelled, emphasizing his words with repeated forward thrusts of the gun. "Now get your goddamned hands over your head."

Don pulled Louise off her stool and pushed her behind him. He then slowly stretched his hands forward and placed them on the cash register. The hammer on the .32 was cocked, and the barrel was pointed directly at his chest.

"OK, calm down now," Don said slowly. "We'll get you some money." Don spun his heel so that the toe of his boot tapped the floorboard of the counter twice, the prearranged signal for Louise to lie on the floor. She continued to stand, however, appearing confused, and tried to move out from behind Don so she could see.

The front door opened again and another man who was older and stockier than the first walked in. When Don saw the weapon this man carried he removed his hands from the register, half-turned his body toward Louise, and again tried to herd her behind him.

"I told you to get those hands up," the younger of the two men shouted, again thrusting the gun toward Don. "Gimme the shotgun," he yelled to the older man.

Ignoring his request, the older man walked by the checkout counter and looked down the last aisle, where built-in refrigerated compartments lined the back wall.

"Let's go," the second man signaled to Don, pointing with his weapon. "Go down this aisle."

Louise started to cry and clutched at Don's arm as he began to move away from her.

"Calm down, now, Louise," Don said quietly. "Just calm down. Stay there and just stand still."

Louise's body started to shake and she began to sob.

Don stared at the pump shotgun the older man held pointed at him and understood he was looking at a dangerous weapon. The standard stock had been replaced with a pistol grip and the barrel had been shortened to produce a scatter pattern for the blast. Don knew from his experiences in Vietnam that a sawed-off shotgun had only one use.

"We'll give you whatever you want," Don said, allowing the man to prod him along. "Just don't hurt my wife."

The front door of the store suddenly opened again. The younger man jerked his body around and thrust the .32 toward a six-year-old black girl holding a quarter. Unaware anything out of the ordinary was happening, the little girl moved through the door and headed for the candy rack.

Don recognized the girl as the daughter of a local brick mason named Robert and instinctively began to move toward her. "Man, let me get that kid out of here," he pleaded.

The younger man wheeled around and pushed the gun in Don's face. "Goddamnit. Get back down there. I'll shoot you."

Don squinted and arched his body away from the

barrel.

The younger man quickly grabbed the little girl, wrapped his forearm across the front of her chest, put the gun to the back of her head, and began pushing her toward the door.

Outside, Robert had gotten out of his truck to get a newspaper from the machine by the front door. Glancing in through the window, he saw Don looking at him and winking. Robert thought how strange Don's behavior appeared and had just put his money in the paper machine when he saw his daughter jerked back away from the door and shoved roughly aside.

Leaving the machine he stepped into the store. "What the hell do you mean pushing my youngun?" he said to the shaggy-headed man. "I'll break you –." He stopped suddenly as a .32 was shoved in his face.

"Shut up," the young man shouted. "Get on inside."

The scene before Robert was confusing as he pulled his daughter close to him. A man with a short, thick-looking gun was pointing it at Don, who kept trying to step in front of Louise, who was screaming and crying. Robert's daughter began to cry as the younger of the two robbers shouted and waved the pistol he was holding.

"This is a hold-up. Get to the back of the store," the young man motioned with the .32. "I want you way in the back of the store."

Robert shielded his daughter in front of him and allowed the young man to push him by the checkout counter. Moving down the last aisle, he heard Louise's voice, pleading in the background.

"Please don't kill us," she said. "Just take the money."

"Yeah," Robert said, turning his head. "You can take my truck. The keys are in it."

"Act like you're shopping," the man with the pistol said. "Pick up something."

"What?" Robert said.

"You heard me, pick up something."

Robert continued to clutch his daughter in front of him and looked at Don.

The young man walked forward and said to his

accomplice who was leaning forward across the beer box beside the front window of the store, "Gimme the shotgun, now."

The older man again ignored the request to swap guns. "Here comes a woman."

At just that moment, Wanda Summers walked in. Her smile quickly faded when she saw the armed men.

The young man motioned with his gun for Wanda to walk over toward the last aisle where Don was holding Louise.

Wanda felt her body flush with heat as she saw Don's anguished face. Louise was near the point of being completely hysterical and struggled against Don's hands as he tried to calm and contain her. Beyond them, she could see Robert holding his daughter, who had continued to cry as she buried her face in her father's shirt.

"Pick up something," the young man ordered. "Act like you're shopping, all of you."

Wanda immediately picked up a can of black pepper. *Thank God, Jimmy and Traci didn't come in with me,* she thought.

Robert exchanged glances with Wanda and reached for a large can of pork and beans.

"Don't get any smart ideas, big man," the young man said, glancing at the little girl. "Get something else."

Robert slowly put the can back on the shelf.

"She's got somebody out in the car," the older man called out.

The younger man moved forward and looked out the front window.

"Who is that?" Turning toward Wanda, he demanded, "Who is that out there?"

"Just wander out there," the older man said. "Act like nothin's goin' on."

"Who is it?" he asked again. "Tell me."

"That's my husband and daughter," Wanda said. Jimmy had stayed in the car with Traci and her new puppies.

"Keep your gun down," the older man said, "and bring 'em in here."

The younger man walked casually out of the store and

across the lot. Jimmy didn't see the man until the driver's door of his car was suddenly jerked open and he realized a gun was pointed at the side of his face at very close range.

"If you move, you're dead," the young man said.

Jimmy's body froze. His right arm slowly floated over toward Traci to partially cover her.

"Get out and come on inside," the man ordered.

Jimmy pulled Traci across the seat and out his door and slowly stood up. He almost tripped over his frightened daughter as he felt a hard shove to his back. His wallet was pulled roughly from his back pocket as he stumbled toward the store. Jimmy felt the gun he had seen jammed into his backbone.

Once inside Jimmy walked directly to Wanda and put his arm around her. Their eyes met as he said, "Everything will be all right, honey. Don't worry."

"I'm OK," Wanda whispered nervously. "You take care of Traci." Traci remained still in her father's arms.

"Somebody else's coming in," the older man said. The young man stepped quickly across the room to a position behind the door.

The front door opened and another frequent customer, Willie, stepped inside. "Somebody's car is boiling over," he said.

Willie felt someone step up behind him. A gun was suddenly pressed against the side of his face and he heard a voice say, "Keep walking." Willie did as he was told, and continued walking to the back of the store.

"Everybody on the floor," the younger man said, his voice taking on an irritated tone. "Damn, this thing's gettin' out of hand." To his partner, he said, "You said this'd be easy."

"It ain't my fault. There wasn't nobody in here," the older man shot back gruffly. "Just get the money." Swinging the shotgun toward the back aisle, he said, "Get down, I said, and spread out."

The small aisle didn't provide a lot of room for eight people to lie down. Jimmy covered Traci with as much of his body as he could, and Robert covered his daughter's head with a large hand.

The young man stood before the cash register and cursed at the closed drawer. He pushed several buttons in rapid succession. "Who runs this thing? Get up here."

Don began to rise from the floor.

"Not you," he snarled. "Her." Louise had been sitting at the cash register when the robbery began.

"She can't, man. She's crying."

"I said her, goddamnit." The younger man aimed the pistol and moved toward Don.

"I can get it, Don," Louise sniffed. She had apparently forgotten that the register was jammed. "Let me get it for them."

"Open it," the young man ordered, pulling Louise's arm to stand her before the register.

Louise's body shook uncontrollably. Finding herself unable to direct the movement of her hand, she pushed clumsily at the buttons. "Oh, no," she sobbed, as the register remained closed. "Please don't kill me."

"Open it," the young man shouted again.

"She can't do it," said Don in desperation. "Please let me help her." Don pushed up with his arms despite the shotgun hovering near his face.

"Stay down and shut up." The older man emphasized his words by thrusting the shotgun forward.

"Calm down, Don," Jimmy said, aware that Don's agitation could provoke the men into shooting.

"Just please don't hurt her," Don said, easing back down.

"Goddamnit, who else can open this thing?"

"I'll carry it out to your car for you," Don suggested.

Wanda suddenly rose and moved toward the front. "I can get it," she said, and stepped behind the register.

Wanda pressed the proper sequence of buttons and opened the drawer.

Shoving her aside, the young man began to remove the bills. "Get their wallets," he shouted over his shoulder.

The older man moved to the register. The younger robber then excitedly began moving over the bodies, collecting wallets. "Get the money bag," he shouted.

"There isn't a money bag," Wanda said. She held Louise

in her arms.

"How do you know that?"

"Because I'm the day manager. I work here, too."

"Well, ain't it lucky that you came along."

The young man moved toward the register. "Let's get out of here, now."

"What about them?" the older man said, looking at the bodies heaped in the aisle.

Both men turned.

"We'll take these two with us," the younger man said, gesturing to Wanda and Louise. "The rest won't do nothing as long as we got them."

The older man hesitated.

"We're taking your women to Georgetown," the younger man said. "If we don't see no police for fifteen minutes, we'll let them go."

The older man began to herd Wanda and Louise toward the door.

Don suddenly rose from the floor and faced the men. "Man, that's my wife," he said, extending his hand toward the young man.

The older man abruptly thrust the shotgun. "Lay back down," he shouted. "Goddamn, I'm getting tired of you. I'll blow you in two if you don't get your ass back down."

Don hesitated, his chest heaving. When the young man put his pistol to Louise's head, he reluctantly lay back down, saying, "I love her. Please don't hurt her. She's been sick."

Don hit the side of his fist to the floor and groaned.

"Calm yourself, Don," Jimmy said sternly. "We got children." Jimmy also watched helplessly as his wife faced the guns of the robbers.

The younger man ripped the receiver from the wall phone and threw it to the floor.

"Trade with me, now," he said, and the two men exchanged weapons.

The older man took Wanda and Louise by their arms and pushed them toward the door.

"Keep your heads down," the young man warned the people on the floor and disappeared around the aisle. The door to the store slammed shut.

Several seconds later, Don began to rise.

"Don't get up, Don," Jimmy said. "Not yet. They haven't left."

Don hesitated. "They got Louise," he said.

"They got my wife, too," Jimmy snapped back. "But we have to think of the children."

Don's body shook as he sucked air, but he stayed down. Jimmy and Robert continued to cover their daughters, while Willie, who was in front of and facing away from everyone, continued to watch the security mirror.

Suddenly, the young, blond robber stuck his head around the corner of the aisle and said, "I'd have given fifteen dollars if one of you sorry sons of bitches had stuck your head up over the aisle. I'd a loved to blown it off."

He disappeared as quickly as he had shown up and the door slammed again. After several minutes passed, Don and Jimmy raised their heads and looked at one another. Jimmy nodded cautiously, and they began to rise.

"They're gone," Don said, peering over the aisle. As everyone else slowly stood, Don raced out the front of the store and ran to the road. After looking in both directions he ran toward his trailer. "I'm going to call the sheriff," he hollered over his shoulder.

Don frantically looked in the phone book. When he dialed the number he finally found he received a busy signal. Slamming down the receiver, he immediately picked it back up and redialed. When the line was still busy on the second try, Don threw the phone and ran back to the front of the store.

There, Jimmy was talking on the payphone to the sheriff.

10

"**G**et in the back seat," Skaar ordered. Wanda and Louise slipped in past the front seat of the two-door car and huddled together in the back.

Louise had begun to sob again and clutched at Wanda as Skaar got in the driver's side and cranked the car. "It's going to be OK," Wanda assured Louise. "We'll just do what they tell us, and they'll let us go."

Several minutes elapsed and the three sat without talking. Skaar began to fidget. He alternately glanced in the rearview mirror and turned his head to look in the back.

Woomer suddenly emerged from the store and hurried to the car. When he opened his door, he leaned forward and looked in. Seeing that both women had gotten in the back, he said, "That's OK, we can change places later."

Before Woomer had closed his door, the tires of the Maverick began to spin and the car lurched forward out of the parking lot and headed north on Highway 17.

"You're going in the wrong direction," Wanda said. "Georgetown is the other way."

"We ain't going to Georgetown," Woomer said, laughing. Turning his body toward the back, he propped the pistol on the top of the front seat and aimed it in the direction of his hostages.

Louise continued to cry.

"There's no need for that," Wanda said boldly. "Not now. We're not going anywhere. So, please, put that away."

Woomer hesitated, then put the pistol down and turned around.

Approximately 20 miles up the road Skaar turned the car off of the main highway onto Highway 544, a dark and seemingly deserted road.

"We're looking for a good place to let y'all out," Woomer said over his shoulder. "We'll need some time to get away."

Skaar slowed the car several times as it approached side roads before finally selecting one.

Relieved that the nightmare was about to end, Wanda said, "You can let us out right here." There were no houses in sight. Though she didn't know exactly where they were, Wanda knew the area well enough that she figured she could find help once she and Louise were released.

"No," Woomer replied. "Not yet. Let's just go on down here and see what we find."

As the car suddenly moved from the pavement onto dirt, Woomer began to climb over the back of the front seat. Nudging Louise with the pistol, he ordered her to move up front. Louise resisted, tightly gripping Wanda's hand.

With her eye on the gun, which was once again pointed at them, Wanda said, "Go ahead, Louise. It'll be all right. Just do as they say."

The car moved slowly on the dark road. When lights appeared ahead in the distance, Woomer said to Skaar, "Turn around. Go back a little ways. I saw a good place."

"Yeah," Wanda said, still under the impression they would be released unharmed. "There wasn't anything back there. Y'all can have a good start."

"Is that what you think?" Woomer said to Wanda, laughing. Pointing the gun directly at her face, he said, "Take off your shirt."

Wanda began to disrobe as Skaar drove the car to the side of the dirt road and switched off the engine.

Wanda was then forced out of the car and down into the wet grass where she was raped. Woomer held the .32 the entire time, off and on placing the barrel to the side of Wanda's head to elicit her full cooperation.

Louise suffered a similar fate in the car at the hands of Skaar.

Standing beside the car in the darkness and drizzle following the assaults, Louise and Wanda attempted to redress. As they huddled with their clothes in their arms, Skaar pulled Woomer aside. Handing him the shotgun, he said quietly, "Walk 'em down the road, and when you hear the car crank, kill 'em. And try not to make too much noise."

"How do I do that?" Woomer asked.

"Don't shoot any more than you have to."

Turning to Louise and Wanda, Woomer pointed down the road and said, "Y'all go on that way. We'll leave when you get down there a ways. Don't look back, though, so you won't know which way we've gone."

"I've been sick, in the hospital," Louise said. "I shouldn't be out here."

"Get going before I change my mind," Woomer ordered.

"Come on, Louise," Wanda said immediately. "We're gonna get some help." Worried about Louise, Wanda wrapped her arm around her friend's shoulders and began to lead her down the dark, country road.

"I'm so cold," Louise said, her teeth chattering. Louise's body began to convulse and she almost fell each time she missed her step.

"Come on, help me, Louise," Wanda said, holding her up. "Hang on."

"I don't know if I can make it." Louise began slurring her words.

"Sure you can, honey." Though Wanda was only partially dressed, her attention was on Louise. "There'll be somebody by those lights we saw."

"So cold . . . ."

"It'll be warm up there. You can do it, Louise."

Wanda stumbled forward, practically carrying the smaller woman. *I'm gonna make it back*, Wanda thought, *to Jimmy.*

"Can't make . . . ."

"Oh, yes, you can, we're gonna make it, I promise." Tears streamed down Wanda's face. "Help me, Louise, come on, honey, you gotta help me." *I know my Jimmy is worried sick.*

Louise stopped trying to talk.

"Come on, baby, here we go. We're almost there. Hang on, now." Wanda tried propping Louise on her hip each time she took a step, and ended up half dragging her.

"You got too much to live for to give up." *I've got to be*

home for my baby's birthday.

"Think of Don, honey, come on, Louise. Think how much he loves you. *I haven't gotten Traci's card yet.*

"You're gonna see him real soon, Louise. We're not giving up now. Not now. It's almost over." *I'll have to go into town tomorrow.*

Wanda and Louise stopped. It suddenly occurred to Wanda that with all their struggling she hadn't heard the sound of the car engine. *Maybe the quiet means it's really over.*

Wanda started to turn her head to look back when a bright light exploded in her face.

11

"**D**id you make sure they're dead?" Skaar asked. "It's a simple question."

"I said I did," Woomer answered. "Let's just get to the motel."

When the Maverick limped into the parking lot behind the motel, Skaar backed it into a spot near the breezeway and the men began to unload the trunk. Besides the cases of coins and the suits stolen from John Turner, there were several rifles and guns wrapped in blankets to be carried into the motel.

On the last trip in, Woomer said hello to a young girl getting a drink from the machine near the door to the room he and Skaar shared. She smiled and said hello back to the nice-looking stranger.

Skaar blurted, "Do you know where we can get some marijuana?"

The girl, surprised, said, "No, I don't."

Woomer quickly said, "Don't pay him no mind. He's cool. We, that is, my father and I, are just getting in from working all day. What are you up to?"

"Nothing much," she said. "Some friends are coming over and we were thinking of having a little party."

"Well," Woomer said, "My name is John, John Wolf, and that sounds like just the kind of thing we like."

"Well, then maybe y'all would like to come up to my room," she said.

"I'd like that," Woomer said, looking at Skaar. "But I'm gonna go to our room first."

"Come on up when you're ready," she said. "Room 12."

Approximately 30 minutes later, Woomer knocked on

the door of Room 12, where several young people were gathered watching television.

When the door opened, Woomer entered and held up a joint. He had some additional marijuana in a baggie in his pocket. "Would y'all like to smoke some pot?" he offered.

"Sure," was the reply, "why not?"

12

$\mathbf{W}$anda awoke unaware of how long she had been on the ground. She was surrounded by darkness and shades of gray. All was quiet.

They're gone, she thought.

Suddenly, the image of an explosion ripped through her brain so violently she sat bolt upright. *Oh, my God.*

Louise. Peering through the darkness Wanda saw Louise lying on the ground and shook her. She knew something was wrong. *Louise. Oh, no. She can't be.*

Wanda looked at the dark smear on her hands and began to pull herself to her feet. A feeling of extreme fatigue, however, washed from her forehead down her face and propelled her forward and back to her knees.

What's wrong? She thought. *I have to get help for Louise.*

Leaning forward on her arms, her chest buckled inward in spasmodic gasps until panic forced her head up and back off of her chest. Wheezing noises as her head fell back were punctuated by the sucking sound a straw makes at the bottom of an empty glass. Using her neck muscles to resist the tugging sensation that seemed to be pulling her head forward again, Wanda struggled to stand. Her body swayed as she looked at the dark form of her friend on the cold, wet ground.

Louise. I'll go for help, she thought.

Wanda stepped out onto the dirt road and stumbled forward again to her knees. Mud squished between her fingers as she once more pulled herself to her feet. With a lurching movement, she set out for the bright lights in the distance. Then, as if she were no longer able to resist an urgent impulse, Wanda began to scream.

● ❖ ●

"Did you hear that?"

The echo of three distinct gunshots, a blast and a pop, and then another pop, rang in Rene's ears. The sounds were quickly absorbed in the thick, night air.

"I did," Dean replied.

Rene and Dean Guyton were on the porch of their home. Rene hurriedly took the last two plants from her husband and set them inside the house. Stepping back out to the porch, Rene stood beside Dean and listened. Several seconds elapsed before a loud muffler and then the barking of tires hitting pavement sounded in the distance.

"That's just down the road," Dean said, his apprehension growing. The anxious couple waited and continued to listen.

The sudden sound of a human voice, half-screaming and half-moaning, propelled them to action.

"I'll get the lights in front," Dean said. "You get the ones in back and find the children."

Floodlights precisely positioned on the corners of the house came on one by one and illuminated the exterior of the house and yard as if it were daytime. Running back around the outside of the house, Dean saw a lone figure emerging from the darkness down the road. "Get in the house," he shouted to his wife.

Rene remained on the porch. "What is it?" she asked.

"It's a woman," he answered when the figure came closer, and then added, "She's hurt." Unsure of who or what else might come down the road out of the dark, Dean again shouted, "Get in the house. And tell the children to hide." Dean moved cautiously in the direction of the drainage ditch separating the yard from the road. He then watched in horror as a shrieking woman tripped and fell face forward into the freezing cold water of the ditch.

Though Wanda tried to keep her neck up and shoulders straight as she ran, her head seemed to bob forward rhythmically with a tugging motion.

The lights . . . I'm closer. I'm almost there, Louise.

Wanda stumbled forward, making screaming noises, but found herself curiously unable to form words to call for help. *Blood on my hands . . . Oh, I must be hurt. I'll have to get a bandage after I help Louise . . . Oh, no, I didn't get Traci's birthday card, yet.*

Wanda stopped running and she turned toward the lights. *The lights. I'm here, Louise.* Wanda saw the silhouette of a man moving slowly across the yard in her direction. *Help Louise,* she thought, and stepped forward. She suddenly began to fall.

The jolt of the cold water stinging her skin jerked her body back up and she found her feet. Wanda moaned as she summoned the energy to trudge up the side of the ditch toward the man. *I have to tell him about Louise.*

When Wanda moved fully into the light, Dean said, "Oh, dear God!" and yelled to his wife, "Call the rescue squad, and get some towels."

Confusion clouded Dean's brain. It was clear the woman was trying to tell him something, but she was obviously unable to talk. Her mouth was gone. Looking directly into the back of Wanda's open throat, Dean watched in horror as gurgling blood arose in a rhythm with each sound she made. Each attempt to talk brought up another surge of blood that spilled down her shirt. Placing his hands on her shoulders, Dean looked into the frantic eyes of the terrified woman.

"Lay down," he commanded.

Wanda reached out her bloody hands toward the man. *Louise,* she wanted to say, but felt instead only a gurgling in her throat. The man's eyes looked strained, urgent. Gasping for air, Wanda grabbed the man's arm and pointed back toward the dark. *I have to make him understand. Louise. Get help for Louise.*

Wanda lay down on the grass on her stomach.

● ❖ ●

Rene came out of the house and ran across the yard with the towels.

"It looks like she's been shot in the face." Dean said, kneeling beside Wanda. Wincing, he grasped her shoulders and lifted. "Here, put the towels under her head." After Rene positioned the towels under Wanda's face, Dean stood up. "I'll get some blankets. She's shivering." Dean ran to the house.

Several moments later, he reemerged with the blankets and his shotgun. Dean leaned the gun against a tree and began to cover Wanda with the blankets. Rene had already begun to take Wanda's pulse.

Six months earlier, and less than a half mile from where Wanda lay, Rene's parents had been brutally gunned down as they tended to their business at the convenience store they owned and operated. The Moons were well known and loved throughout the area. Their store had been a gathering point for local residents for years. The senselessness of their deaths had stunned the small community. That they had apparently pleaded with their killers made their murders even more of an abomination. Since the incident Dean and many of his neighbors kept guns fully loaded and handy.

"You're not going down there, are you?" Rene asked. Her husband had been looking down the road every few seconds and had walked to the edge of the yard twice.

"No, I'm staying here with you and the kids." Dean said, picking up his shotgun. Taking several steps toward the road, he added, "But if anything comes out of the dark . . . ."

13

The first to arrive on the scene was an EMT who quickly assessed that the largest bandage she had would be insufficient for the woman with the gunshot wound to the face.

"Where did she come from?" the technician asked as she began to work.

"She wandered down the road," Rene answered. "She's been trying to tell us something, but she can't talk. We think she telling us there's someone else down the road."

Jodell Johnson had been at the scene of some gruesome accidents since becoming an EMT, but neither she nor her husband, "Hoss," who drove an ambulance as a volunteer, had seen anything to compare to what they saw that night.

"An ambulance is on the way," Jodell said. When the call for help came in, she had been able to leave a moment before Hoss and an additional EMT, who would arrive shortly. "The towels were a good idea," she added.

"Yes, ma'am," Rene said. "We've stayed with her to keep her calm. Her pulse has dropped to nothing several times. I thought she might pass out. But she hasn't."

"You're doing fine," Jodell said to Wanda. "Stay with me now." Jodell used her hand to prop up Wanda's head. "Let your head rest," she said.

Wanda's eyes were wide open.

"Why did you lay her on her stomach?"

"We didn't, really," Dean replied. "I just told her to lay down. She did that by herself. She keeps pointing and trying to rise up. Something must be down that road. We heard shots and then screaming."

"Have you been down there?" Jodell said to Dean, noting his grip on the shotgun he held.

"No, ma'am," Dean said. "I've stayed with my family."

Within a couple of minutes, Dean saw the flashing lights of an ambulance and ran out to the road to flag it down.

"This is it," Dean said loudly to the EMT who jumped out of the passenger side of the ambulance. Hoss, the driver, quickly stepped to the rear of the vehicle, opened the doors and pulled out a stretcher.

Though the first impulse of the men had been to place Wanda on her back, it became apparent from her gesturing that she wanted to lie on her stomach.

As Wanda was loaded into the ambulance, she continued to make mumbling noises and point down the road. Jodell crawled in the back and resumed holding up Wanda's head.

"I'm going to see what's down there," the other EMT said, and ran toward the dark.

Hoss backed the ambulance out of the drive, drove part of the way down the road and got out and stood on the running board.

Several moments later, Hoss heard the EMT shout, "It's another woman."

"Can she wait for the other ambulance?" Hoss yelled back.

"No," the EMT emphatically replied. Louise had been found lying unconscious in a pool of her own blood. "She needs immediate attention."

Louise was then loaded into the ambulance with Wanda and both were transported to the hospital at the Myrtle Beach Air Force Base.

14

Which is your wife?" the general medical officer at the base hospital asked of Don. Cursory examinations had provided the doctor with better news for one of the distraught husbands than for the other.

"Mine's the little bitty one," Don said. He searched the doctor's face for a sign that Louise was OK.

Don and Jimmy had stayed at the store and talked with the officers until word came over the police radio that the hostages had been found and transported to the nearest medical facility. When the alarmed husbands arrived at the air base hospital, they didn't know the condition of their wives.

Colonel Manley was the doctor in charge.

"When I first saw your wife," Manley explained to Don, "she was semi-comatose, or partially unconscious."

Fear gripped Don as the doctor carefully continued.

"Sir, I'm not sure what you know about bullet wounds, but your wife's been shot through the head."

Don knew about bullet wounds. He had spent two years of his life in Vietnam looking at them on a daily basis. He knew that nothing good comes from a head wound. "Is she alive, doc?"

"Yes, she is. She showed a response to the IV we put in her to get some fluids started. That's a good sign. I called Specialty Services and a surgeon came immediately and began an examination."

"Can I see her?" Don asked.

"She's leaving for Charleston, going to the Medical University."

"Is she gone already?" Don asked. He appeared ready to run out the door.

"Wait just a moment, if you would," said the doctor. "I need to tell you something."

Don hesitated.

"She has to go to Charleston because she needs a neurosurgeon. We've prepped her for the ride down. But you need to know that her condition is very serious."

Don thanked the doctor over his shoulder as he turned to look for the deputy who gave him and Jimmy a ride to the hospital.

"I need a ride back to Pawley's to get my car," Don said loudly. "I really want to follow along."

The deputy ran with Don outside as the ambulance pulled away.

The only route to Charleston took the ambulance right by Jack's Mini-mall, which looked deserted compared to just minutes before. Most of the officers who swarmed the store had left. Robert and his daughter and Willie had gone home to their waiting families.

Don quickly retrieved his car and then pulled out when the ambulance sped by. In his emotional state, however, he hadn't noticed that his gas gauge was on empty. When Don reluctantly stopped for gas, the ambulance tail lights disappeared in the distance.

The long, dark highway seemed to stretch to eternity in front of Don as he pulled back onto the road and punched the gas pedal.

"Oh, Louise, please don't die on me," he said. "You know you're my life, baby." Don clutched the steering wheel and fought tears welling in his eyes.

Don and Louise had met almost four years earlier in Chesterfield, South Carolina, their hometown. One day when Louise stopped at the gas station where Don worked, he summoned his courage and asked the petite brunette for a date. Louise initially turned him down.

"I've heard about you," she said.

Don had years earlier acquired a well-earned reputation as a wild man, though he was perceived to be more full of mischief and fun than meanness. The stories he brought back from Vietnam had only added to his reputation.

"Well, was what you heard good?" Don asked

hopefully. He was more than attracted to Louise's curly brown hair and sparkling eyes.

"No," Louise answered, laughing. "I can't say it was."

Not easily dissuaded, Don said, "All right, but you're missing some fun."

Louise didn't miss it for long. She and Don soon became constant companions and eight months later were married in a friend's garden. Louise had been married once before, at age fourteen, to escape being sent to an orphanage after her mother died. A mother twice over by the age of twenty, Louise had, just four months before the robbery at Jack's Mini-mall, become a grandmother at age thirty-three.

Don knew Louise as a quiet, unassuming woman. Others also recognized the honest, straightforward, nothing put-on or fancy qualities she exuded and knew that she was the best thing that ever happened to Don. He agreed and doted on her at every opportunity.

When Don reached Mt. Pleasant, just north of Charleston, he came upon flashing lights and was forced to pull over. A highway patrol roadblock, one of several, was in place for the manhunt for Woomer and Skaar.

"Did an ambulance come by here?" Don asked loudly out his window.

"Yes, sir, about ten minutes ago," the officer replied.

"I'm with the ambulance. My wife is in it. I have to go."

"We'll need to see some identification, sir," the trooper said.

Don realized at that moment that his identification was in his wallet.

"I don't have any," Don said. "I was robbed in Pawley's Island. My wife is in that ambulance. She's been shot. Now get out of my way."

"Sir, you'll have to get out of the car."

"Listen, I've got to go," Don pleaded. "My wife's been shot. Call somebody if you need to, but I'm going. The only way you're gonna stop me is to blow my head off."

The trooper hesitated, then said, "Sir, give us just a minute to verify, please."

Don revved the engine as he waited. Within a couple of

minutes, he had a blue-light escort into Charleston.

Don was mistakenly led to Roper Hospital. His frustration was apparent as he jumped from his car when he finally arrived at the Medical University parking lot. Running through the large medical complex, Don asked for directions as he approached nurses' stations and thanked the nurses as he passed by.

When he finally found the right hall, he was asked to wait for a doctor. The wooden seat outside of the room where Louise was being treated offered little comfort to the frightened man. Don's nightmare had begun four hours earlier and now threatened to stretch into forever.

"Are you the husband?" a doctor asked quietly as he emerged from the treatment room.

"Yes, sir," Don said, rising quickly. "You got my wife in there?"

"Yes. She's still hanging on right now," the doctor said.

"Doc, do everything you can for her," Don pleaded. "I love her so much."

"We will," the doctor assured him.

Fifteen minutes later, the doctor reappeared at the door. Stepping out into the hall, he said, "Mr. Sellers, her blood pressure is dropping. We're doing all we can. I want you to know that. But she's in a very serious condition."

Don sank back into his chair. "I'll be sitting right here."

Several minutes later, just after midnight, the doctor again entered the hall. Don stood as the doctor pulled the mask from his mouth.

"I'm sorry, Mr. Sellers," the doctor began . . . .

"I need to see her, Doc," Don said, trembling.

"Of course."

Don stood over the lifeless body of his wife and wept. For several minutes his plaintive cry echoed through the tiled room and down the sterile, deserted hallway. Clutching her still-warm hand, Don slipped the wedding ring he'd given Louise from her finger. This was the first time the ring had been removed since their wedding.

Clutching the ring tightly in his fist, Don made Louise a promise. "Honey, if God's willing, I'll see the men dead that did this to you."

15

It was just after ten o'clock when Jimmy ran into the emergency room entrance of the Grand Strand General Hospital.

"I believe my wife's here, Wanda Summers?" he blurted to the woman behind the counter. The little information that Colonel Manley, the doctor in charge at the air base, had given him wasn't encouraging. Jimmy was told that Wanda had been rushed to Grand Strand General for immediate surgery. He hadn't been told she had been shot in the face.

"Where is she?" Jimmy demanded, before the nurse could answer his first query.

She had been alerted to Jimmy's arrival and said, "You're Mr. Summers?"

"Yes, I am," Jimmy answered. "How do you know that?"

"Your wife is here." The nurse slid a clipboard across the counter in Jimmy's direction. "I've prepared the necessary paperwork so we can get started."

"What?" Jimmy looked at the papers. "What's this?"

"We'll need you to fill these out. It's just the usual: medical history, insurance –"

"What the hell are you talking about? Where's my wife?"

Several other personnel on duty stopped what they were doing and watched the nurse's reaction.

"Mr. Summers, if you could just take a minute –"

"Lady, I don't give a damn who's gonna pay for what. Right now, I don't know what's happened to my wife. You better get somebody out here quick who can give me some answers."

"Please give me a moment, sir," the nurse said. "If

you'd like to sit down, the doctor will be right with you."

"Sit down? What the hell are you talking about? Where is she?" Jimmy asked, looking at the door leading to the treatment area. "Is she in there?" Jimmy moved toward the door.

The nurse stepped from behind the desk and blocked his path. "You can't go in there, Mr. Summers. Please, you'll have to work with us."

"Can I just find out what's happened to my wife, please?"

When the doctor appeared at the treatment door, Jimmy practically ran to him. The look on the doctor's face was frightening.

"Mr. Summers?" the doctor asked. He appeared to be in a hurry.

"Yes," Jimmy said, looking around the doctor down the hallway. "Can I see her?"

"No, not at this point, Mr. Summers. Please just let us work." Jimmy had no way of knowing that Dr. Edward Eckert was a surgeon who specialized in the jaw and teeth, the lower face.

"Please tell me what's happened," Jimmy said.

"Your wife has been shot in the jaw. It's very serious, but another specialist and I are here to help. We're both plastic surgeons. We work on faces, and we're going to work now. Please bear with us, and we'll keep you informed as well as we can."

"I can't see her?" Jimmy asked again. When Eckert had received the call from the air base and he recommended the gunshot wound victim be transported to Grand Strand General, he'd not been given any details. When Wanda was wheeled into the emergency room and he got his first look at the extent of her injuries, Eckert realized he was in for a long night.

"No, Mr. Summers, please, not now," Eckert said. He then added, "I'm sorry. I have to go," and walked back through the swinging door.

Visitors to the hospital that night would include Wanda's brothers, the police, and even Jimmy's boss. But in spite of the phone calls and well wishing, Jimmy would remember only the feeling of being alone.

Jimmy watched numbly as the door swung shut behind the doctor. The last several hours were beginning to take their toll. Bowing his head, he folded his arms tightly across his chest.

In one sense, Jimmy had been prepared for the long wait that night by years of waiting as a child: waiting to eat, waiting for hand-me-downs, waiting to grow up. Having nothing as a child made emptiness seem normal. Now that he had Wanda, though, the thought of losing her was unbearable. For one split moment, Jimmy felt as if he were again becoming that little barefoot boy, alone and vulnerable to the bullies.

Jimmy blinked hard, as he had a hundred times before, and the image in his mind of the lonely little boy he had once been started to fade. He had started to believe that person no longer existed. He knew he wasn't alone any longer. He had also believed, however, that no one could disrupt the life of his growing family.

"Damn you," he muttered as the image of the robber leading Wanda at gunpoint out of the store flashed through his brain.

Jimmy turned to the empty waiting room and chose a seat.

Oh, Wanda, Jimmy thought, his arms still folded tightly across his chest. *You've got to be OK.* As the hours ticked by, Jimmy couldn't remember anything more difficult than having to wait for the doctor to reappear.

Oh, no, Jimmy suddenly thought. When he had returned to his car following the robbery he realized that the car door out of which he and Traci had been forced had been left open. The thought that he had next, a thought that he had not had earlier as he drove to the hospital, made him despair. *Where are the puppies?*

16

Earlier that evening, at about 7:30, Detective Ellis Bellamy of the Horry County Police Department (HCPD) received a call to go to a dirt road off Highway 544 where two hostages from a robbery in Georgetown had been shot and left for dead. The 20-year veteran was needed to work the scene. Bellamy noted with dismay as he arrived that the scene was a dirt road, and the rain that had fallen intermittently during the day was now steady. Donning his rain gear, Bellamy grabbed a flashlight and got out of his car.

Arriving immediately after Bellamy was Corporal Ralph Vaught, also of the Horry County Police. The two officers began their grisly work, and despite the rain, quickly found two big blood spots, one larger than the other, in the middle of the dirt road. Extending the search to the area immediately around the blood spots, the officers found several teeth, apparently human, and pieces of bone, one large enough to identify as a jawbone.

In addition, bits of meat, some type of flesh, were scattered over a large area and down in the ditch adjacent to the road. Vehicle tracks along the road were later determined to belong to the ambulance that transported the female hostages to the hospital. The teeth and bone particles that Bellamy gathered were put in a blue, white and green Dixie cup and turned in later as evidence from the scene.

While Bellamy and Vaught worked the crime scene, Chief of the Horry County Police, Herman Enzor, huddled with several other officers for a brief strategy meeting at their cars parked alongside Highway 544. Enzor provided his men with additional information garnered from the hospital. One of the hostages had been conscious when she arrived and had the presence of mind to know she had information the police wanted and needed. Asking for a pen, the young woman had written on the paper of the examination room table where she lay face down. In addition to providing good descriptions of her assailants and the car they drove, the woman had written, "WE WERE RAPED." Enzor was positive the descriptions were of the very same men sought by the Colleton County and Georgetown County Police.

Now that the manhunt had moved north into Horry County, Chief Enzor was in charge. As officers from other jurisdictions arrived, the order was given to begin a systematic search of the 60-mile-long beach area. In addition to officers from the Myrtle Beach, Conway, and Horry County Police Departments, and state officers from the State Law Enforcement Division, the Highway Patrol, and the Department of Wildlife, the canvass would require the cooperation of the Georgetown and Colleton County Police Departments. Since their chiefs and some of their officers had been following the manhunt all day, Enzor knew that all involved were eager to continue the pursuit of the criminals.

Earlier that afternoon, Officer Glen "Buddy" Causey of the Horry County Police Department thought that he might get to go home early. Things had been quiet at the station. Since it was February, "early" meant after dark but before the wee hours of the morning. In 1979, shift work hadn't caught on in the largely rural jurisdiction and Causey was accustomed to working "from-until." His wife had long ago adjusted to seeing him when she saw him.

At approximately eight o'clock that evening, the dispatcher relayed a call just received from the Colleton County Sheriff. "Be on the lookout," the caller requested, "for two unidentified, white males driving a brown, Ford Maverick with out-of-state tags, possibly Louisiana."

"Holy cow, look at this, Buddy." Detective Enoch Smith hurried into the room with the bulletin. "Just in. It's going on now."

Causey looked up from what he was doing. Just then,

the phone rang. Causey grabbed the receiver as he took the report from Smith.

"Yes, sir," Causey said into the phone and mouthed, "Enzor," to Smith.

"We just got it." Causey looked at the report. Several seconds later, he said, "We're on our way, Chief," and hung up.

• ❖ •

Causey and Smith connected with Enzor as soon as they reached Highway 544. Police cruisers and unmarked cars rolled in continually while Enzor updated the two senior officers. Additional reports indicated that the two suspects were driving a tan Maverick with West Virginia tags. One of the white males was middle aged and stocky. The younger man was thinner, with blond hair. The suspects were now not only sought for a robbery and murder in Colleton County, but for two murders and an attempted murder in Georgetown County, and armed robbery and kidnapping in Horry County. Two hostages that had been taken in Georgetown and transported into Horry had just been found and were being treated for gunshot wounds to the head. There was no question that the heavily armed suspects were very dangerous and headed north. It was believed that the suspects would either try to make a run for the North Carolina border or, more likely, hole up for the night in one of the hundreds of motels in Myrtle Beach. In addition, given the magnitude of the crimes committed, capturing the heavily armed men would not be easy and might involve a shoot-out. It had been 75 years since an officer had been killed in the line of duty in Horry County.

Approximately an hour into the search, Lt. Causey responded to a call from Captain George "Buddy" Fowler for assistance. "I'm tailing a car matching the suspect's description on 544. The car's carrying two white males, headed northbound toward the beach."

Causey looked down at the shotgun on the front seat and responded. "This is Lt. Causey. I'm about a mile and a half from you." Causey felt his heart begin to pound as he pressed the pedal in the unmarked Crown Victoria and the large engine came to life. Causey had made hundreds of arrests and had been in more than one fist fight, but he had not had to draw and use his weapon in all of his years with the force.

"I'm on them," Fowler said.

"We're about a mile and a half away," Causey radioed back. Causey, Smith, and two officers riding in the back seat of the car checked their weapons.

"If this is them," Causey said, primarily to the officers in the back, "they got nowhere to go." The long stretch of Highway 544 where Fowler had sited the Maverick didn't intersect with any other major roads. "Nothing but woods out here. The dogs'll get 'em if we don't. Remember your families."

Causey glanced again at the shotgun and thought of his wife, Janice. Rarely had she ever complained about his dangerous work. That didn't mean she was comfortable with the occasional talk she heard around town of her husband's exploits. She had gotten a little ornery, Buddy recalled, when he failed to tell her about the time he had to wrestle a shotgun away from a man inside the police station when the man showed up angry because his sister had been detained. By and large, though, Buddy and Janice agreed that she didn't need to know about the day-to-day events related to his job.

Honey, I'm gonna be sure to make it home to tell you about this one, Buddy thought.

Rounding the last curve, Causey's car came upon Fowler's car and the Maverick.

"What's wrong with this?" Causey asked of no one in particular. Fowler's car and that of the potential suspects were traveling at 35 miles an hour, not exactly the pace one might assume desperate fugitives would adopt.

"I see you," Fowler said to his approaching colleagues. "I know what you're thinking. This is it. Nothing erratic, the same speed the whole time. Carolina tags, too."

"I'm coming up beside you," Causey said. "Just around this curve, hit your blue light. It's a good spot. No houses. Let's see what they do."

When the blue lights flashed, the driver of the Maverick immediately slowed and pulled the car to the shoulder. Causey and Fowler hit their spotlights. The two heads of the occupants of the Maverick, clearly visible in the bright lights, didn't move.

"This is it, boys," Causey said, and opened his door.

"You in the Maverick," Fowler said over his loudspeaker. "Do exactly as I instruct. Get out of your car slowly, holding your hands up where we can see them."

As the doors of the Maverick opened, officers wielding shotguns rushed up from behind the car on both sides.

"Out of that car," Causey shouted to the driver. An obese young man held his arms out of the car and tried to rock forward to get up. It was apparent to Causey that the fat man would either have to use his arms to pull himself out or he would need assistance. Without hesitation, Causey grabbed the man's left arm and in a rush of adrenaline jerked him out of the car.

"Lay down on your belly with your hands stretched up over your head," Causey yelled.

"It's wet," the young man protested, but began getting to his knees anyway.

Within seconds, Detective Smith had the passenger out and lying close to the driver on the wet asphalt.

"These look like kids," Causey said. "You boys have identification?"

"Yes, sir," the boys said nervously. "Did we do something wrong?"

Causey looked at Fowler. "Goddamnnit," he said.

For the next several minutes, while additional officers arrived, the boys continued to lie in the rain while Fowler confirmed their identities. The boys were local teens out in a parent's car, the same make, same year, and same color as the criminals' vehicle. Causey apologized to the boys for the inconvenience and the scare.

"You boys have to get this car off the road. One of these officers will escort you. We're looking for a car just like this. You understand? You can't be out tonight in this car."

The wet teens took their identifications and got back into their car.

Causey, Smith, and the two officers piled back into the cruiser and sat for a moment, exchanging relieved glances. "Did you see the looks on those ol' boys' faces?" Causey finally said. The officers chuckled to break the tension and then continued to sit silently. Having nervous fingers on the triggers of loaded shotguns pointed at teenagers out in daddy's car was a frightening experience for everyone.

A short while later, just as the officers had calmed down from their close call, the radio suddenly sounded. A couple of Myrtle Beach police had spotted a tan Maverick on the south end of the beach, parked behind a motel on the boulevard.

Pressing the gas pedal, Causey glanced over at Smith, and then in the rearview mirror at the officers in back. "Hang on, boys," he said. "Here we go again."

17

"**W**here's your father?" Beth asked as the man she knew as John Wolf sat down. Woomer lit the joint he was carrying.

"He ain't coming," Woomer said. "He's got some business to attend to. You might can meet him later, though."

Beth and a few others were watching television. Woomer engaged in small talk, primarily with the males at the impromptu party. Alcohol and marijuana were used freely, and several persons moved in and out of the small room throughout the night.

"What'cha watching?" Woomer said. "Wanna listen to some jams?"

"All I got is a radio, but if y'all want to," Beth said.

"OK by me," Sheila said. Turning to Woomer, she asked, "So you and your father been doing construction work?"

Woomer fiddled with the radio until he found what he liked.

"Yeah, we been doing some construction work," Woomer said, then added, "and some hustling."

"Hustling?" Sheila asked.

"That's right." Woomer replied. "Just today we took some people for nine hundred dollars."

"Nine hundred?" Sheila laughed. "Well, you'll just have to tell me and Beth how you did that. I don't have any money myself."

"Shoot," Woomer said, "I ain't even gonna begin to waste my time telling a woman about it."

"You and your father must be two enterprising fellas," Sheila quipped. "C'mon, tell us the secret."

"No, I can't tell you," Woomer said. "But I will tell you one thing. If you're willing to hustle for money, you got to be willing to do anything."

"Anything?" Sheila asked.

"That's right," Woomer said matter of factly. "Go to no limits, even if it means killing somebody. You just go out and do it."

Sheila stared at Woomer.

"Why, who have you killed?" Beth asked.

Woomer put up his hands, sat back, and said, "Don't pay any attention to me. I've been drinking too much, that's all."

The radio traffic of the police cars taking part in the search for the murderers was light, especially considering that several dozen cars were creeping slowly about. Back roads and dirt lanes were searched, and spotlights were shone in nooks and crannies, anywhere big enough to hide. The key was to find the Maverick.

Just before midnight, Detective Bellamy got a call to go to the south end of Myrtle Beach. Two Myrtle Beach officers, Corporal Ray Lewis and Patrolman Donald Vaught, had spotted a 1972 Maverick fitting the description of the wanted vehicle right down to the broken taillight.

When Bellamy arrived at the Komo Mai, he received instructions to sit tight and wait.

Meanwhile, the conversation at the party had turned to money again.

"We do, too, have a lot of money downstairs," Woomer said. "Two stacks of it." He was having a hard time convincing his new friends.

"Oh, I bet you don't have that much money," Sheila teased.

"Shoot, girl, I'll take you down there and show it to you."

"No, that's OK," Sheila said. "I'm just working at McDonald's. It'd probably just make me cry to see all that money."

"You don't believe me, I can tell. We got guns and money down there. C'mon, I'll take you down there. What do you mean, you don't believe me?"

"No," Sheila said again, "that's OK. I don't want to see it."

"Damn," Woomer said in disgust. "I tell you what. You come down with me, bring Beth with you, and if the money's not there, I'll give you both twenty dollars."

"Your father probably wouldn't let us see it," Sheila teased again.

"My father? Shoot, I'll pull a pistol and put it on him. He'd show you the money. C'mon, I'll give you twenty dollars."

"No, that's OK. We believe you."

Woomer sat by the radio during the party and periodically turned the volume down so low that the others complained. Each time someone heard a song he or she liked and turned the volume up, Woomer would eventually turn it back down again.

When the partiers ran out of mixers for the liquor, Woomer suggested that Sheila and Beth go down to his room and ask his father for some change for the drink machine.

"It'd be all right," Woomer said. "Ask him about the money, too."

"Wanna go?" Beth asked Sheila.

"Wait a minute," Woomer said. "On second thought, you'd better not. If somebody my father doesn't know comes to the door, with all the money and everything, he might shoot you."

"Shoot us?" Beth said. "We don't need that."

Woomer stood up. "Better let me go with you."

"Well, if he's going, y'all just go ahead," Sheila said, looking around for a clock. "I got to go to work in the morning, early. I'm gonna be going soon."

Beth and Woomer went down the stairs to Room 8. Woomer stuck his head in the cracked-open door. "Hey, man," he said. "We need some change for the drink machine."

Skaar came out of the room several seconds later with a handful of change.

While Beth, Woomer, and Skaar were still standing in the drink machine alcove at the base of the stairs, Fred Whitehead suddenly rounded the corner. Dressed in a sport coat, Whitehead stopped, grimaced and looked slowly at all three, but said nothing. Skaar returned Whitehead's stare with a menacing look of his own. Whitehead then turned and walked directly into Woomer's and Skaar's room.

Skaar leaned over to Woomer and said, "I'll take care of this. You go on back upstairs for a while and stay there."

"Let's go," Woomer said to Beth and turned to climb the stairs.

"That fella looked kinda mean," Beth said when they got out of earshot. "Staring like that."

"Who? My father?"

"Well," Beth said, considering that was also true. "I meant the other one."

"Don't worry about that. It ain't nothing," Woomer said. "Some business is all."

"Thought you said y'all were new in town, didn't know nobody," Beth said. "He seemed to know right where he was going."

"Just best you forget about that," Woomer replied. "I'm telling you. My father'll handle it. He knows what's what. He's cool."

Woomer continued to brag about Skaar and his tolerance for liquor and drugs when they got back upstairs. "Shoot, he drank near two fifths of whiskey today, by hisself," Woomer said matter of factly. Not to be outdone, Woomer then added, "Course I've done plenty of drugs, myself. Did some Quaaludes today." As further evidence of his drug savvy, Woomer stated, "I can get you some cocaine, too. Pretty soon some men are coming down from West Virginia, and we'll be doing some business. If you want some, I can get you all the cocaine you want."

"I don't think so," Beth replied.

The party moved down the hall to the room of John, another young person staying at the motel for the winter. Beth left for about half an hour to go to the nearby Gaslight Tavern to see her brother but, when she returned, she rejoined the group.

"Damn, long as you was out, we should've got you to get some papers," Woomer said. The group still had marijuana but no way of rolling joints. "I got five dollars if you'll go get some. You can take my car if you want."

"Oh, man," Beth said. She wasn't sure she wanted to go back out. "Why don't you go with me?" she suggested to Woomer.

"No, I ain't going. You can take my car, but I ain't going." Woomer shook his head. "Take him with you," he suggested, pointing to John. "Me, I'm gonna sit right here and wait. Here's five dollars to get 'em." Woomer held out the money.

"Five dollars for a pack of rolling papers?" Beth asked. "They're only fifty cents."

"Go ahead and pick up some munchies, too, then. It don't matter."

"All right, I'll go," Beth said.

Beth did not take the Maverick as suggested by Woomer and instead drove Sheila's car a couple blocks to a convenience store. On the way back with the papers and some potato chips, Beth noticed, but didn't think anything of, a police car sitting at the back of the motel.

18

From where he was parked at the Komo Mai, Detective Bellamy couldn't see most of the additional officers arriving on the scene. But he knew from his radio that dozens of police had surrounded the building and cordoned off nearby streets. There was no escape route for the fugitives.

Several of Bellamy's colleagues, including Buddy Causey, Buddy Fowler, and a SLED agent named Michael Carter soon arrived. Agent Carter was the son of Sheriff Carter of Georgetown County and along with his father had followed the crime spree since Georgetown. Agent Carter had also earlier viewed the bodies of Arnie Richardson and Earl Dean Wright and, in addition, visited Jack's Mini-mall following the robbery.

Causey, Carter, and Fowler slipped into the motel office and met with the motel manager and his wife. The manager told them that two men from West Virginia fitting the descriptions the officers provided had been registered at the motel for two days under the names John Fisher and John Wolf. Consulting a floor plan of the motel, the manager pointed out Room Number 8, an end room on the first floor.

Back-up units were called to move in closer. More than fifty officers, most armed with rifles and shotguns pointed at doors and windows, had the L-shaped building surrounded.

The door to Room 8 was cracked open as the officers quietly moved into place. When the signal was given, Carter and Causey slipped up to the door. Carter tapped on the door using a long flashlight and stepped to the side.

"This is the police," Carter said loudly into the door crack. "We have the motel surrounded. Give yourself up."

● ❖ ●

Beth had gone back up to John's room on the second floor and had given Woomer the rolling papers. Woomer prepared to roll a joint when a noise from outside caught his attention. Woomer quickly turned the radio down and went to the front window.

"What is it?" Beth asked.

Woomer was unable to see out of the window and opened the door. When he stepped on the landing for a better view, a voice boomed, "Get back in your room and stay there."

Woomer quickly stepped back into the room.

"What was that?" Beth asked, her voice registering alarm. "What's going on?"

"Looks like four men in black coats with sawed-off double-barrel shotguns," Woomer answered. "Damn. I bet they're gonna rob somebody."

● ❖ ●

Downstairs, the window curtains to Room 8 parted briefly as Skaar peeked out. The officers stayed back away from the windows. Carter reached around the concrete partition that shielded him and tapped the flashlight on the door again. The crack in the door widened.

"We have the building surrounded," Carter repeated. "Come out and give yourself up."

Several seconds later, the door was slammed shut.

Skaar broke the bathroom window and attempted to flee out the back of the building but retreated into the room when he saw the line of armed officers behind the motel. Approximately fifteen seconds later, a muffled blast was heard coming from the room.

"That's a shotgun," Carter said. "One shot only, though."

"Misfire, maybe. In any event, there's gotta be another one," Causey said. "Tell 'em to go ahead with the gas."

While the other officers provided cover to the back of the motel, Detective Bellamy crept to the kitchen window of the room to toss a tear gas grenade inside. The first grenade hit the sill, bounced back and spent itself on the ground.

While the police in back waited for the gas to clear, Causey became irritated when the blond man again stuck his head out of the upstairs room. "I told you to stay inside," he yelled.

Woomer again ducked back and shut the door.

Bellamy's second grenade toss smashed through the kitchen window and filled Room 8 with tear gas. Causey watched as gas seeped out of the eve on the front of the building. "Nobody could stand that," he said, his shotgun ready.

Upstairs, Woomer paced the small room and cursed. "Calm down," he ordered the group. Several persons were talking at once. They thought they had heard a popping noise outside.

"I got to think," Woomer said.

"I heard a gunshot," John said.

"No," Woomer said, straining to listen, "That weren't no gunshot."

Woomer headed for the light switch. Over his shoulder he told John to turn off the television. Woomer opened the door a third time. Tear gas began seeping in the room and Woomer was again ordered to go back inside.

As he slammed the door, Woomer said in frustration, "Damn, here I am, and I'd even have me some hostages."

"What's going on?" Beth began to cry.

Woomer sat beside Beth and put his arm around her. "Don't worry," he said. "If anybody's gonna be in trouble, it's gonna be me, not you."

Woomer thought for a moment and then said, "I got an idea. What's your last name?"

When Beth told him, he said, "OK, if anyone asks you, I'm your husband."

Beth looked at him with uncertainty. "What?"

"You heard me. If anyone asks, I'm your husband."

"Why would anyone ask me that?"

Ignoring her, Woomer asked, "Where's the key to your room, Beth?"

"Why do you want –"

"Where's the key?" Woomer asked insistently.

"It's in my coat pocket," she said, still crying.

Woomer got the key, took Beth by the arm and began pulling her toward the door. "C'mon, we're going to your apartment."

Woomer opened the door and pulled Beth out of the room and down the hallway. He was unable to get the key quickly into the door and handed it to Beth.

"You, up there, hurry up," boomed the voice from below. "Get in that room and stay there."

Once in the room, Woomer took the bag of marijuana out of his pocket and put it on the windowsill. He then removed his shoes and socks, put his wallet on the bedside table, and sat back on the bed.

Woomer made Beth sit quietly and listen with him to the commotion outside.

A few minutes later, police wearing gas masks moved into Room 8. Skaar had turned the .20 gauge sawed-off shotgun on himself and lay on his side between the second double bed away from the door and the wall of the bathroom. Detective Causey's flashbulb memory of the event was of Skaar's brain tissue dripping down the wall beside the bed. The blast dislodged Skaar's false teeth and pushed them forward so that they protruded eerily out of the dead man's mouth. Scattered about the room was evidence that someone else had been staying in the room. Several guns and rifles lay on one of the beds on an old spread. The television was still on.

Following a cursory search of the gas-filled room, the shotgun-toting officers filed back out into the fresh air.

"Where's the other one?" Carter asked.

Causey looked across the courtyard. "I think we just saw him. Jobe, come with me." Jobe Blain and a third officer accompanied Causey to the upstairs room that the thin blond man and the young woman had just entered.

The officers rapped on the door.

"Go to the door, Beth," Woomer ordered. "Now, remember, tell 'em I'm your husband."

Beth nervously crossed the room and opened the door. She saw several police officers down in front of the motel but saw none at her door.

"Watch it," Beth heard someone say that she couldn't see. "He's got a girl with him."

Beth stood in the doorway and trembled.

Causey took a step out from the wall so he could see Beth. To him, she looked like she was just a young girl. "Ma'am, the man who entered this room a few minutes ago, where is he from?"

"West Virginia," Beth replied. Tears welled in her eyes.

"Send that young man out here, now," Causey ordered.

Beth turned and said, "Johnny, they want you outside."

"Who is it?" Woomer asked.

"It's the police," Beth said.

"What do they want?" Woomer asked.

"Go out there," Beth said loudly. "Get out of my room."

Woomer got up and started toward the door. "You would know it," he said to Beth as he passed by. "This is the one and only time I haven't had a gun in my back pocket."

When Woomer appeared at the door, Blain and Causey reached into the doorway, grabbed Woomer's arms, pulled him out of the room, and bent him forward over the rail on the landing.

"Is that your room down there, Number 8?" Causey asked as he frisked Woomer.

"Yes, sir."

"What's your name, son?"

"John Wolf."

Woomer was handcuffed and led barefoot down the stairs to Causey's unmarked car. Woomer and Causey got in the back. In the presence of Sheriff Brown, the man calling himself Wolf was read his rights. When asked who the man in Room 8 was, Woomer identified him only as "Gene."

19

J immy was sitting alone at 2 a.m. when the police called the hospital. Standing by the nurses' station, Jimmy got the news he'd hoped for: the kidnappers had been caught. One was already dead. The other one, the skinny, mouthy one, was in police custody. *Don't suppose they'd let me and Don have him for a while,* Jimmy thought.

Jimmy thanked the nurse and began pacing again. He'd already established a routine of sitting, then pacing, then asking, and then doing it all over again.

Jimmy was pacing later when Sheriff Woodrow Carter and his son, Agent Michael Carter, walked in with a couple of additional officers. Jimmy listened quietly to the explanation of how the capture had occurred. The sheriff relayed that the police thought Jimmy had a right to know.

"It's just so hard to believe," Jimmy said. "Why would these guys want to do something so senseless?"

"We're still trying to figure it out ourselves," Agent Carter said, and then added reassuringly, "but don't worry, we will."

"I feel so helpless," Jimmy said. He knew better than to blame himself, but couldn't help feeling that things might have been different if he'd – if he'd what? He knew there was nothing he could have done.

"You're not responsible, Mr. Summers," Sheriff Carter said. "That's one of the reasons we came, to let you know that these were bad men." Carter held out pictures for Jimmy to see. "Here's what they did right before they got to y'all."

Jimmy was astonished. The pictures showed a man and woman who had been shot. Blood appeared to be everywhere. Tiny slippers rested in a pool of blood and a little girl's pocketbook lay on the floor nearby.

Carter quickly added, "Those men wouldn't have hesitated to kill every one of you, children and all. You did the right thing, the only thing you could have done. I wish we could tell you something better than that."

Jimmy felt himself becoming angry again.

Sheriff Carter spoke to calm Jimmy. "How's your wife?" Carter probably knew more about Wanda's condition than Jimmy.

"I don't know," Jimmy said. "She's been in surgery for a few hours. They've got to be fixin' to tell me something here, soon. At least, I hope so."

Don Sellers suddenly walked in the emergency room entrance. When Don left Charleston he had driven straight to Grand Strand General to check on Jimmy and Wanda.

Jimmy rushed over and the two men embraced. The look on Don's face told Jimmy the worst had happened.

"She didn't make it," Don said, wiping his eyes. "Son of a bitch put a bullet in her brain. She died in the hospital in Charleston."

The numbness Jimmy felt suddenly became an ache. "Oh, God, Don," Jimmy said. The two men stood awkwardly and embraced again. Jimmy felt as if Don might squeeze the breath out of him.

"I didn't get to see her, man," Don stammered. The tall man wiped his eyes on his shirtsleeve.

Jimmy realized that Don's last image of Louise was essentially his own last image of Wanda. Both men had watched as their wives were pushed roughly toward the door of the store. Only now Don would never get to see his wife again. That terrible image of tiny Louise crying as she was being shoved by the gunman out of the door into the dark night would forever be Don's last memory of his wife alive.

Oh, God, please, Jimmy prayed, *don't let that be the last time I get to see Wanda alive.*

"How's Wanda?" Don asked.

"She's still in surgery. She was shot in the head, too, from what I gather, but she's alive. They tell me they're doing everything they can."

"That's what they told me, too," Don said.

Jimmy stared at Don, and then suddenly asked, "Did you hear? They got 'em."

"They did?" Don replied.

Agent Carter had been standing nearby. Stepping up, he said, "Guys, if we could ask you a few more questions, we'd appreciate it. And we might could answer some of yours."

"You got 'em?" Don asked quickly.

"Yes," Carter said. "One of them killed himself at a motel in Myrtle Beach. We captured the other one and he's in jail now."

"Which one's dead?" Don asked, his eyes narrowing.

"The older one, shot himself when we moved in. The younger one didn't have a gun on him. We caught him without a fight."

"Should have shot him, too, the son-of-a-bitch," Don said bitterly. "He's the one – why didn't you shoot him?" Don's face appeared hard. "At least one of 'em is dead," he said, and then added, "I'll answer any questions you have."

Don and Jimmy spoke with the police for several minutes, and then, after stopping by the nurses' station, went to the cafeteria for a cup of coffee.

"I got her ring," Don said when they sat down. He held Louise's wedding ring in his hand, nervously flipping it from side to side as one might a coin. When he tried to poke his finger through it, the small ring would only fit the last joint of his pinky. "I promised Louise that I'll see 'em dead, both of 'em," Don said. A gleam suddenly appeared in his eyes. "And they got 'em," he said excitedly, "and one's already dead. Good." Don clutched the ring tightly in his fist. "That other son-of-a-bitch had better fry. And when he does, I'll be there."

Jimmy listened as Don told him of his trip to Charleston. Jimmy ached for his friend and, for moments at a time, began to experience Don's sadness over losing Louise.

What if it had been Wanda? Jimmy thought, and then had the horrible realization of, *What if it is Wanda?*

At 4 a.m., Jimmy was told that Wanda was out of surgery and that she was stable.

"Mr. Summers," Dr. Eckert said, "your wife's been hurt

real bad. She's had extensive damage to the lower part of her face. We've done what we could for now."

What does that mean, "for now"? Jimmy didn't understand. Was he being told that Wanda wasn't going to recover from the surgery?

"She's gonna live, isn't she, Doctor?"

"Yes, we think so. We were able to stop the bleeding, which is good, but there's a lot that remains to be done."

Jimmy felt relief flood through his body. He took a deep breath. "Is she gonna be okay?" Jimmy searched the doctor's face for a sign - any sign – indicating that the worst was over.

"We don't know for certain," Eckert said. "We had to put about two hundred stitches in her tongue. I'm afraid I can't guarantee that she will ever be able to talk again. But we're optimistic. Let's just take this as it goes."

"But, sooner or later, she'll be okay?"

"Right now she's stable," the doctor answered. "Like I said, let's just take this one day at a time."

20

The man who called himself "John Wolf" was driven to the Horry County Jail in Conway. A uniformed guard stood outside the holding cell where he was placed.

Approximately two hours later, Detectives Causey and Smith took the prisoner into an open area and sat him down to talk. Several minutes into the conversation, Causey received a phone call from Michael Carter.

Following the arrest, Agent Carter had gone back into Beth's room and found the marijuana on the windowsill and the wallet Woomer put on the bedside stand. The wallet contained the identification of John Wolf.

When the police searched Room 8, however, and the Maverick, other items were found that tied the suspects to the crimes. These items included several silver coins belonging to John Turner and an assortment of firearms; four of the guns had belonged to Arnie Richardson. In addition, identification cards belonging to Richardson were found, plus photographs of his wife and two children, photographs of Earl Dean and her parents, and other items from Richardson's wallet. Apparently Skaar had a practice of saving identification cards of his victims, putting the cards he intended to use in his wallet, and placing the others in a bag. The police would later tie Skaar to unsolved crimes in several states.

Most relevant for Causey were documents found by Carter that clearly identified the suspect as Ronald Raymond Woomer of Huntington, West Virginia.

"I do believe our boy's real name is Woomer," Causey said as he rejoined Smith and the suspect. When Woomer was confronted with the new information, he conceded his name and said that people called him "Rusty."

It was apparent to Causey that Woomer was sleepy. He could barely keep his eyes open, and he slurred his speech. Causey wasn't certain but thought Woomer was under the influence of some type of drug or drugs. Recognizing the legal implications of interrogating an obviously drugged suspect, Causey ordered that Woomer be taken back to the holding cell. A few minutes later, Woomer was relocated to yet another cell where he was allowed to sleep.

Causey remained at the station for a few hours exchanging stories with other law enforcement personnel and tying up loose ends. He knew when he went home around dawn that sleep would be hard to come by.

● ❖ ●

Seven hours later, at approximately 1 p.m., the official interrogation of Woomer began. Just prior to entering the interrogation room, Causey was asked by the sheriff of Colleton County if Woomer would be questioned about the entire day of criminal activity and not just about the crimes committed in Horry County. Causey assured the sheriff that he and Chief Enzor had discussed the issue and agreed that a comprehensive confession made sense, given that the crimes involved all three jurisdictions.

Causey had heard about the death of Louise Sellers the previous evening, but he wasn't sure of the status of Wanda Summers. He had not seen Wanda or had contact with any of her family either the night before or that day.

When the interrogation began Woomer appeared refreshed and alert. Dressed in an orange prison suit, he sat with his wrists cuffed closely together in front of his body. The interrogation took place in a private room, sparsely furnished with only a table and two chairs, and included only Woomer and Causey. A tape recorder sat on a nearby table but was not turned on for the first hour of the session. Causey was armed and dressed in plain clothes. The stress of the previous night's ordeal had not yet revealed itself in his facial expression.

Causey's interrogation technique was tried and true to

his personal style. He worked with an easy, ol' boy manner, often matching or at least familiar to that of the suspects he faced. Beginning with casual questions, Causey's aim was simply to get the suspect talking. Causey believed that somewhere deep down in their hearts, criminals wanted to tell what they'd done. His job was to make them comfortable enough to do just that.

Causey tossed his cigarettes on the table in front of Woomer. "Help yourself whenever you want," he said, reaching into his shirt pocket. "I got some matches here."

Woomer immediately reached out and began to maneuver the pack as it lay flat on the table. Grasping the first cigarette to stick out, Woomer raised both wrists to his face. Causey lit his own cigarette and extended his hand with the match across the table. Woomer leaned forward, his eyes meeting Causey's as the tip of his cigarette began to glow.

"Is this your kind?" Causey asked. They both glanced at the pack.

"No, sir. But they'll do," Woomer said. "Long as it's not menthol."

"Were you able to get some rest?"

"Yes, sir. I woke up and didn't know where I was. It took me a minute to remember everything."

"But you do remember?" Causey asked.

In other cases, Causey had to work on suspects for hours getting them to loosen up before they'd begin to talk. Then they often had to be painstakingly coaxed through every admission. Maybe this time would be different. *Woomer might be cooperating already*, Causey thought.

"Yes, sir," Woomer said. "It don't seem like it was me doing all those things, but I do remember."

Causey thought Woomer seemed to be relaxed. *Why not give it a shot?* Causey thought. *See if he's ready to talk.* "Let's talk about yesterday," Causey said.

Thus began the confession of Ronald R. Woomer to the events of February 22, 1979, that resulted in the deaths of John Turner, Arnie Richardson, Earl Dean Wright, Louise Sellers, and the wounding and maiming of Wanda Summers. Woomer did not know during the interrogation that Wanda Summers and the five-year-old daughter of Arnie Richardson were still alive. In an effort to keep Woomer from a blame-it-on-the-other-guy strategy, he had also not been told of Skaar's suicide.

"Woomer was very polite," Causey recalled. "Yes, sir – no, sir. He cooperated from the beginning. I took notes and when I felt I had gone through everything, I asked Rusty if I could turn on the tape recorder. He said he didn't mind."

Relying on his notes, Causey led Woomer through the day's activities. Woomer spoke calmly about the crimes he and Skaar had committed without blaming Skaar and without attempting to minimize the role that each man had played in the day's tragic events. According to Causey, Woomer displayed no remorse, nor did Woomer falter when speaking of raping and killing.

"His voice was even," Causey said. "I'm telling you. He didn't display nervousness of any type." While relaying this story Causey shook his head slowly, lost in his thoughts for several seconds, and then added, "I'll never forget it. He was the most cold-blooded killer I've ever seen."

Causey stated that Woomer seemed relieved after confessing. Woomer thanked the detective for the cigarettes as the interrogation ended and was taken back to the cell where he had slept earlier. In 1979, suicide watches were not posted.

Causey immediately took the 45 minutes of taped conversation to the office of Chief Enzor and, together with the chief and a few other officers, played it back. The tape was then taken to a secretary to be transcribed.

Exhausted, but needing to see the crime scene, Causey left the police station and drove to the desolate area where Wanda Summers and Louise Sellers were raped and shot less than 24 hours earlier. The memory of the scene of the brutal attacks on the two women would forever remain with the detective.

21

J immy talked to the doctor early that Friday morning, then cleaned up as best he could. He hadn't found any time to sleep. Although he tried to address the questions that everyone calling the hospital and coming in and out seemed to have, he found he didn't have any more answers than anyone else. Late in the afternoon he entered the intensive care unit.

Wanda was strapped to the bed. Her face was completely bandaged except for one large hole around her eyes that extended to the tip of her nose; a tuft of Wanda's hair pushed up by the wrap-around bandage stuck up on the top of her head. Standing quietly by her bedside, Jimmy listened to the breathing sounds that his wife made through the tube that was inserted in her throat. The tube in her nose was for feeding.

According to the nurse, Wanda had been delirious and in and out of consciousness all day. Her fingernails had been hastily trimmed short, Jimmy had been told, to prevent her from hurting herself, as persons who have experienced trauma sometimes do. Jimmy stared at the blood beneath the ragged nails and knew Wanda would hate how they looked.

Jimmy knelt beside Wanda. Holding her hand in his, he bowed his head and began to pray.

That evening, Walter Cronkite began the CBS broadcast with news of the crime spree that had taken place the day before in South Carolina. Millions of Americans listened to the tragic story of a manhunt that had ended with the storming of a motel in Myrtle Beach and a suspect killing himself. A second suspect, Cronkite reported, had been caught and jailed; it was expected that he would be tried for murder.

For the public and many of the police involved in the manhunt, the storming of the Komo-Mai and Woomer's arrest had ended the nightmare. For the families of the victims, the nightmare had just begun.

22

Jim Dunn had barely been in office two months as the solicitor for Horry and Georgetown Counties when he had an opportunity to make good on a campaign promise. Dunn had assured voters that if elected he would seek the death penalty for any murder committed in his jurisdiction that involved aggravating circumstances. In a hastily prepared press release, Dunn announced Friday afternoon that the state would seek the death penalty against Ronald R. Woomer for the kidnap, rape and murder of Louise Sellers. Additional charges depended on whether Wanda lived or died.

Just a couple of years earlier, in 1977, Dunn had been appointed as the first public defender of Horry County. A local man, Dunn served in the Marine Corps before attending Wofford College and then The University of South Carolina Law School, graduating in 1963. Following law school, Dunn established a practice in Winston-Salem, North Carolina, and served on the legal staff of the National Labor Relations Board. By 1971, when Dunn returned to Conway to open a private practice, he was clear in his conviction to serve the public. The highly personable attorney moved easily among persons he perceived as the regular folks of society. Dunn professed a special affinity for farmers and African-Americans, persons he believed had worked particularly hard and struggled to make ends meet. Dunn was profoundly affected by the civil rights movement of the early 1960s and was often heard quoting Martin Luther King, Jr.

In the public defender's office, Dunn quickly established a reputation as a bulldog in the courtroom. The tenacity with which he performed his duties wasn't always appreciated, however. As the public defender he often represented politically unpopular clients. He was once accused of being anti-police as a result of a case during which he mercilessly grilled police officers who tried to defend evidence that Dunn thought had been sloppily gathered. In another instance, Dunn's clients were black men accused of raping a white woman who was a member of a prominent local family. Though his defense of the men was unsuccessful, Dunn put forth the same effort as he did for any other case. Jim Dunn was first and foremost a champion of the law.

Dunn did not find the work of a defense lawyer personally satisfying, however. Although he recognized that even guilty clients deserved an effective defense, he increasingly began to feel that he wasn't the best person to provide that defense. He had always believed strongly in the death penalty for certain crimes and began to question whether he was willing to continue to defend persons charged with aggravated murder and rape. By the early spring of 1978 Dunn made an important decision. Holding a campaign photo of himself taken as he stood next to the electric chair at the Death House in Columbia, Dunn announced his intention to run for the solicitor's position. The reaction to his decision in the community was positive. Many persons reasoned it would be better to have the powerful attorney arguing to put criminals in jail rather than arguing to keep them out.

Prior to the election for the solicitor's position, however, a chain of events initiated by a double-murder propelled Dunn to take decisive action and resign from the public defender's position after having served only ten months. William and Myrtie Moon of Socastee were found murdered in their convenience store on Saturday, March 18, 1978. Dunn was reportedly a friend of the Moon family. Early the following Monday, before he could be officially appointed to defend the two persons responsible for the Moon murders, Dunn resigned as public defender. As reasons for his resignation he cited his candidacy for the solicitor's position and his public stand in favor of capital punishment. Dunn thought it was possible, if not probable, that the conflict of interest between his political stance and the requirements of his job as public defender would enable persons he might defend to appeal on grounds of inadequate representation.

As a private attorney, Dunn assisted the lawyers hired by the Moon family in the successful prosecution of Rudolph Tyner in August of 1978. Tyner was given a death sentence. Dunn was subsequently elected solicitor and, two weeks after Woomer was arrested for his crime spree, Carlton Davis, Tyner's partner in the Moon murders, was successfully prosecuted. Dunn had the Davis case relocated to Georgetown and handled by Assistant Prosecutor Carroll Padgett.

The arrest of Woomer shortly after Dunn assumed office as solicitor signaled the beginning of a personal crusade for the colorful attorney that placed him at the forefront of a movement that is only now, 20 years later, beginning to garner widespread attention. Dunn's work in the public defender's office revealed to him an increasingly large segment of the population who he believed was being ignored by the American justice system. Within hours after the arrest of Woomer, Jim Dunn was able to ask in public for the first time, "What about the victims?"

23

The police had all they needed after Woomer's confession to go after at least one of the accomplices. At 7 p.m. Friday, Fred Whitehead was arrested at his coin shop. Not surprisingly, the story he had to tell differed significantly from Woomer's story. Whitehead had an advantage that Woomer didn't have, however; he knew that Skaar was dead. That information was repeated in newspapers and television stories. On the other hand, Whitehead knew very little of what had happened to Woomer. Whitehead felt sick to his stomach while watching the newsbreaks during the day as the motel where he'd engaged in illegal activities just the night before was shown from every possible angle. The reported activities made Whitehead cringe: rape, murder, kidnapping, robbery, Skaar dead, Woomer in custody and telling who knows what – it was all a nightmare.

The police let Whitehead sit in jail for a few hours while the rest of the contents of Room 8 at the Komo-Mai were examined.

The evening before, Officer Bob Riddle of the Myrtle Beach Police Department was at home watching the story unfold when he received a long distance phone call from Whitehead's wife. Calling from Kentucky, Ms. Whitehead said that she believed her husband was in trouble. She told Riddle of her husband's involvement with Woomer and Skaar and asked if Riddle would help her husband, if necessary.

Riddle had first met Ms. Whitehead when she called the Myrtle Beach Police to report a theft. Following an investigation during which Riddle and the wife of the coin dealer had several interactions, Riddle acted on a hunch and provided her with an opportunity to establish a relationship with the police. As the relationship developed, and without her husband's knowledge, Ms. Whitehead supplied Riddle with information about crimes involving persons her husband knew. Riddle credited the woman with helping to solve crimes the police might not have solved otherwise.

Whether Whitehead knew of his wife's plea for Riddle to intervene on his behalf following Woomer's and Skaar's crime spree is unknown. In any event, the Horry County Police were handling the case, and Riddle was asked to conduct the interrogation of Whitehead.

"I prefer that this conversation not be taped," Whitehead said immediately as he was seated in an interrogation room. Riddle agreed and let the machine sit idle. Riddle noted the time of 11:45 p.m. and then quickly steered the conversation to Whitehead's relationship with Fisher.

"This all goes back to John Fisher of Huntington," Whitehead said disgustedly, and then added, "He talks, but he don't do nothing." Whitehead had cursed Fisher all day. Where was the slick, con man now that the shit was hitting the fan?

"When did you last see Fisher?" Riddle probed.

"He was here with Gene over a month ago," Whitehead said.

Skaar and Fisher had stayed in Myrtle Beach for two days in January. Only Skaar had stayed at the Komo-Mai, but he had registered under the name John Fisher.

"Did they come to your shop?" Riddle asked.

"We were out of town," Whitehead said, referring to himself and his wife. "We went to the Atlanta Flea Market."

"So, you didn't see them in January?"

Whitehead had seen Fisher and Skaar. He bought a used Lincoln Continental from Fisher, an easily traceable transaction.

"Well, they were still here on Monday, when we got back," Whitehead admitted. "We saw them then. I bought his car so they would have money to get home on. I loaned them my Toyota to drive back up to Huntington. We wanted to get it up there so my stepdaughter could have it."

"So, you had been in contact with them?" Riddle asked. Phone traces would show a flood of calls had been made back and forth between Whitehead and Fisher on Whitehead's home phone and his business phone.

"Yes."

"So, did they come by your shop?" Riddle asked again.

"They were looking for something to do." Whitehead shifted in his seat.

"What do you mean, 'something to do'?" Riddle continued.

"They wanted me to tell them who had coins."

"Why would they ask you about who had coins?"

"Ah, you know," Whitehead said, aware the police knew of his extensive record, "when thieves get together they talk about who can be robbed." Whitehead's attempt at humor fell flat.

"What did you tell them?"

"I didn't tell them anything. Just talk, you know, there's nothing to it."

"Do you know what they did while they were here in January?"

"As far as I know, they didn't steal anything, if that's what you mean," Whitehead said.

"Do you know a John Turner?" The police had found two of Whitehead's business cards in Room 8. One was in the stolen wallet of Turner and the other was in Eugene Skaar's wallet.

Whitehead stiffened. Things were taking an ugly turn. "Yeah, I know John Turner. I met John at an antique show."

"Do you know where John Turner lives?"

"No," Whitehead said emphatically. "I don't know that."

"Don't know at all, huh?"

"I always took for granted he lives in Charleston."

"Did you know he's dead?"

"I heard that on the news."

"Tell us about Gene Skaar," Riddle said.

"I know Gene Skaar," Whitehead said, suddenly sure the police would try to tie him to the murder. "OK, Wednesday, day before yesterday, they came into my shop."

"Who're 'they'?" Riddle asked.

"The other guy was there. He wasn't introduced that I remember. We talked about coins they had. Well, they said they were going to get coins. That's how talk is, you don't believe them, it's just talk."

"Did you talk about John Turner with them?"

"No, John Turner was not mentioned. I didn't know about John Turner, what they were going to do."

"What did they do?" Riddle asked.

"It's been all over the TV. I did not buy any coins from them."

"Who said anything about buying coins?" Riddle asked.

"Look, they wanted me to buy coins from them. I did not buy coins from them."

"We know that wasn't the only time you saw them. Tell us what happened at the motel."

Whitehead hesitated, then said, "They didn't tell me where they were staying. Last night, Gene Skaar called, seven o'clock or eight o'clock, right before *Roots* comes on. He said he wanted to come to my house, that he had some stuff. I told him I would meet him wherever he was, and he told me he would meet me at the motel. When I got to the motel, the other guy was talking to a girl at the Coke machine. Gene told him to go upstairs, to stay out of the room for a while, that we would be talking."

Whitehead folded his arms and then sat forward. He looked at the floor.

"What did you talk about with Skaar?" Riddle asked.

"We went in there and Gene said they robbed and killed seven people between Wednesday and when they got back to Myrtle Beach. He's telling me all this. It was five, then six, then seven. He told me they robbed and killed Turner. He said they left no witnesses. Gene said he didn't do it, that the other guy blew them away."

"Did Skaar appear to be drunk?"

"No, Gene was not drunk. He said he wanted me to help him. They didn't have any money. He was persistent."

"Did you help him?"

"It boiled down to either I was going to help him out or he would have the other guy kill me. He mentioned that he knew where my family was. He ate at my house with John Fisher once in January."

"What did you do?"

"I got scared. I really didn't know what to do. He told me they didn't have much money, twelve or fifteen dollars, something around that. I went home very nervous."

"You just left then, after he told you about robbing and killing all those people?" Riddle asked. "That doesn't make sense."

"I got the feeling from Gene that they were not interested in robbing; they just wanted to kill. I went home and got some money and came back. It might have been two hundred dollars."

"Why would you get money?"

"I had to. Gene was really insistent. They were out on a limb."

"Did they say anything about coins at that time?"

"You got to understand, I was willing to agree with anything," Whitehead said, his voice beginning to sound desperate. "I knew he knew where I lived. Gene told me they killed John Turner. Gene told me John Turner knew he was going to die. He said south of Georgetown the other guy killed just to be killing. No witnesses, he said. They said they were going to leave and get some more stuff and I agreed to run it through my shop. He wanted me to line Myrtle Beach up as a drop off for all his coins."

"What did you say to that?"

"I told him I wouldn't handle it."

"Just like that, they tell you all about killing and you admit you're scared and you just say, 'No, I won't handle it'?"

"That's right. I was not going to give them any more money."

"What did he say to that?"

"He told me they were going to leave town, and I hoped they would."

"Did they have coins with them? You mentioned they had coins."

"I did not buy anything from them. There was stuff laying around, three or four guns, a sawed-off shotgun."

"What about coins?"

"There were coins on the bed partially covered by clothes – pinstriped suits. He wanted me to handle the coins. That's where the money came into the picture."

"So, he wanted money for the coins?"

"I told him I wouldn't handle blood money," Whitehead insisted. "We don't need stolen goods at the shop. We're doing too good."

As the interview concluded, Whitehead authorized the police to search his home and his coin shop. The coins stolen from Turner were not found during the thorough search of Whitehead's property or the exhaustive search of Room 8 at the Komo-Mai. The coins remain missing to this day.

24

"There you are, honey," Traci's Aunt Paula said as she got the last button through the loop. "You look so pretty."

Traci put her hands on her hips and turned to look admiringly at the white birthday dress in the full-length mirror. Her small hand ran down the crease of a ruffle. She knew smoothing was important; she had watched her momma do it many times.

"Momma's not gonna be here," Traci said, shaking her head and repeating what she had been told.

Paula took a deep breath. "That's right, Traci," she said. "Your momma can't be here, but she sends you all her love and kisses." Traci had been told that her mom wasn't feeling well. Paula's eyes misted and she turned her head. "Where were those other ribbons?" she said, as she tried to conceal her tears by appearing busy. "Do you like the ones you have?"

"I like the white ones," Traci said. Matching was another important rule about getting dressed that her mother had taught her. With short, little fingers spread wide, the soon-to-be six-year-old gingerly patted the looping bow of ribbon holding one clump of her dark blond hair in a pigtail on the side of her head.

Paula tugged gently on the left pigtail. "Turn a little bit, honey. Let me straighten this one."

"Don't undo it," Traci said, suddenly concerned.

"I'm not," Paula said reassuringly. "I'm making the bow a little bit bigger so it matches the other one."

"Good," Traci said. She turned her head and looked at each bow and smiled with satisfaction. "Daddy is going to be here," Traci said, nodding her head. She hadn't seen her

father since the incident, either, two days earlier. The night of
the rapes and the abduction, when Jimmy left the store to go
to the hospital, he had to know Traci was safe. He instructed
a close friend to take her to her granddaddy. Jimmy knew
Reggie would watch after Traci with his life. Jimmy had been
at the hospital since Thursday night.

"That's right," Aunt Paula replied. She looked at her
watch. "We're gonna see him in just a few minutes, when we
walk over to your house. I think he might have a birthday
surprise for you." Paula felt her eyes misting again. Neither
she nor the darling child smiling into the mirror had any
idea what life held in store for their family.

"A surprise?" Traci said excitedly. "Do you think I have
to wait until tomorrow to see it?" Traci's birthday was
actually Sunday, the next day, but the surprise party had
been planned for Saturday all along.

In a singsong voice, Paula said teasingly, "I-don't-
knowww." She grabbed Traci and pulled her closer for a hug.
"What do you think? You think you want to see some
presents today?" Paula nuzzled Traci's neck. It was almost
noon and time to go.

"Careful," Traci said, giggling. "You'll mess it up." Traci
turned to look in the mirror and again smoothed the front of
her dress, relieved that it still looked perfect.

Jimmy had instructed family members by phone where
the decorations for the party and the presents from Jimmy
and Wanda would be. Paula, Wanda's mother, and several
friends close to the family had spent some time the afternoon
before blowing up balloons and hanging crepe paper
streamers. Traci's new purple bicycle was adorned with a big
bow and placed under the banner that read, "Happy
Birthday, Traci."

Traci finished admiring her birthday dress and ran to
show her granddaddy and grandmomma. Her classmates
from kindergarten and most of the children from the
neighborhood were gathering at her house.

Scribbling on a legal pad from her hospital bed, Wanda
had given barely legible instructions that Traci's party could
not be marred by thoughts of sorrow or uncertainty. Staying
alive for Traci had been Wanda's primary reason to keep

going toward the lights down that cold dirt road. Trudging through the dark, covered with blood, Wanda's guiding thought was survival so her daughter would not grow up without a mom. As Wanda lay on her bed in the intensive-care unit, in spite of her drugged thoughts, she had to know that the party was a success.

Traci held her Aunt Paula's hand and walked along the dirt road separating her house from that of her grandparents'. The arrangement had been perfect for a child. Before Traci was born, her granddaddy and grandmomma decided to build a new house on their land and offered the old house to Jimmy and Wanda. The newly married couple accepted the offer and borrowed money to have the house moved to a piece of land just adjacent to the small farm on which Wanda had been raised. The loving care that Jimmy put into the restoration of the original family home helped to cement his relationship with his father-in-law. Night after night, after having already worked a full day, Jimmy and Wanda toiled until bedtime refurbishing the small house to make it a home. Wanda's father began to understand that Jimmy could accomplish anything through his determination and hard work. When Traci was a baby, her proud momma and daddy were able to take her to her new home – to their new home. Being able to walk on a seldom traveled dirt road to the grandparents' house was a country luxury; the arrangement had allowed Traci to grow up under the loving care and watchful eyes of her kin.

Traci looked at all of the cars at her house as she and Paula approached. Paula smiled, knowing the perceptive little girl was aware that something was going on.

Jimmy waited eagerly at the door. "Here they come," he said. "Everybody get ready."

Traci moved up the steps and into her daddy's arms as a cheer went up.

"Surprise!"

Traci hugged her daddy's neck.

"Thank you," Jimmy said to Paula. He followed Traci to her new bicycle.

Traci's eyes widened. A broad smile broke across her face and she hugged her daddy's legs.

"There you go, baby girl," Jimmy said above the din, smiling. Turning to the adults standing nearby, he added, "Now I won't have to carry her so much."

Jimmy and Paula stood and watched the happy crowd.

The joyous sounds of 50 kindergarten-age children singing "Happy Birthday" filled every square inch of the small house. Jimmy sat down with Traci and read aloud every card. When necessary, he helped her with the wrapping on the presents.

With all of the hugs and kisses, with the cake and ice cream and presents and friends and noise, Traci was sure this was the most special birthday ever.

Several hours later, as the last of the children prepared to leave, Traci climbed up on her father's lap and sat quietly for a minute. She was finally exhausted, as the adults had been for some time. "I wish Momma could've been here," she said softly in her father's ear.

Jimmy's arm reflexively tightened. "So do I, baby girl," he said quietly. "So do I."

25

Irby Walker barely raised his head off of the pillow at the sound of his wife's voice.

"Honey, it's Judge Floyd on the phone," she said into the darkened bedroom.

Walker would normally have been up with the sun on a Saturday morning, but a bout of the flu starting the afternoon before had driven him to bed early and kept him there, alternately sweating and shivering through the night.

"What is it?" he asked weakly. "Did he say?" In the three years Walker had been with the public defender's office, he had never gotten a work-related call at home on the weekend. He couldn't remember ever having gotten a call from a judge.

"No, but he said it's important," she replied. "I told him you were sick, and he apologized, but he said he had to talk to you anyway."

"OK, thank you." Walker picked up the receiver by the bed.

"Irby?" Judge Sidney Floyd said. "Sorry you're sick, but I need somebody down at the jail. The murder suspect – I'm sure you've seen the news – he needs y'all's services."

"All right," Walker said and sat up slowly. A throbbing feeling in his head washed down his body and made his ears ring. Judge Floyd's voice sounded distant as he relayed what he needed Irby to do. Walker agreed to be at the jail in a couple of hours, thanked the judge and hung up. He didn't think to ask why he and not Cleveland Stevens, the public defender and his boss, had been called. Only three years out of law school, Walker still retained an urgent sense of duty to the job. Though he didn't plan on remaining in the defender's office, he knew that time spent there would be invaluable when he later returned to private practice.

"Have I ever felt so bad?" Walker asked and then realized that his wife had gone to hang up the other phone.

Until he got the flu, Walker had watched along with everyone else the events of the preceding days. Judge Floyd's reference to a murder suspect had to mean Woomer. Walker didn't know of Whitehead's arrest and wouldn't learn of Woomer's confession until arriving at the jail.

"Are you going in?" Mrs. Walker said upon her return to the bedroom. "Did they call Steve?" she added, referring to Stevens.

"I don't know," Walker said, trying to avoid an explanation. Still sitting, he tried to assess whether standing would produce nausea. "I think I'm gonna need your help," he said a moment later. "Can you drive me?"

The jail where Woomer was held was located next to the Horry County Courthouse in Conway, the county seat of Horry. From the Walker home in the town of Surfside Beach, Conway was 18 miles and, depending on traffic, a half hour away.

"Sure," she said, looking at her watch. "You need help getting ready?"

"No, I'm just going to sit here a bit, though. I need to be there by one."

"OK," she said. "I'm ready when you are."

Irby had enjoyed his time spent working for the county and felt he owed a debt of gratitude to Cleveland Stevens, a man whom he considered a true mentor. Stevens taught Walker that individuals make a difference if they are willing to dedicate themselves to a task, regardless of public opinion.

One of the first African-American lawyers to set up shop in Horry County, Cleveland Stevens successfully brought legal services to the poor of the region. After completing military service and law school, Stevens spent ten years in Washington, D.C., with the U.S. Department of Agriculture, and then a few years working in Charleston, South Carolina, as Director of Legal Aid Services. When Stevens finally moved back to his home county of Horry in the 1960s, he established a law office in Conway. There he served anyone who walked in his door, regardless of ability to pay, and predictably he built a thriving practice.

Stevens grew up in Horry County during the depression and told Walker of injustices that were committed, he thought, not out of malice but rather as a result of tradition. Stevens had witnessed how black and white individuals who were poor faced discrimination in a legal system that favored persons with money. Stevens told Walker of former clients who he believed were convicted not based on guilt or innocence but rather on personal characteristics that made them underdogs. Stevens loved the underdogs. In 1978, when Jim Dunn resigned from his position as the first public defender for Horry County, Stevens quickly accepted the appointment as Dunn's successor. He was then officially paid for serving a clientele with whom he was familiar and comfortable. Though Irby Walker had joined the public defender's office under Dunn in 1977, he easily made the transition to working for Stevens and quickly grew to admire the energy and passion with which Stevens served the public.

Walker's first impression of Woomer at the jailhouse was formed as two officers led the young-looking, blond-haired man into the conference room where Walker sat reviewing paperwork. Walker remembers that Woomer didn't look at all as he imagined he might. Dressed in a yellow shirt and army fatigues, Woomer looked thin and tired, but also relaxed and calm and not like someone who had just savagely murdered several people. Woomer nodded politely to Walker and sat down.

Walker explained to Woomer that he had been asked to act as his attorney during the hearing at 2:30 that afternoon. Walker noted from the documents he was given that Woomer had been formally charged the evening before with kidnap, rape, and murder. After cautioning Woomer about making further statements to anyone until legal representation was established, Walker asked his new client if he understood what he had been told. Woomer politely said he understood.

That afternoon, after Woomer told the court he did not have money to hire a lawyer, Judge Floyd appointed the public defender's office and a private attorney from Conway to provide his defense. Following a brief court appearance,

Walker addressed the press, explaining that no legal strategy had yet been discussed, and then went back home to bed.

After a quick review of the evidence, Woomer's new attorneys privately noted that their client had confessed to the crimes for which he was charged. It was apparent that Woomer would need all of the help he could get. The confession would need to be examined carefully, of course, but Buddy Causey was known to be something of a specialist in obtaining confessions. Causey's careful and systematic attention to detail had held up under scrutiny many times. There was probably little that could be done with Woomer's confession, particularly if the tape of Woomer describing his activities was played in court. Strike one. There were also witnesses, at least to the robbery and kidnappings in Georgetown and, if Wanda Summers lived, possibly to murder. Strike two. Then there was Woomer himself. Maybe strike three, maybe not. Irby Walker had watched with concern at the jail as Woomer sat quietly across the table with no more emotion than if he were waiting for a bus. That wasn't good, Walker considered, but perhaps Woomer could be coached on how to act and appear in court. Woomer's slow manner of speech with a thick, West Virginia drawl shouldn't be a handicap, Walker reasoned, given a good mix of local citizens on the jury. Many persons in South Carolina prided themselves on their accents and made a game of listening closely to an acquaintance to figure out where the individual was from.

It seemed apparent to Woomer's attorneys that the goal was simply to save his life.

Another significant obstacle for the defense in the opinion of Walker was the person of Jim Dunn. Walker had watched Dunn in the courtroom and had been amazed at his presence. Walker said he once read that, all other things being equal, large people make more of an impression on others than small people. By that measure, Walker concluded, Dunn left quite a wake as he moved about every inch of the front of the courtroom, marking the space as his territory. A former college football player, Dunn was tall and had big hands and a large upper body. Accentuating the appearance of the flamboyant attorney were piercing eyes that shone brightly beneath a thick pompadour of coal-black hair. Walker remembers that women on juries sometimes blushed as Dunn leaned forward on the railing of the jury box and looked directly into their eyes. Always a meticulous dresser, Dunn had his measurements for the jet-black suits he wore when he appeared in court on file at the mortuary. Once when questioning an expert witness, Dunn noticed and admired the coordinated tie and top-pocket handkerchief of the out-of-town man. Dunn appeared in court later that day with a pocket handkerchief that matched the tie he wore. When asked by a coworker how he had managed that, Dunn smiled and unbuttoned his coat. He had cut the bottom off of his tie and stuffed the severed piece in his pocket to produce the matching accessory look, a habit he maintained for years, until pocket handkerchiefs were no longer in style. Jim Dunn had the gift of making people in a room feel as if he were there just for them, and Walker knew that Dunn would be a powerful adversary.

Balancing the equation somewhat, though, was Cleveland Stevens. Walker remembers that Stevens had been practicing law for 25 years when he was appointed to Woomer's case, and he was "a great and experienced lawyer by the standards of anyone." Stevens had developed a tough skin by experiencing rough times of humiliation, insults and racial remarks. He wasn't concerned that he would be criticized for fighting to save Woomer's life. Stevens saw Woomer as an underdog and therefore similar to many of his previous clients. Stevens thought Woomer deserving of all of the skills and cunning he could muster as lead attorney for the defense.

In the courtroom, Stevens' style was different from that of Dunn. While Dunn was dramatic and loud, the gray-haired Stevens moved about the courtroom calmly and quietly. Stevens knew when to step very closely to a witness for effect and when to look to the jurors for sympathy. The crisp crease Stevens kept in the pant legs of his gray and pinstripe suits was testament to his attention to detail. Stevens listened intently to witnesses, often jotting quick notes, and didn't hesitate to raise objections to the often-exaggerated antics of Dunn.

In more than one case, Dunn had loudly instructed a bailiff to go out to the graveyard and ask a victim if a witness was telling the truth. Once, while working as public defender, Dunn suddenly grabbed a female defendant accused of murder and forcefully wrestled her to the floor. The stunned jurors watched as Dunn dramatically made his point that it was unlikely that his client had overpowered and murdered a much larger man. The jurors were notably impressed by the unconventional display and found in favor of Dunn's client. No doubt, Jim Dunn could ratchet up the tension in the courtroom to a fever pitch.

But would that work in the Woomer trial, wondered Irby Walker, when considering possible defense tactics. In the Woomer trial, the nature of the crimes involved was horrific and jurors exposed to the sordid details would experience great personal stress. Perhaps the even, unchanging expression of Stevens would provide a balance for Dunn's flair and also provide for jurors an emotional respite, an anchored place from which to watch as Dunn hammered home the brutality of Woomer's behavior. Perhaps just one juror would be overwhelmed and inexplicably find a deep-seated need to put an end to the violence.

Irby Walker was convinced that if anyone could find that juror and save Woomer's life, it was Stevens. What scared Walker, though, was his feeling that, given the evidence, it would not take all of Jim Dunn's expertise to convince a jury to convict and condemn Woomer to die.

26

$\mathbf{M}$onday afternoon, February 26, Woomer was arraigned in Georgetown and charged with two counts of murder, assault and battery, two counts of kidnapping, and four counts of armed robbery. Standing before the court in a sport shirt and green fatigues, Woomer heard his name spoken aloud in association with heinous crimes. Judge Sidney Floyd was at the bench in Georgetown, as he had been for Woomer's arraignment in Horry County, and appointed two attorneys to represent Woomer. If two arraignments in three days and a total of fourteen charges brought against Woomer were not enough to indicate to the West Virginian that he was in serious trouble, the following day Woomer was transported to Walterboro, in Colleton County, and was there arraigned and charged with armed robbery and an additional murder. From Walterboro, Woomer went straight to the Central Correctional Institute (CCI) in Columbia.

Woomer was transported to Columbia for psychiatric evaluation, but the transfer was also beneficial for another reason. There were serious concerns for Woomer's safety in all three counties.

"We had to send him to Columbia for his own protection," one of Woomer's attorneys told a reporter. "No county jail in the state is secure enough to adequately protect a defendant of Woomer's importance against someone attempting to kill him. We'd hate to have another Jack Ruby kind of thing."

That type of sentiment wasn't inconceivable either, given the circumstances that surrounded Woomer's crimes. A little later that same year in Horry County, another high profile case that involved Dunn resulted in vigilante action by the family of victims against a criminal.

During the trial of Rudolph Tyner for the murders of local convenience store owners William and Myrtie Moon, Tyner laughed in the faces of two men from the Moon family and was attacked on the spot. The Moon relatives were led away in handcuffs while Tyner escaped the skirmish with a bloodied lip and a torn shirt. The ill feelings against Tyner didn't end there.

Shortly after Tyner's conviction and relocation to death row at CCI, a son of the slain couple managed to circulate information regarding a contract to kill Tyner among the prison population. Notorious serial killer Pee Wee Gaskins accepted the contract and did kill Tyner, a feat for which he was proud. Gaskins ingeniously rigged an explosive in a radio and laughed as he coaxed Tyner to put one of his ears directly on the radio as the device was turned on. Gaskins received a death sentence for the murder and he was later electrocuted. The son of the Moons who paid for the hit was allowed to plea-bargain and received a year in prison. At the end of the year, the son was welcomed back into the community.

Dunn was confident that Woomer was as safe as possible in Columbia at the maximum-security facility, but was also aware that citizens of Horry County could and would take matters into their own hands.

Dunn directed his energies toward solving logistical problems he faced. Woomer was charged with three sets of crimes in three counties and had three sets of attorneys. Aside from the problem of the expense to the taxpayers of three separate trials, Dunn found that he had to mediate among political forces in each county that demanded justice for their respective constituencies. Since the 46 counties of South Carolina are divided into judicial circuits, with Horry and Georgetown Counties comprising the Fifteenth Circuit and organized under a single solicitor, Dunn had more say about matters in Horry and Georgetown than in Colleton County.

It seemed obvious that Horry County would get Woomer first, but coordinating access to Woomer for his other lawyers while maintaining his security loomed as a problem. Within two weeks after Woomer's arrest, the *Georgetown Times* printed an article under the headline, "Defender: I Can't Get to Woomer." The public defender in Georgetown called the access problem a "bad situation" and said, "The only thing I know about the case is what I read in the newspapers." To further complicate matters, it was clear that each set of lawyers had their own political agenda as to how to handle the important case. Despite Dunn's initial statement, that "Woomer will be available to his attorneys at any time," it would be at least 30 days before he was available to anyone other than his Horry County attorneys.

Meanwhile, Woomer sat in Columbia at the state prison-affiliated hospital where he was undergoing mental testing and a competency evaluation. Buddy Causey had listened again to the tape of Woomer's confession and was again stunned by Woomer's nonchalance. "One would have thought from his lack of concern that he had just been issued a traffic violation," Causey said. It seemed possible to the seasoned detective that Woomer hadn't fully realized the magnitude of the senseless crimes he committed. Perhaps the sessions with the psychiatrists at CCI would help Woomer understand the trouble he faced.

In late March, when Woomer was returned to Horry County to begin preparing for his first court appearance, something happened to suggest that the series of sober sessions with prison psychiatrists had influenced the troubled young man to think about the futility of his life. One evening at the Horry County Jail, Woomer began a series of dialogues with a volunteer chaplain. Woomer confessed to the woman that he had never felt so alone. Though he had been in serious trouble before, two things were different. Never had he faced public scorn and hatred for his crimes as he now did each day. Woomer had no illusions that he was safe in jail. He had been raped and beaten in a West Virginia prison while incarcerated for crimes considered by the prison population more acceptable than his current crimes. The way his movements were monitored at

CCI constantly reminded Woomer of efforts to provide for his security.

Also, Woomer recognized that he was further from home than he had ever been. South Carolina was as foreign to Woomer as distant countries are to most other people. No matter how the trials came out, there would be no friends or family coming by on visitation days in South Carolina. Woomer began to realize that his crimes potentially meant being alone for the rest of his life among people who hated him.

One evening in the presence of the chaplain, Woomer reportedly experienced a Christian conversion and accepted Jesus Christ as his personal savior. The following day when defense counsel Cleveland Stevens heard of Woomer's experience, Stevens asked a Conway Baptist minister to visit and pray with Rusty to validate the sincerity of the act of repentance. Stevens reasoned that a jury would ultimately consist of persons from the local area, considered the "Bible Belt" by outsiders because of the ubiquity of fundamental religious beliefs, who would respond to a sincere conversion experience. Stevens was stunned and then angered by the response he received. The minister sent word back that he didn't believe in jailhouse conversions and would have nothing to do with Woomer.

27

"**W**anda, I'm really sorry about this. It's just going to take time." Dr. Calhoun Cunningham stood quietly by the hospital bed.

Although Wanda's doctors actually felt optimistic about her chances for improvement, the day-to-day realities of the developing treatment plan only seemed to mean more heartache and misery for the struggling woman.

Tears streamed down Wanda's cheeks onto her bandages as she scribbled furiously on her pad. "I have a family at home! I can't stay here!"

In the two weeks since the accident Wanda felt as if she had died and gone to hell. She was in constant pain and, now facing an unknown amount of surgery to repair her face, she had to stay in the hospital for at least another month. The doctor had just confirmed her new worst fear: She wouldn't get to see her little girl anytime soon.

"I have to see my baby!" she wrote emphatically, over and over.

After two weeks of intensive care, Wanda was transferred to critical care and placed directly across the hall from a nurse's station. Visitation was better – one immediate family member allowed at a time for two hours – but children were still not allowed in to visit at all.

The doctors had discussed the possibility that Wanda might become despondent and as a result suffer a major setback. She was doing as well as she could, so far, but if she lost her will to continue, she could die.

"I don't see why we can't bend the rule a little," Cunningham said and began writing out the special order. "I'm going to authorize some short visits with your daughter and we'll see how it goes. She'll need to be with an adult though."

"Thank you!" Wanda wrote in large letters. She looked immediately at Jimmy.

"You want me to go get her right now?" Jimmy asked. He had already picked up the phone. The look in Wanda's eyes said it all.

"Mr. Reggie," he said a minute later. "How about have Betty get Traci ready, if you would. The doctor just said she can visit now, so I'm coming to get her."

Traci had been with her grandparents since the "accident," as it was now called. She did not know what had happened to her mother, or the seriousness of it, and had barely seen her father for two weeks.

Traci arrived at the hospital in a cute floral print dress and white shoes. Her hair had again been arranged in pigtails, which was her favorite hairstyle. In her tiny fist, Traci carried a single purple flower. The mystery of the visit stretched out in front of her as she walked down the long hall holding her daddy's hand. Why was her momma here? Why had she been gone so long? An important process was beginning for the little girl that would last into her adult years.

Wanda was reportedly overjoyed to see Traci but dismayed by the frightened look on her face. Traci remembers being confused as she stood quietly and examined the array of tubes running into Wanda's body. The last time she had seen her mother had been in the store two weeks earlier. Unaware of even the notion of violent acts, Traci had calmly watched her mother as she interacted with the gun-wielding men; she had a clear view of everything that happened from underneath her father's arm as she lay on the floor. She knew her mother left the store with the men, but she did not know why. At her grandparents' house later that night, Traci had slipped out of bed and watched as her grandmother cried. Traci was unaware that following a miscommunication with the air base hospital, the Georgetown sheriff's office had called the Altman home and reported that Wanda had died. By morning, Traci thought her grandmother seemed calmer, but she was still not as calm as she normally was. From that morning until she stood before the bed in which Wanda lay, Traci had been told very little about her mother and nothing about what to expect at the hospital.

Traci climbed upon her mother's bed and stared at the bandages covering her face. Traci asked her mother if her face had been wrapped because it was bleeding. Wanda fought back her tears as she nodded her head. Traci remained quiet for the rest of the visit and mostly kept her questions to herself.

Following the accident Jimmy stayed by Wanda's side, sleeping at night on a roll-a-way bed that was placed beside Wanda's bed, and he left the hospital only to take care of business, shower and change clothes. He maintained that routine for close to a month, through the most critical phase of Wanda's early surgeries, before he returned to work. During this time his boss drove 40 miles one way from Georgetown to the hospital every Friday afternoon to give Jimmy his paycheck. Wanda's mother came to the hospital each morning and stayed until suppertime. The names of other "family" members were put on a list and given to the hospital staff. Wanda said later, "My family grew when I was in the hospital." Wanda's real father, whom she had not seen since her adoption at age six by the Altmans, showed up unexpectedly. His name was added to the list, but he never visited Wanda a second time.

A few days after Traci's first visit, a big moment for Jimmy and Wanda occurred when the breathing tube was removed from Wanda's throat. As the tube was slowly slipped from the tracheal ring, Jimmy sat close to Wanda and wondered. Would the woman to whom he was deeply committed ever be able to talk again? The doctors had given no guarantees. When the nurse was finally satisfied that Wanda's breathing was unobstructed, she stepped back. Following the instruction given by the nurse, Wanda placed her finger over the hole in her throat and, looking into Jimmy's eyes, made croaking sounds distinguishable as the words, "I love you." Tears ran down Jimmy's cheeks and he laughed. Carefully leaning in, he looked into Wanda's eyes and said softly, "I love you, too."

The minutes stretched into hours and then days and still Jimmy sat beside Wanda and held her hand. Each day, new cards were taped to the wall until the entire room was papered with wishes for Wanda's speedy recovery. Bouquets of flowers began to take up too much space and were given away.

At the end of the third week of Wanda's stay in the hospital, Dr. Cunningham asked Jimmy to step into the hall for a few minutes. The process of changing the bandages had become routine and Jimmy rose to leave.

"Today's the day," Cunningham said to Jimmy.

"What do you mean?" Jimmy asked.

"The bandages come off today. We're going to leave them off, let everything air." The doctor studied Jimmy's face for a response. "I think it'd be better if you could stay nearby," Cunningham added.

Jimmy had expected this moment. He had prepared himself but the doctor's words still sent a shiver through his chest and arms. His forehead burned. Jimmy stepped back into the room and moved to the side of the bed; the nurse was already at work, talking gently to Wanda. After giving Wanda's hand a brief squeeze, Jimmy walked out into the hall again. *Please, God. Help her be strong,* he thought.

Jimmy knew when the doctor first told him that Wanda had been shot in the face that his life had taken a turn. The road he now walked led in an unknown direction, but he never doubted that his walk was still beside Wanda. He didn't need to be warned about Wanda's appearance when the bandages were removed. His concern all along had been for how Wanda might respond.

Jimmy entered the room again when the nurse called and walked directly to the side of the bed. "There we go," he said.

Wanda's eyes rolled momentarily, a result of the medications for pain and anxiety, and then focused on Jimmy. "How is it?" she asked in a voice barely above a whisper. Her mouth remained still.

"You look fine, honey," he said. Jimmy's face appeared calm as he looked at the folds of skin laced together where Wanda's chin used to be. Large red scars ran at angles opposite to the irregular contours of her face. Her lower lip protruded where it had been sewed back in place.

"You wouldn't tell me a lie, would you?" Wanda asked slowly.

"You know I've never lied to you." Jimmy smiled. "Doctor says it's gonna take some time is all, and we've got plenty of that. Everything's gonna be just fine."

"I think I'm going to sleep now," Wanda said, her voice trailing off.

"I'll be right here," Jimmy said as Wanda's eyes fluttered and then closed.

Jimmy stepped into the hall for a word with the doctor.

"She's out of danger," Cunningham said. "She's strong. Take my word for it, things are moving along better than they look."

"Anything I should do?" Jimmy asked.

"Just what you're doing. She might have a rough moment when she sees herself for the first time, but you can assure her we're going to work at this. It's step-by-step from here, a series of operations, each making her look more and more normal. For now, though . . . well, you saw her. She's going to want to look."

Jimmy tried to anticipate Wanda's response. In every scenario, he imagined Wanda lying in bed holding a mirror. He finally concluded that he didn't have a clue how she might respond. Nor did he correctly anticipate the circumstances when she would see her damaged face.

That night Wanda woke suddenly to the deep sound of Jimmy's breathing. Everything else was quiet. Light trickling into the room from the crack in the door mixed with the soft glow of the light over the top of the bed. Wanda lay still, listening to the rhythm of Jimmy's soft snore and then remembered. *The bandages are off.* She raised her hand but stopped short of actually touching her face. The feeding tube in her nose was now taped to the side. *Jimmy,* she thought. Jimmy continued to sleep, the roll-a-way bed just out of her reach. *Jimmy. I'm gonna look now.*

Wanda gripped the raised railing on the side of the bed and pulled herself to a sitting position. Her head felt heavy, but the thought of lying back down passed quickly. *The mirror over the sink,* she thought. Wanda pushed on the bedrail fixed in place and then slipped forward toward the bottom of the bed. Continuing to hold the rail, she turned and leaned forward off the side of the bed until her feet touched the floor.

The struggle for Wanda to reach the mirror was quickly forgotten when she took the first look at what used to be a pretty face. The image of the stranger looking back would have been utterly horrifying had Wanda not been under the influence of heavy medications. As it was, she simply stared for a minute and then turned away. The thought that she took back to the hospital bed where she would spend another week was, *It's worse than I thought. I look like a monster.*

28

Not long after the crime spree, the community began to rally in support of the victims. Day after day, as the newspapers reported details of the assault, a picture familiar to independent-minded citizens of South Carolina began to emerge. Unwanted outside influences had disturbed the calm. Unfortunately, when the full image of Woomer's and Skaar's day of senseless violence took form, it was apparent that the two West Virginians had wreaked a havoc that wouldn't just fade away in a matter of months. When it became apparent that a trial would not end the nightmare for the victims and their families, anger swept like a brushfire through the lowcountry. The media fueled the flame with several articles dramatizing the plight of those left behind.

The *Georgetown Times* carried an article under the headline, "Violence Shatters Everyday Lives," that cut to the core of the human side of the story. "Three average, hard-working families were minding their own business and following everyday routines when their lives were suddenly shattered." Attributing the victimization to fate, the article also described the randomness of the assaults. "It didn't have to be Arnie Lee Richardson, Wanda Summers, Earl Dean Wright, and Della Louise Sellers. It could have been anyone." The violence had been so brutal and widespread, covering three counties, that the newspaper used the article to provide a service normally reserved for the obituary section: a listing of over two dozen names of surviving family members of the victims gave readers who perhaps had missed some of the coverage another opportunity to pay their respects.

Citizens went into action. Focusing on something tangible that could be done, a fund-raising drive was set into motion, largely due to the efforts of the owners of Jack's Mini-mall, Jack and Connie Clemmons, to help offset the enormous costs of treating Wanda. Though Jimmy's insurance would ultimately pay most of the bills, persons close to the violence needed an outlet for the anger they felt toward Woomer and for the frustration of having to wait for justice. A heartfelt letter to the editor of *The Sun News* from a concerned citizen expressed the sentiment that many persons shared. "My understanding is that the financial situation is such that we as a community cannot ignore it."

In addition to funds to help finance long-term treatment options, funds were needed for immediate expenses as well. Jimmy's wallet, which was stolen in the robbery, contained money from his paycheck that he and Wanda normally used to buy food and pay bills. Sympathetic business owners throughout Georgetown, Pawley's Island, Litchfield and Myrtle Beach set out gallon jugs for donations. Many of the jugs had to be emptied daily, and the money was transferred to an account established as the Wanda Summers Fund at a bank with branches throughout the Myrtle Beach area. Churches took up collections, received mail contributions and sponsored car washes.

Four hundred persons paid one dollar and fifty cents apiece to attend a musical benefit at the Georgetown National Guard Armory to show support for the Summers' and listen to rock 'n' roll, country, disco, and gospel bands. "Some fifty groups of volunteers donated time, money, personnel and supplies for the concert," the *Georgetown Times* reported. Wanda, Jimmy and Traci made an appearance at the concert. Though Wanda had been out of the hospital less than two weeks, the family felt they needed to express in person their gratitude for the outpouring of sympathy and support from the community. Following an unsuccessful attempt to find a veil to cover the lower portion of her face, Wanda made the decision to go to the concert anyway. "It doesn't bother me when friends see my face the way it is now," she said. "But when I go somewhere and strangers stare at me – that hurts."

The Sun News published a promotional article prior to the concert under the headline "Tragic Changes Mark Wanda

Summers' Life." Wanda admitted that her life had become very difficult and included nightmares, special diets, and sedatives to get through the day and the night. An additional note was both positive – "her injury has forced her to quit smoking" — and sad, when Wanda used humor to try to find the silver lining. "When people tell me to keep my chin up, I reply, 'How can I? I don't have one'; she laughed."

Following the concert, the *Georgetown Times* published an upbeat piece, "Walking Tall: Wanda Summers Is Determined to Rebound." The article provided the first description available for the public of details of Wanda's ordeal. Speaking optimistically of the medical side of her story, Wanda said, "Doctors have said that they can fix me nearly as good as new. It'll just be a long, long time." On a realistic note, she said, "I try to hold up in the daytime, and I do my crying at night. You've got to let it out sometime." With no teeth or lower lip to catch her saliva, during the interview for the newspaper Wanda had to constantly dab at her mouth with tissues. "Sometimes," she said, reflecting on her uncertain future, "I don't think it will ever be the same." Wanda paused. "I couldn't stand it if it weren't for my God, my wonderful family, and my friends. Especially Jimmy, he's been wonderful."

Jimmy, for his part, simply said, "My wife's alive, and the three of us are together. That's the most important thing."

With the court proceedings scheduled to begin the following month, Wanda knew she faced perhaps the most difficult challenge of her life. Who could blame her for saying, "I know that we are all supposed to be God's children, but it's hard to forgive them. I don't think that man who shot me had any feelings. I'm bitter towards him and just hope he has to suffer like I'm suffering. He messed up a fine life."

29

Wanda first found out about the preliminary hearing for Woomer from Buddy Causey, but received a call from Dunn shortly thereafter who explained that the hearing was simply a formality. Preliminary hearings, she was told, are to determine if there is enough evidence to take a case to a grand jury. Having just been recently released from the hospital, Wanda was feeling better, but still spent much of her time in bed. Since the hearing was the first step in the process of making sure Woomer got what was coming to him, she agreed to attend. The hearing should have been Wanda's first encounter with Woomer since he shot her. Something bizarre occurred, however, to put Wanda and Woomer into face-to-face contact in a situation that is still unexplained.

Wanda has this remembrance of the incident. Just before the hearing, Wanda received a call from the police asking if she would come to the jail. Assuming the trip was necessary, Wanda made arrangements and rode to Conway with Jack and Connie Clemmons. When Wanda arrived at the jailhouse, officers positioned themselves on either side of her and took her arms to lead her down a corridor. Wanda assumed the officers were operating to protect her and said nothing about the procedure as they walked along. Just before they reached an intersecting hall, the officers suddenly pulled her to a stop and held Wanda's arms tightly. Two officers holding Woomer by his arms appeared from the intersecting hallway and hurried past as Wanda looked on in shock. Wanda immediately experienced a flashback to the night of the robbery and rape and began to scream. In her mind, she was once again with Woomer on that cold and dark dirt road and was unable to get away. The officers were alarmed by her reaction, and they continued to hold Wanda as she screamed and struggled furiously. Wanda was pulled into a side room, and a call for help was placed to Eckert. The doctor instructed the officers to give her some of the Valium he knew she should have in her purse and ordered them to stay with her until she calmed down.

When Wanda's terror eventually subsided, she became very angry and confronted Dunn. What had he known of the "ambush"? Why had one officer said, "Well, I guess there's no more doubt about that."

Wanda eventually believed Dunn when he swore to her that he had no prior knowledge of the meeting. Dunn, in turn, expressed his fury to the police, insisting that no further manipulations of his client take place.

When asked about the incident during the preparation for this book, Buddy Causey said that while he didn't remember that specific incident, it could have happened, but he did not think it was a contrived meeting to put Woomer and Wanda together. The old two-story building that housed the Horry County Police Department had rooms where prisoners had meetings with police and lawyers on the first floor and the jail was on the second floor. Prisoners were often led through the downstairs portion of the jailhouse on their way to various meetings and court appearances, and there were tense moments on the rare occasion when a criminal and victim accidentally met. Causey further stated that he doesn't have any recollections from all of his years on the police force of police tactics that would have purposely put a victim in harm's way. Wanda, in turn, remembers Buddy Causey as a caring and considerate officer and though she is still sensitive to the incident, doesn't feel he had anything to do with her unexpected encounter with Woomer.

Wanda made it through the preliminary hearing and her second face-to-face meeting with Woomer. The case was forwarded to the grand jury, which indicted Woomer, and the date for the trial was set for July.

After the hearing, Dunn sat with Wanda to explain the timetable of the unfolding events and her involvement in the process. Using phrases such as "When you testify . . ." and "Your testimony will . . .," Dunn made it clear to Wanda that he expected her to testify. Wanda was sure that Dunn was her strongest supporter. She also believed that he would not force or coerce her to testify if she felt unable to do so. Dunn knew the case he had was rock solid, even without Wanda's testimony, and Woomer would never be a free man again. Dunn wanted Woomer to die for his sins, though, and for that, he might need Wanda. He believed correctly that Wanda's appearance before a jury would cinch the case against Woomer.

Wanda insisted that Dunn continue to provide for Traci's security. "Jim Dunn knew that if anything happened to Traci, I was out of it," Wanda said, indicating that she would have been emotionally incapable of testifying.

Skaar was dead and Woomer was in jail, but no one knew what Whitehead and Fisher were capable of. Whitehead hadn't been happy sitting in jail for two months especially knowing that Fisher remained a free man. Fisher was eventually arrested in West Virginia late in April on a fugitive warrant and was extradited to South Carolina, but the police weren't taking chances. From February 22 until school let out for the summer, an officer was stationed at Waccamaw Elementary, where Traci attended kindergarten. The children at the school became used to the presence of the policeman as he shadowed Traci through the day. "Every afternoon, my granddaddy's car would be parked behind the police car that would escort us home. Once I was with my granddaddy, of course, I was probably safer than when I was with the policeman," Traci recalled.

As the time for the trial approached, Dunn's behaviors became obsessive and sometimes irritated his staff. His normal habit was to focus on a single big case and turn all other cases over to assistants. A death penalty trial naturally consumed Dunn and thereby allowed for the full expression of his eccentricities. For example, Dunn might call a meeting of staff persons and ask for input on the wording of a motion. The meeting could last minutes or hours, sometimes even continuing off and on for days, taking staff persons away from other duties to spend what some thought was an inordinate amount of time on minute details. Ralph Wilson, a Conway attorney who worked closely with Dunn and who would succeed Dunn as solicitor, said, "There was no question about his brilliance in the courtroom, and a lot of it was due to the intensity with which he attacked a case. Every line, every word, every syllable meant something to Jim Dunn."

The attention to detail wasn't a waste of time for Wanda, though. She appreciated the personal attention Dunn offered in the way of explanations and alerts when something relevant to her case came up. Dunn knew how an overextended court system, as it grinds slowly forward, can often overlook the people it is designed to serve.

Dunn understood the concept of victimization to include the individuals directly affected by crimes and the families and close friends of those individuals, who also experience upheaval as a result of the careless acts of criminals. Dunn tried to learn the names of all of the persons directly and indirectly affected by a particular crime and spent his personal time off the job going to their homes and getting to know them. Since there were no formalized services available for victims of crimes in South Carolina in 1979, nor would there be until many years later, Dunn's initial efforts at attending to the needs of victims were small scale and personal. There was nothing small about his efforts, however, to the individuals and the families for whom he labored. With the Woomer case, Jim Dunn, the champion of the law, became, in addition, the champion of the victim.

30

The Woomer trial generated considerable excitement in Horry and Georgetown Counties, and for nearly two weeks in July of 1979 the 100-year-old courthouse in Conway was packed almost every day. The media reporting of the crime spree, both while it was taking place and for a few days afterwards, didn't approximate the nonstop coverage that a similar event today would receive. Nonetheless, everyone in the area devoured newspaper articles and television newsbreaks about the killing spree in disbelief. The unprecedented criminal activities brought people together to shake their heads and wonder what was happening in the community. Everyone wanted to know what was going on at the courthouse.

An attractive two-story building with a widow's walk, the rectangular courthouse sits solemnly on several acres of well-tended grass and is a centerpiece of the downtown area of Conway, the county seat of Horry. Large moss-covered oak trees frame the skyline on all four sides of the courthouse. People with business inside bustle along the cracked sidewalks, their arms loaded with documents.

Prior to the 1970s most of the squabbles and disputes settled in the Conway courthouse were between local interests. Even criminal activities in the coastal area tended to involve persons living in the lowcountry and known to local law enforcement. As the coastline of South Carolina began to flourish in the 1970s as a tourist destination, Horry County began to witness problems that accompany rapid growth in population, including an increase in hard-core criminal activity. The Woomer trial provided an upclose examination of one of the inevitable results of progress for the citizens of the small communities that dot the county map. When summer rolled around and the trial began, more people walked beneath the stately white columns of the old brick courthouse to see justice wrought for Woomer than for any other criminal in decades.

● ❖ ●

The first actual testimony of the trial began on Monday morning, July 16, 1979. The summer morning heat was only partially offset for trial attendees by the air conditioning in the courthouse. Three months earlier, when the judge who would preside over the case, David Harwell, asked whether the air in the courthouse was conditioned for a summer trial, Dunn responded quickly. "Absolutely," he had said. But the heat of the summer combined with the cramped conditions as people packed into the old-fashioned theatre-style seats in the courthouse put a strain on the system. Paper fans on wooden sticks waved throughout the large room.

The few empty seats the week before, when the jurors had been selected, were gone when testimony began. Similar to a theater, the courtroom had two tiered sections in the back separated in the middle by a sloping walkway. The seats in the front were reserved for family members and close friends and were positioned in a row just in front of a rail that served as a boundary between the back two-thirds and the forward third of the courtroom. The long tables where the defense and prosecution teams sat were side by side in front of the rail. The witness stand and the jury box were located to the right of the judge, and he could survey the courtroom from his elevated perch.

Each and every remaining day of the trial would begin the same way. When the doors opened, the thunderous shuffling of feet on the thinly carpeted wooden floor soon gave way to the creaking of wooden seats as excited spectators made quick choices concerning where to sit. Elbow space was politely determined with nods and smiles as 300 persons slowly found their spots and began to settle in; seatmates made introductions and established who knew what so far in the trial. Bailiffs pointed out the few remaining empty seats to latecomers who had not anticipated having to wait in a long line. The sharp sounds of the occasional loud voice or cough echoed off the high ceiling as attention shifted to the front of the room. Lawyers spread materials and asked assistants to account for witnesses. Pitchers of iced water were placed strategically about the front of the courtroom. The court reporter readied and checked her equipment. Officers posted along the walls began pulling the doors to, blocking the entrances with their bodies. As the last few individuals were allowed to enter on a one-by-one basis, disappointment spread back through the cavernous halls among those who could not enter the courtroom that day.

Several newspapers in the area printed stories of the expected testimony. Informed sources, said *The Sun News*, had revealed that early testimony would include the husbands of the kidnap victims. Interestingly, and perhaps a topic of conversation as trial attendees waited, *The State* newspaper carried side-by-side articles on Monday of two other trials taking place. The trial of Dr. Jeffrey McDonald, the former Green Beret, who stood accused of killing his wife and two daughters nine years earlier at Fort Bragg, was finally beginning in Raleigh, North Carolina. In addition, serial killer Ted Bundy was being tried in Florida for several of the dozens of kidnappings and murders for which he would ultimately be known to have committed. Unfortunately, persons in Horry County didn't have to look too far beyond their morning papers to see a real life version of the mass murder they shook their heads over as they had their morning coffee. All they had to do was look in the their own courthouse.

Woomer's entrance to the courtroom with an officer evoked murmurs. Standing five feet eight inches tall, Rusty looked pale and thin from the five months he had been in jail waiting for trial. His blondish hair, though still collar-length and shaggy, had darkened. Cleveland Stevens provided the street clothes Woomer wore, perhaps achieving the desired effect. Woomer looked boyish as he shifted restlessly in his seat at the defense table.

For all the murmuring and attention given Woomer, though, when the trial began, even the rustling of clothes stopped when Wanda Summers entered the courtroom. Outfitted in Sunday clothes, Wanda held her head up as she made her way through the courtroom. The irregular contours and scars from the reconstruction of her face were clearly visible. Accompanied by her husband, a police officer, and John Breeden, one member of the prosecution team, Wanda found her spot marked by a large box of Kleenex tissues and she settled at the prosecution table. As the trial wore on, Wanda's movements received less attention, enabling her to mingle a little and interact with family members and friends who had taken time off from work to show support for her by attending the trial.

Seated directly behind Wanda was Jimmy and, seated beside him, Don Sellers. Jimmy leaned forward each day and rested his hand on Wanda's shoulder. Don spent the entire two weeks of the trial glaring at Woomer, who, for the most part, appeared oblivious to the animosity.

The trial was unlike any that could be remembered in the history of Horry County. Wanda's agony over her decision to appear in court was felt by every person in the room. Most persons were transfixed by her presence. Dunn knew the jurors would respond emotionally to the sight of Wanda. Had she not been present, their only images of the savagery inflicted by Woomer upon her flesh and bone would have been mental images resulting from word descriptions alone. Pictures of Wanda might have been considered too prejudicial for display. The fact that Wanda was seated a mere few feet from where Woomer sat throughout the trial added to a palpable feeling of embarrassment jurors felt as they were forced to witness Wanda's humiliation and pain.

• ❖ •

Jim Dunn began his opening statement as he traditionally did using the metaphor of an artist's canvas. Each witness would paint a little, Dunn instructed, until the full picture emerged. Confident that the verdict in the first phase of the trial, when guilt or innocence was determined, would go against Woomer, Dunn began preparing jurors for the sentencing phase and a recommendation of death. "You will hear evidence," Dunn said, "of how Ronald Woomer cold bloodedly, with ice water in his veins, hell in his hand, and death in his heart, just blew people away." The metaphorical picture on the canvas, Dunn said, would be a real picture of a "cold-blooded, brutal slaying of a human being. I hope that won't upset you too much." Dunn expected the jury to wield the brush for the final stroke and complete the picture by sentencing Woomer to death.

Cleveland Stevens found he could do little in the opening for the defense but plant seeds for the second phase of the trial, when he hoped to save Woomer's life. Admitting that the trial was Stevens' first death penalty case, he said, "We're not going to sit here at this table and try to tell you that Woomer is not guilty of a crime, that he did not take the life of Mrs. Sellers, that he did not rape this lady. Yes, he went wrong. No question about it. He went wrong somewhere." Stevens paused strategically and gave the jurors a glimpse of the defense strategy. "I don't know who to blame," Stevens said resignedly. "Do I blame his mother who sits behind him, who is poor from West Virginia, whose husband left her with four children? I don't want to put the blame on her. Do I want to put the blame on Rusty Woomer that he voluntarily took some wine, some coke, or whatever he took that messed up his mind? Does the blame lie there? Or does it lie with all of us?

"I know what poverty is. I know what crime is. I know what deprivation is. All of these things affect the lives of people. How can you isolate him from the society he was born in?

"I'm talking about behavior patterns, how things and forces can get hold of them and make them do things that none of us can understand.

"The State says, 'Kill him; take him away from society. He's no more good to nobody.' That's a copout. Is the solution to what he's done to kill him?

"I'm not trying to condone what he's done. I'm making no excuses, Mr. Foreman. I don't excuse him for what he did. I'm just trying to save his life."

The tension in the courtroom accelerated through the

first several witnesses as Dunn recreated the robbery in Pawley's Island, highlighting through testimony the callous treatment the victims received at the hands of Skaar and Woomer. During the selection of the jurors, Woomer had been allowed, as was his right in a capital case, to make a statement to the prospective jurors. The resulting image of the timid, soft-spoken Woomer, who asked the jury panel to "Please pay attention, it's important to me," was not an image to which Dunn would allow the jurors to cling for long.

Don Sellers stood for much of his testimony and used his hands to gesture as Woomer had that night at the mini-mall. Sellers repeatedly thrust his clasped hands forward as a mock gun, all the while shouting as Woomer had, "I want money, money!" and "Get your Goddamn hands over your head!" Don's voice faltered when he told the court how he pleaded with Woomer, saying, "That's my wife and I love her. Please don't hurt her."

During cross-examination, Stevens tried to use Sellers' demonstration to show that Woomer was out of his mind that night.

"Mr. Sellers," Stevens said. "Did I understand you to say that when you first saw this young man he was acting crazy like a wild man?"

"No, sir," Sellers said bluntly, "I didn't say that."

"Would you explain to me what you said because I don't want to misunderstand you?" Stevens asked, looking at the pad on which he wrote constantly during the testimony of the various witnesses.

"He was very cool," Sellers said, his eyes becoming slits as he remembered. "When he first walked in, he was shoving the little girl around."

"I believe the State asked you if you had heard him talk this week, and I believe you said you did?" Stevens asked.

"Yes, sir," Sellers answered coldly. "He talked a lot louder the night of February 22, very much louder. He had a lot of authority that night when he had that pistol in his hand."

The testimony of the second witness, Robert Thomas, the father of the little girl shoved by Woomer, supported

Sellers' recollections of Woomer and Skaar as tough-acting that night. The man testified that having a child with him had influenced his behavior. Recalling when Woomer had ordered him to, "Act like you're shopping," Thomas testified, "I picked up a can of pork and beans, and I was thinking, if I could cram it up side his head once, I'll get on him." When Woomer threatened his daughter again, though, Thomas put the can down. "I figured I'm just going to mess around and get killed or get somebody else hurt, so when they told us all to hit the floor, I hit the floor."

The story Dunn created for the jury took an ominous turn with the testimony of Dean and Renee Guyton, the couple who called the rescue squad when Wanda stumbled into their yard.

"When we finished eating supper that night," Mr. Guyton said, "we sat down to watch Andy Griffith on T.V., and this program went off at 7:30. My wife has a lot of potted plants that we move in and out of doors that time of year. And about that time, I heard some shots."

The jurors sat quietly and alternately looked at Woomer, and then at Wanda, as Guyton described in vivid detail how Wanda had come out of the dark. "I could see down her throat," he said. "She had one side of her face left, no jaw. And the side of her face that was left was busted open like it had been cut from the corner of her mouth all the way up to her hairline." Dunn hammered home the brutality of the crimes.

The testimony of the ambulance driver, Hoss Johnson, added a sad note to the horror being described in the courtroom. Johnson, a boat captain during the day, supported his community by serving as a volunteer for the rescue squad and for the fire department.

"Did you know Wanda before this happened?" Dunn asked the life-long resident of the area.

"Yes, sir, I did," Johnson replied. "I've known her for a couple of years, seeing her around Jack's Mini-mall. Her brother at that time worked for me on the boat. I've seen her when she used to stay at the river. I launched my boat there. I've talked with her before, but I didn't recognize her that night."

"You could not recognize her at all?"

"No, sir, I could not."

Though the defense attorneys had known that the jury would no doubt find Woomer guilty, they hoped to inject some reason for mercy into the description of the crime. Stevens and Irby Walker found, however, as they watched Dunn methodically paint the vivid case for the State that they could do little for their client besides object occasionally when a witness started to report what someone else had said.

Dunn liked to be physically close to the jurors so they could see him clearly, smell him, and feel his presence. Dunn also liked to be able to get in the face of a witness to use his imposing size as necessary. He solved this dilemma of how to be in two places at once by standing at an angle at the front of the courtroom. With just a quick side step and a turn of his head, Dunn could appear to be directly in front of both the witness stand and the jurors' box.

When the charismatic solicitor was building testimony for a strong point, Dunn would nonchalantly ask questions over his shoulder and then look directly at the jurors as the witness answered. At the right moment, Dunn would then turn his head and say, "What?," as if he were incredulous and couldn't believe the response. When the witness answered again, Dunn would repeat the answer and bend his knees, managing to deliver the punch of the line while straightening his body. The mesmerizing effect, which sometimes included voice inflections and gesturing, was similar to what one might see while watching a very good evangelist. Each time something particularly horrible was said, Dunn would turn and look at Woomer and once even walked over and placed his hand on Woomer's shoulder. Next to Dunn, Woomer looked small and frail as he slumped in his seat with his head down.

Dunn applied one more macabre stroke to the canvas before leading the testimony in a more clinical direction.

At sunrise the day after Louise's murder, G.B. Shelley of the Horry County Police Department had gone to search the area near where Wanda and Louise had been shot.

"I figured that maybe some of the other officers might have missed something," the officer said.

"As a result of your search there, what, if anything, did you find?" Dunn asked.

"I proceeded down a dirt road on foot and I came to a patch of blood."

"Came to a what?" Dunn asked, looking at Shelley.

"A patch of blood. Also, there were particles of what looked like meat laying around. We ran a dog off which had licked the blood some and stepped on the particles of bone."

The highlight of the long, gruesome morning was the testimony of Dr. Edward Eckert, one of Wanda's doctors with whom she remained closely associated for years after the trial. Eckert testified as an oral surgeon and a specialist in plastic surgery.

"Let me ask you this," Dunn said to Eckert. "How did she look on the evening that you saw her, on the twenty-second of February?"

"I'd have to say that she was in a state of shock," Eckert said. "She was conscious, and the fact that she remained conscious probably was the thing that kept her alive, because she had no support of her lower face. Your lower jaw, your mandible, supports the muscles coming up from your neck, so it maintains your airway. She had to remain on her stomach so that her head was forward so that she could maintain an airway and breathe. If she had lain on her back, everything would have fallen back, and she would have obstructed herself and died."

"Tell us, please, sir," continued Dunn. "What else in reference to the parts of the body were injured?"

"When I saw her, they brought her into the Emergency Room of Grand Strand General," Eckert said. "She was lying in the prone position, on her stomach, and she was propped up by a pillow. She had her hands up on her forehead maintaining her head up, and there was just a mass of tissue. Essentially, she had no lower jaw from where your wisdom teeth are on either side all the way forward. Her tongue was in a couple of pieces, and her lip was hanging down. She had no consistency to her lip at all. The upper lip was intact. The lower lip was hanging down. It's just like if you took a razor blade and cut at your right corner and let it dangle. Essentially, she had no chin at all. The force from the gunshot wound had extended it down into her neck, and it looked like somebody had taken her chin and put it in a blender."

Eckert had color photos in his lap that he offered, to show how Wanda looked when she first entered the hospital. Dunn said that the photos weren't admissible.

"You didn't know Mrs. Summers at that point in time, but have you come to know her since?" Dunn asked.

"Yes, sir," the specialist replied. "I've seen her quite a number of times. The surgery that night and the surgical procedures that have followed."

"Let me ask you, Doctor, the condition that you see her in today. Is that the same or different than how you saw her on that night?"

"Well, it's quite a bit different. What you're seeing today is after four surgical procedures. The first night, we debrided what was left of her lower jaw on either side."

"What does that mean?"

"Took out the fragments of bone and teeth, areas of tissue that we knew that if we tried to bring back up and suture would die because they had not enough blood supply."

"Did you remove any foreign particles from her jaws?"

"Yes, sir. There were numerous fragments of metal, fragments off of either a casing or pellets. We didn't know at the time what type of gun had been used."

"What did you do with those particles of metal?"

"Those were sent to the pathology lab."

"Now," Dunn continued, "you say it took about four hours that night?"

"Yes, sir. We had to do a tracheostomy on her, which is a procedure to make a cut in the neck and put a tube in the airway. Then, we started taking out the fragments of bone and teeth and metal that were in the area of trauma, and then started trying to close the soft tissue and bring everything back together as much as possible."

"All right, sir. And, thereafter, she remained in the hospital for some time?"

"She was in the hospital for about three and a half weeks the initial time after the incident."

"Thereafter, what procedure did you follow, Doctor?"

"Before she was out of the hospital, part of her lip which had been brought back together had separated and had to be revised. And since that time, she has been admitted twice: once for removal – her teeth. She has three teeth in the lower jaw, and she had some in the upper jaw blown out, also. Her teeth were wired together for approximately eight to ten weeks. And she was taken back [into surgery] one time and all the wires taken off. And then on the fourth operation, she was taken back to give her more room in her lower jaw and in the floor of her mouth. We had to take skin off her leg and put it into her mouth."

"Transplanted that?"

"Yes, sir."

"All right. To what extent, if any, does she have control over her saliva?"

"Well, she still produces because she still has her glands. The trouble is, since she has no support, she has no chin in front, no support for the soft tissue, it's very hard for her to swallow because her tongue is bound down. So, she tends to drool quite a bit. She faces several other surgical procedures which will be quite extensive."

"Thank you, Doctor."

Eckert's testimony ended the grueling morning for the jurors and spectators alike. The reprieve was short-lived, though, for more horrible, though riveting, revelations awaited the end of the lunch break.

Dr. Michael Walsh was the Director of Pathology at Grand Strand General Hospital. Walsh had performed the autopsy of Louise Sellers the morning following her death.

"Doctor," Dunn began, "did you have an occasion on or about February 22 of this year to see Della Louise Sellers?"

"Yes, sir," Walsh answered. "The body of Mrs. Sellers had been transported back from the Medical University of South Carolina from where she had been pronounced dead following a gunshot wound to the right side of the head."

"All right, Doctor, what physical wounds did you observe on or about her body at that time?"

"Mrs. Sellers had been sent to Charleston, and they had attempted to decompress the brain. She had been shot in the head, and the skull encases the brain. So, when the brain starts to swell from any sort of injury, much like a bruise, there's no space for the brain to swell because of the bony cavity. The attempt of a neurosurgeon is to drill what they call a bur hole, a little hole in the skull to allow the pressure within the brain, due to the gunshot wound, to be somewhat alleviated. This was not successful, and she died very soon after that procedure.

"Immediately above it in the region we call the parietal bone, there was a contact gunshot wound. In a contact wound, we can demonstrate that the muzzle of the pistol was in direct continuity with the skin. In other words, it was placed directly up to the skin and held in that position the moment the trigger was pulled and the projectile fired. The way you can tell that it was contact is that the muzzle of the gun will actually kick back, and you will see a bruising and you can trace the pattern of the muzzle of the gun, including the barrel site, so that the exact replica of the weapon was imprinted on the skin of her scalp.

"This is in contradistinction from, say, firing a shot from any distance away from the body from which you would see powder around the wound. The further away you get, the less powder. Once you get up to the skin, you will actually see bruising and no powder, because when the gasses explode, they go underneath the skin and lift it off the bone. So, we could unequivocally say that the gun was in direct continuity with the skin of the skull at the time of the firing.

"The cause of death was directly related to a .32 caliber gunshot to the brain with extensive destruction of brain tissue, swelling of the brain, and subsequently, the brain just sort of gets pushed down to the base of the skull, which cuts off the ability of the heart to beat and the respirations to be continued."

Dunn then produced an envelope containing a plastic container. After demonstrating chain of custody for the sealed envelope, Dunn handed the evidence to Walsh.

"All right, sir," Dunn said. "Would you open that up and look in it and tell us whether you had an occasion to see the contents before?"

Walsh removed the container and examined the contents. "This is a significantly distorted projectile, the base of it can still be quite well described, so that rifling marks could be obtained from this. We have distortion of the tip that's secondary to the distortion of a soft coat on this metal as it penetrates with high energy into the bone of the skull. This was the projectile that I recovered from the brain of Mrs. Sellers."

"Is this the condition it was in when you removed it from her brain?" Dunn asked.

"Yes, sir," Walsh replied. "We removed the top of the skull and then took the brain from the casing and examined it for extent of the injury. Then, as we find the bullet, we extract it using fingers rather than any sort of metal object. If you use, say, a forceps or tweezers, you're very likely to scrape the metal and induce false markings, so it would be difficult to trace to a particular gun."

"All right, sir. Go ahead, please, Doctor, and tell us what other physical findings that you observed about Della Louise Sellers."

"Besides the wound, there was significant bruising around the face, and this is secondary to the fact that when the bullet goes through, it's under such a high velocity that it cracks the skull.

"Additionally, she had multiple abrasions; the skin had been abraded, like with sandpaper. It's been injured and somewhat oozing beneath. These were present along with what we term lacerations, which are basically cuts. Two of them were present over the right chest, and then on the right upper arm, there were two distinct patterns of injury. One was in somewhat of a circumferential shape due to the placement of the fingernails. And the second was a dentition mark, or a bite mark, located immediately above it.

"Furthermore, she had a significant number of abrasions and bruises around both of the front parts of her hip. And they were most marked over the right side. She had presence of recent evidence of or attempts at sexual intercourse. There was a considerable amount of dirt, including a gold cigarette wrapper, or at least the little pull cord that's present around cigarette packs, present between the gluteal folds; that is, the back part of your buttocks."

Walsh additionally testified that a pap smear of the cervix of Louise Sellers indicated that she had sexual intercourse sometime within the last 72 hours of her life. The time range couldn't be narrowed, according to Walsh, given that additional tests that would normally be performed for a living woman wouldn't be appropriate for someone who had been dead for more than 12 hours, as had Louise at the time of the autopsy.

● ❖ ●

The cross-examination of Walsh by Irby Walker for the defense revealed something that was quite interesting, considering the whole context of the crime spree, something that Dunn had failed to bring out during his examination.

"Dr. Walsh, was any alcoholic content done as to Mr. Skaar's blood?" Walker asked.

"Yes, there was," Walsh answered. "Results did show he had consumed alcoholic beverages, but he was not presumed to be under significant influence."

"What do you mean by 'significant influence,' Doctor?"

"Well, legally, that's 100, but my definition is about 150 milligrams percent."

"Would that be like blowing 15 on the breathalyzer?"

"That's correct. Drunken driving is a hundred," Walsh replied.

"All right, sir," Walker continued. "Any evidence of drugs in his system?"

"No. We looked for drugs in the urine, the stomach contents, and in the blood, and we did not detect any abnormal substances."

"Just alcohol?"

"That's correct."

The defense would later contend that Woomer was under the influence of Skaar when the pair killed, raped, and robbed on February 22. Skaar, it would be argued, fed, clothed, and provided drugs for Woomer, who, in turn, did whatever Skaar told him to do.

● ❖ ●

Following the testimonies of Beth and Sheila, the two young women staying at the Komo-Mai for the winter, a series of witnesses were presented to establish the necessary chain-of-custody for many of the pieces of evidence for the case. The emotional toll from the morning and early afternoon testimony must have weighed heavily through the courtroom as the crowd periodically became impatient during the less than exciting testimonies. Speaking for the court, Dunn called for order, and when he deemed it necessary, told individuals to sit down.

The long first day of testimony ended at 6:15 p.m. and the tired spectators filed out quietly, many perhaps shaking their heads over their decisions to subject themselves to such horrific subject matter. Little did they know what was in store for the following day. Though there would only be one more day of testimony in the first phase of the trial, that next day would end with what was described by one of the attorneys present as, "Easily, the most dramatic moment I've ever witnessed in a courtroom."

31

The next morning, Dunn began with less than exciting but necessary technical testimony. The Crime Scene Specialist of the HCPD, Sgt. Dennis Gallant, and a SLED firearms expert, Lt. Bill Anderson, provided detailed information concerning the several firearms and hundreds of live- and spent-rounds of ammunition found in Room 8 of the Komo-Mai following Skaar's suicide.

Interestingly, Anderson spoke of the .25 caliber pistol that was known from other testimony to have been the gun that Woomer carried into the Turner home in Cottageville. Woomer had reported to Skaar that the .25 was missing, which necessitated the use of the .32 at the Richardson's residence and at Jack's Mini-mall. Apparently, during the robbery in Cottageville, when Woomer carried Turner's coins and suits to the Maverick, he had laid the .25 on the car seat, from where it slipped to the floorboard beside the door and became wedged against the bracket bolting the seatbelt to the floor. When the police who were experienced in such matters began their careful search of the Maverick, the loaded .25 was found in a cocked position, with the hammer back.

This revelation prompted Judge Harwell to caution the jurors. "Mr. Foreman and ladies and gentlemen, I know this is probably not necessary, but I don't want any tragedy to happen in your jury room. You have live ammunition and weapons that are in evidence for your inspection, but no experimenting now, such as loading and unloading these in the jury room."

The testimony following Anderson's included a statement that, despite being hotly contested by the defense, was repeated by Jim Dunn several times during the remainder of the trial. A trustee where Woomer was incarcerated had an opportunity to speak with Woomer on several occasions when the trustee made his rounds through the jail to get refreshments for prisoners.

"Go ahead, now," Dunn said, during direct examination. "Just look over at the jury and tell them what conversation you had with Woomer."

"We was sitting there talking, and I got to asking him what happened. So, he started telling me. He said, 'We went to a store at Pawley's Island. We didn't have no cigarettes, so I told my partner to stop and I'd go in and get some cigarettes.' So, he went in the store and every time he'd go to rob the place, more people would be coming in. So, he said he had to carry them out. And said, 'There were two women there with their husbands,' and he got them and told their husbands if they wanted to see their wives again for them not to call the law. So, he said that probably gave them about 30 or 35 minutes head start. So, they got going to Conway, and his friend says, 'I want a piece of lay,' and so they end up raping them. And I said, 'Well, did the women argue with you or anything like that?' He said, 'No, the women didn't give us no trouble whatsoever.' He said, 'After we got through raping them, I looked at them for a few minutes, they was standing side by side, and I just picked the gun up and blew their shit away.' And he started, you know, just snickering, laughing."

Under heavy cross-examination by Stevens, the trustee admitted he had been in jail on several occasions prior to that time and that he had, in fact, that day been transported to court from the jail where he had been incarcerated for yet another offense.

When court recessed a little later for the two-hour lunch break, Jimmy and Wanda ran an errand in their car. On their return, Jimmy parallel parked in front of a restaurant, next door to the courthouse to pick up some take-out lunches. Jimmy had just stepped in the front door of the restaurant when a car with West Virginia tags pulled up and stopped close to where Wanda sat as she waited for her husband. Wanda became alarmed when three men exited the out-of-state vehicle and approached the passenger side of her car.

Slipping across the seat, Wanda jumped out in traffic and ran into the restaurant. The owner of the restaurant quickly called the courthouse and within minutes a Conway police officer appeared on the scene.

The three men from West Virginia subsequently drove over and parked at the courthouse. While two of the men waited in the car, one man walked inside the building. The men claimed to be friends of Woomer and said they had driven to South Carolina to deliver some clothes. The police had heard a rumor from the jail of a planned escape attempt and decided not to take any chances. The man inside the courthouse was detained while the men outside were searched. The man inside was arrested for being drunk and disorderly and violating state liquor laws. The other two were arrested for violations of state liquor and drug laws. A long-bladed hunting knife was the only weapon found in the car.

When court resumed after lunch, spectators noted that several additional officers were present in the courtroom. Judge Harwell announced, without further explanation, a change in the security procedure allowing persons in to watch the trial. Once testimony got under way, Harwell said, bailiffs would lock the doors and no one would be allowed to enter or leave the courtroom for any reason until a break was called.

From the moment of the harrowing incident at the restaurant, Jimmy and Wanda were under heavy guard everywhere they went, including on bathroom breaks and in the evenings, when they were now to be sequestered at the Conway Motor Inn with the jurors. A policeman Jimmy described as "really huge" was permanently assigned to sit beside him in the courtroom and protect him and Wanda at all times for the remainder of the trial.

The afternoon included several dramatic moments. Prior to playing the tape of Woomer's confession for the court, Stevens called Woomer to the stand for direct testimony in a motion to suppress the confession.

"Would you tell us what happened when Mr. Causey arrested you, Rusty?" Stevens asked.

"He knocked on the door and I went to the hotel room

door, and I walked out the door, and they put the handcuffs on me and started me down the steps, and we stopped and they asked the manager of the hotel, said, 'Is that him?,' and he said, 'Yes.' And they took me down and put me in the police car."

"Did you have any conversation with him?" Stevens asked.

"While we was in the car, I never had no shoes on, and I asked him if they could get my shoes, and they said they'd get them to me later."

"Did Mr. Causey give you any type of warning of any sort?"

"Read me my rights," Woomer replied.

"And did he go further and ask you any questions while you were en route to the jail?"

"Something was said about I was in a whole lot of trouble," Woomer said, "and I was asked who was in Room 8."

"All right," Stevens continued. "When they got you to the jail, tell me what happened?"

"They took me in one of those rooms, and I was asked several questions about what I was locked up for. I don't remember really a whole lot right then. They talked to me for a few minutes, and they took me and put me in a holding tank."

"All right. Did you make a statement to them before you were put in the holding tank?"

"I told them that I felt I was in quite a bit of trouble, and I thought that I should have a lawyer there," Woomer stated.

Stevens continued to lead Woomer through the evening's events. Woomer said several additional times that he had requested a lawyer. The police acknowledged his request, he maintained, but then ignored it.

On cross-examination, Dunn ascertained that Woomer remembered having been read his rights several times during the course of the evening. Dunn also demonstrated that Woomer's memory for the events of that night differed in many respects from the statement he gave several hours after his arrest. There was no further mention of Woomer's supposed requests for a lawyer, not even in the closing remarks made by his attorneys.

When Woomer was dismissed from the stand he returned to the defense table. Just as he turned to slip in his seat, Woomer looked directly at Jimmy and contorted his face. Jimmy's anger rose in disbelief. *That little son-of-a-bitch smirked at me*, Jimmy thought. At just that moment, Jimmy felt a heavy arm across his chest hold him to the back of his seat. The officer seated beside Jimmy had witnessed Woomer's insult and responded quickly to restrain Jimmy.

"I don't know what I might have done, but I certainly wasn't going to do it then. That big officer had me," Jimmy remembered. "I'm not sure if he grabbed Don or not."

Prior to the introduction of the taped confession, Dunn carefully laid the foundation for the chain-of-custody for the damning evidence. Leaving no stone unturned, Dunn called Buddy Causey back to the stand and walked him through much of the same testimony that had previously been given.

Dunn followed a similar pattern for Sheriff Brown. Brown had witnessed the arrest and the first reading of the Miranda warning at the Komo-Mai, and he had personally read Woomer his rights at the jail at 10:30 the next morning. One of the few wrinkles in the trial occurred during Brown's testimony. When Dunn asked Brown to describe the conversation he had with Woomer, Brown said, "He told me his name was Ronald Rusty Woomer. And I explained to him that at the time I gave him the Miranda warning that all I was there for was to establish his identity, that I wasn't going to ask him any other questions except that pertaining to his identity."

"And that was the extent of the conversation that you had with him at that time?" Dunn asked.

"Well, that's not the extent of it," Brown said. "It went further than that."

"Very well, what else did he say?"

"It went so far as he remembered his probation officer's number in Huntington. And I made a phone call."

Stevens was immediately on his feet with an objection.

Harwell dismissed the jury.

"Your Honor," Stevens argued, "at this time, on behalf of the defendant, we would move for a mistrial on the grounds that these statements by the sheriff, even though Your Honor may ask the jurors to disregard them, have so prejudiced the minds of the jurors that we feel that no instruction from the court is going to cure the statement of the sheriff, the inference being of some prior criminal record." In the event of a guilty verdict for the murder charge in the first phase of the trial, the defense intended to argue as a mitigating circumstance that the defendant had no significant criminal history involving violence. The sheriff's statement planted a seed that could potentially damage the ability of the defense to mount a successful argument.

Harwell called for a brief recess and went to his chambers to study the matter. Some 20 minutes later, citing the State versus Charlie Robinson, 1961, South Carolina Supreme Court, a precedent that mirrored the case at hand, Harwell denied the motion for a mistrial. Though the evidence of commission of another crime would not be admissible, he explained, no such evidence of an independent crime had become testimony. Further, Harwell explained that for reversible error to have occurred, prejudice against the defendant must be shown. Harwell stated that he would explain the matter to the jury in a manner to avoid such prejudice.

"Mr. Foreman and ladies and gentlemen," Harwell said, when the jury returned to the courtroom, "inadvertently, the sheriff testified regarding some requests to call a probation officer. I instruct you now, as a matter of law, the defendant is not and has never been on probation. I instruct you now to disregard that portion of the witness' testimony relating to any requests to call a probation officer. It is not a matter for you to consider. Wipe it from your minds."

It seems likely that even if the jurors weren't able to completely forget the remark at that time, they would shortly afterwards when the tape of the confession was played. The remark about the probation officer meant nothing compared to the incriminating evidence of the tape.

"Your honor, at this time, the State would move to introduce the tape and submit it to be played in the presence of the jury," Dunn said.

Nancy Booth, a secretary with the Horry County Police

Department, prepared the tape on a Dictaphone machine and handed out written transcripts.

"All right," agreed Harwell, "I think it's admissible."

"Would you, please, now, Miss Nancy, play the tape?" Dunn asked.

32

The foreman of the jury, Raymond Finch, described the macabre fascination of listening to the tape that he and the other jurors experienced. "It's similar to a situation where you know something is going to happen and you want to turn away, but you don't, and then it's too late. You are left with an indelible image that haunts you. That's what we felt. Sometimes I think if I listen, I can still hear the sound of that voice."

Not only had Woomer already spent an hour with Causey prior to the taping reviewing the particulars of the confession, but Woomer had also spent time prior to that with Enoch Smith, one of the Horry County officers who assisted Causey with the arrest. Woomer said the same things to Smith that were recorded by Causey.

While the tape was played, Woomer sat quietly without expressing emotion.

"Ronald R. Woomer questioned by Buddy Causey at the Horry County Jail on February 23, 1979, 1:55 p.m.," Causey began.

"Ronald, what's your address?"

"Huntington, West Virginia."

"Now, how old are you?"

"Twenty-four."

"How much education do you have?"

"Ninth grade."

"Ronald, do you understand the rights that we have read and explained to you?"

"Yes, sir," Woomer said.

"Do you understand you have the right to remain silent?"

"Yes, sir."

"Do you understand that?"

"Yes, sir."

"Anything you say can and will be used against you in a court of law. Do you understand that?"

"Yes, sir."

"You have the right to talk with a lawyer and have him present with you while you're being questioned. Do you understand that?"

"Yes, sir."

"If you cannot afford a lawyer, one will be appointed to represent you before any questions if you wish one. Do you understand that?"

"Yes, sir."

"If you desire to make a statement or answer any questions, you have the right to stop at any time. Do you understand that?"

"Yes, sir."

"Now, do you also understand that no one has promised you anything or threatened you in any way in order for you to give us a statement concerning the trouble that you're in now?"

"Yes, sir."

"Now, at this time, do you mind giving me a statement on tape concerning the trouble that you're in now?"

"No, sir. I don't care."

"Ronald, now in Huntington, West Virginia, who did you stay with up there?"

"Wanda Matthews and Linda Sowders."

"Now, is Wanda Matthews your girlfriend?"

"Yes, sir."

"And how long have you been staying with her?"

"About eight months."

"Now, what time did you leave Huntington Tuesday?"

"It was in the early evening."

"Early evening?"

"It was early. It was in the afternoon, cause we got to the motel almost down here, not very far from here – it was 9:30 when we got to the hotel."

"All right. Now, who did you leave West Virginia with?"

"Gene."

Determined to be together, Jimmy (age 16) and Wanda
(age 18) stand before a preacher on their wedding day.
When Wanda's father asked Jimmy of his intentions,
Jimmy assured the concerned man that he loved Wanda
and that nothing would ever come between them.

With the birth of
Traci, seventeen
months after
Jimmy and Wanda
married, Jimmy
felt he had the
family he'd
always wanted.

The
proud
couple with Jimmy's
father holding Traci.

Traci wondered aloud
at the party planned
for her sixth birthday
why her mother
wasn't there.

Eugene Skaar (age 42) had a
long history of felonies
committed in several states
when he recruited Woomer
for what they thought would
be a simple robbery.

Ronald "Rusty" Woomer (age 24)
had already been in prison
twice before he traveled with
Skaar to South Carolina to
steal a valuable coin
collection.

As often happens, the "simple plan" went wrong and caused tragedy for many innocent people, including Wanda Summers and her family, whose misfortune was to encounter Woomer and Skaar during their day-long crime spree.

Fred Whitehead, owner of
a coin shop in Myrtle
Beach, helped Fisher devise
the ill-fated criminal plan
that led to four murders
and the deaths of five
people.

John Fisher of Huntington,
W. Va., sent Skaar and
Woomer to do his and
Whitehead's dirty work.

The motel room where Skaar killed himself.

An assortment of weapons and stolen property were found when the police searched the room and the Maverick.

The rain and the mud at one of the crime scenes made the job of the police more difficult.

Refusing to die on the isolated dirt road, Wanda Summers, largely unaware of the severity of her own injuries, struggled to find help for her friend, Louise Sellers.

Woomer being escorted by Detective Buddy Causey in for one of the arraignments. In contrast to the mild appearance of Woomer, his behavior indicated him to be a mean and cold-blooded killer.

The stately Horry County Courthouse in Conway was packed each day of the trial of Woomer. Wanda's appearance in court and her testimony was described by an attorney as "easily" the most dramatic event he had ever witnessed in a courtroom.

Dressed in one of his trademark black suits, the charismatic Jim Dunn stands before the courthouse.

Cleveland Stevens championed the cause of the underdog. Believing that Woomer understood discrimination because of his poor upbringing, Stevens developed a bond with Woomer that lasted until Woomer's death.

Wanda holding Jamie. Jimmy and Wanda held fast to their love through the difficult years of struggle for their family. Rather than ending the nightmare, the trial and conviction of Woomer was only the beginning of the family's recovery process.

Traci with Jamie at the mall on picture day. Traci's love for her brother is revealed by the sparkle in her eyes.

Wanda's journey on behalf of crime victims took her to the state capitol (Wanda is shown in the left photo with then-Lt. Gov. Nick Theodore) and to Washington, DC, with Senator Strom Thurmond, where she testifed about the impact of crime on her family. Wanda's beautiful smile, admittedly hard for her to find for many years, is evident in this picture taken in March, 2001.

The announcement that Jim Dunn placed in the newspaper of the victims' memorial service. Dunn's vision for the rights of victims was formed many years before legislation began to address the impact of crime on the lives of hard-working citizens.

The tombstone where it stands today in the yard of the Horry County Courthouse.

Jenny Chisholm (left), Wanda and Traci appeared on a Geraldo Rivera television show that examined the long wait for justice experienced by crime victims. Both Wanda and Traci were touched by the sincerity expressed by Geraldo, off-camera, after the taping had concluded.

Don Sellers (left) and Buddy Causey with the tombstone outside of the prison on the day Woomer was executed, eleven years and four months after Woomer's crimes. Dunn carried the monument in the back of his truck to remind people of his belief that a significant emphasis of the legal process should be on the victims that criminals leave behind. The media event of Woomer's electrocution turned into a "circus" before the night ended.

Wanda's work with animals helped heal her wounds.

Wanda loves flowers and often chooses scenes of natural and serene environs for her paintings. Wanda finds her artwork to be therapeutic and fulfilling.

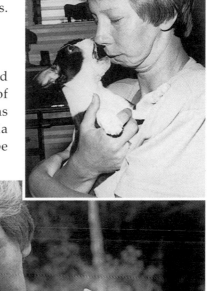

One of Wanda's paintings. The scene shown is familiar to persons living in the low-country of South Carolina. Wanda's renewed sense of purpose is a result, in part, of her blossoming talent as an artist. Wanda's work has been accepted in competitions and is on display at the Georgetown Art Gallery (Georgetown, SC).

Jimmy and Wanda at the wedding of Traci and Olin.

Wanda steps into the post-race, Winner's Circle photograph with her family and friends. Jamie is on the left with his arm in the air. Jimmy is being hoisted by David Henderson, the driver of the #27 OBR racecar sponsored by Summers' Roofing. Olin is holding the victory flag.

Traci is just behind Olin.

"Do you know what Gene's last name is?"

"Skaar."

"And why did y'all decide to come to Myrtle Beach?"

"He called me at Wanda's house one evening, and I was out on bond, and I wasn't going to go to court, and I was planning on leaving town, and he called me and asked me if I wanted to make some money, and I said, 'Yeah.' And he was just joking with me and told me to get some swimming trunks and stuff cause we was going to go to Myrtle Beach."

"And did he say how y'all was going to make some money when you got down here?"

"Stealing old coins."

"And how long have you been knowing Gene?"

"About a year."

"All right. Now, and you left Huntington about what time Tuesday?"

"Around in the early – right after noon, around noon or after noon."

"And how were you traveling?"

"In a Maverick, a brown one."

"Whose car was it?"

"It belongs to Gene's son."

"All right. Now, so you left Huntington on Tuesday. Did you stop somewhere Tuesday night and spend the night?"

"Yes, sir. We stopped – it took – the day we left, we stopped at a hotel that night. It's 175 miles from here, cause I remember him telling me that's how far that we had to go."

"Was that somewhere in the state of North Carolina?"

"Yes, sir. I believe so."

"So, you got up Wednesday morning and come to Myrtle Beach then?"

"Yes, sir."

"Now, about what time did you arrive at Myrtle Beach?"

"About – I don't remember. It was after dark."

"That was after dark Wednesday night?"

"Yes, sir."

"All right. Now, what, did you get you a place to stay here in Myrtle Beach then?"

"Yes, sir, at the Komo-Mai Hotel."

"At the what?"

"Komo-Mai."

"And what room did you get?"

"Room 8."

"All right. Who registered for the room?"

"Gene did."

"Do you know the name he registered in?"

"No, sir. I set – I set in the big brown chair over side the window while he was registering."

"Now, when you left Huntington, West Virginia, how much money did you have?"

"We had about three or four hundred dollars. I had about a hundred and fifty."

"And Gene had the rest of it?"

"Yes, sir."

"So, when you got down here, now, Wednesday night and got your motel room, what did you do after you got in your room that night?"

"Just laid in the motel and watched television. We went to the store and bought some food and put it in the refrigerator, and we just stayed at the hotel."

"All right. Thursday morning, what time did you get up?"

"About 10:30."

"And you was in what room?"

"Room 8."

"And you and Gene was sharing the same room?"

"Yes, sir."

"And about what time did you leave the motel Thursday?"

"Around 12 o'clock."

"And where did you leave the motel to go?"

"To this guy's house that we was supposed to steal coins off of."

"Now, are you talking about the – "

"The first house that we went to."

"John Turner, John Turner house?"

"Yes, sir. That's his name."

"That's in Colleton County up near Walterboro. Is that correct?"

"Yes, sir. I know it's near Walterboro."

"Okay. Now, did Gene know this Mr. John Turner?"

"Yeah, evidently, cause he – only thing he didn't know, he knew the town he lived in, and he knew he had a bunch of old coins, but he didn't know how to get to the house, and that's why we stopped at that white house, and I asked that boy where he lived."

"Now, about how old was this little boy that you asked where Mr. John Turner lived?"

"He looked like he was about 13, 14."

"Thirteen? So, you got to Walterboro and found Mr. John Turner's house. Now, what kind of guns did y'all have in the car?"

"A .32."

"A .32 pistol?"

"Yes, sir. And a .25 pistol and a .20 gauge pump shotgun."

"Who did the guns belong to?"

"They all belong to Gene."

"And did y'all have these guns when you left Huntington?"

"Yes, sir."

"All right. Now, when you found out from the little boy where Mr. John Turner lived, how far from Mr. Turner's house were you then?"

"Just three houses."

"Three houses down?"

"Right across the street. It's a Y where that big white house was setting, and right across the street, there was two houses beside each other and then a driveway beside it, and his house sets back in the woods."

"All right. Now, when you pulled into the driveway of Mr. Turner's house, what happened? Did you see, see – "

"A car was coming out of the driveway and – "

"Do you remember what kind of car it was coming out of the driveway?"

"I think it was a little blue car."

"Do you know who was driving?"

"No, sir."

"Was it a man, woman, or – "

"I couldn't tell. We backed up. When they started out,

we just pulled in. And when we backed out the driveway, he drove back down the road towards that other big white house where we asked where he lived, and they cut left when they come out of the driveway and then went out a road beside that school."

"All right. Now, was Gene doing the driving?"

"Yes, sir."

"Now, at the time, where was the guns in the car?"

"I had one of the pistols, and he had one of them, and the shotgun was underneath the seat."

"OK. So, is this when you turned around and went back to the Turner's house?"

"Yes, sir."

"Now, tell me, Ronald, what happened when y'all pulled up in Mr. Turner's driveway the second time?"

"He told me when we went up and knocked on the door, said, as soon as you open the door to pull the pistol on him so he wouldn't try to shoot us or nothing."

"Now, which pistol did you have?"

"I had the .25, I think, then."

"And which gun did Gene have?"

".32 pistol."

"So, when you went up, who knocked on the door?"

"Gene and I both did."

"Knocked on the door?"

"Yes, sir."

"And what happened then?"

"The guy opened the door up."

"The old man opened the door up?"

"Yes, sir."

"What was the first thing that was said when the man opened the door?"

"I asked him where the old, where – if he had any old money."

"Now, did you have the guns pointed on him then?"

"Yes, sir."

"You and Gene?"

"Yes, sir."

"And tell me what took place then."

"We just – he said he didn't have no coins, but old

foreign coins, and Gene told me to make him set there in the chair and he went in the back, and he found the coin books in a back bedroom, and he laid them out on the bed. And then he come back in there and he told me he found the coins, and I carried the coins out, and Gene asked him if he had any guns, and he said he had a .357 out in his car, and he give me the keys and I went out to the car."

"Now, when you went out to the car, where was Gene?"

"In the house with the man."

"Holding the gun on the man?"

"Yes, sir."

"And when you went out to the car, did you take something out to the car then?"

"No, sir. I went to his car to see if I could find that gun."

"Did you find the pistol in his car?"

"No, sir. He told me it was under the seats, and I – well, I made two trips and I come back in, and he told me it was in the trunk, and it wasn't in there either."

"All right. Now, had Gene already took the old coins out and put them in y'all's car?"

"No, sir. I took the coins out and put them in the car."

"You did?"

"Yes, sir."

"And after you went and looked for the gun in the man's car, did you go back in the house then?"

"Yes, sir. That was when I got the coins."

"All right. When you went back in the house, tell me what happened then."

"I carried the coins out, and Gene got a whole bunch of suits, and I carried them out, too, and came back in the house, and I was standing in a hallway off the living room, and the man was setting in the chair with his back to me, and Gene come over there and told me, said, 'Wait 'til I start the car and tell him to walk in the back of the bedroom so he can't see the car and,' he said, 'as soon as you hear the car start, shoot him and come out to the car and get in.'"

"All right. So, did Gene go out to the car then?"

"Yes, sir."

"When he went out to the car, what did you do then?"

"I told him – well, he was already getting up. Gene had told him – you know, he told me what to do: take him in the back bedroom. And he was setting there when he heard it, when he said it, and he got up and started towards the back bedroom in the hall, and I heard the car start, and I shot him."

"Where did you shoot him?"

"In the head."

"In the back of the head?"

"Yes, sir."

"And you shot him with which gun?"

".32."

"You shot him with the .32?"

"Yes, sir. We lost the .25 somewhere."

"So, when you shot him with the .32, what happened?"

"I just shot him and turned around and took off running."

"Did he fall then?"

"He was falling when I turned around and took off running."

"And you went out and got in the car?"

"Yes, sir."

"And what was said after you got in the car? What did Gene ask you?"

"Just asked me if I shot him, and I said, 'Yes.' And he asked me where I shot him at, and I told him in the head. He said that was the way you're supposed to do it, cause that way couldn't nobody tell on you."

"And then, y'all left and went where?"

"We started driving back home, back to Myrtle Beach, back to the hotel. And he was driving down the road and there was a big brick house, and I think it was a brick house. There wasn't nobody home – well, there was people there. I don't know if this was the first or second place we stopped at. We stopped at one house on the way back down the road, and we got out and – well, both of us got out. And the back door was open. All that was there was the screen door. And we knocked on the door and pulled the pistols on the man."

"Now, the man come and answered the door, and both of you was at the door then?"

"Yes, sir."

"The back door?"

"Yes, sir, the back door."

"And you done what then?"

"We pulled the pistols on him and went in the house and went in his closets and got all of his guns and – "

"Well, let me ask you now, what gun did you have then?"

"I had the .32 pistol, cause we only had one pistol then."

"And Gene had the .20 gauge shotgun?"

"No, sir. He left it in the car. I don't know, because I didn't – I was – I just – I don't know if he brought it out of the car or not. He brought it in the house after we got in the house. No, sir. After we got in the house, I pulled the pistol. We only had one pistol. And after we got in the house, he told me to give him the pistol, and I went out and got the shotgun."

"Now, who all was at the house besides the old man?"

"A woman and a girl."

"How old was the man? Was he an old man or a young man?"

"Middle age."

"How about the woman?"

"Forty."

"How about the girl?"

"I don't know. She was young."

"Do you know about how old she was?"

"About 12 or 13, something like that. She was little."

"Now, what did you do when – after you got in the house with those people? What did you and Gene do then?"

"Gene asked him if he had any guns, and he said – and asked him if he had any old money or any money in the house and told him, you know, not to lie to him. And he told us, told us that the guns was in the closet. And I went in the closet and got the guns and took them out and put them in the car, and we come back into the house. And I went back in the bedroom to see if there was any more guns, and he just told me to do the same thing that we done at the other house."

"Now, were they sitting down or – "

"Yes, sir."

"All three of them?"

"Yes, sir."

"And, so, what kind of weapon did you have at that time?"

"The shotgun."

"And did Gene go get in the car?"

"No, sir. Not – I shot the man and the girl and then he left and went out to the car."

"You shot the man first?"

"I shot. I just shot. I shot the man and the girl together, yes, sir."

"You're talking about the little girl?"

"Yes, sir."

"And did the man fall when you shot him?"

"Yes, sir."

"Did the little girl fall?"

"Yes, sir."

"And what about the woman?"

"And then I shot her."

"With the shotgun?"

"Yes, sir."

"Did she fall?"

"Yes, but she was still screaming."

"All right. Now, were they standing up or sitting down then?"

"Setting down. On the couches."

"You say Gene was in the room when you shot the man and the little girl?"

"Yes, sir. And after – as soon as I pulled the trigger, he took off and went out of the door."

"How many shots did you fire in the house?"

"Three."

"Three shots?"

"Yes, sir."

"And after you shot the woman, what did you do?"

"I shot her again, because she was screaming."

"And what else did you do then?"

"Then I just left and went out and got in the car, and we left and started back down the road."

"Now, again, tell me what all y'all took from the house."

"Four guns and his billfold."

"Anything else?"

"No, sir."

"And you say you went back out to the car?"

"And a light."

"What kind of light?"

"The kind you plug into a cigarette lighter. A little sealbeam light."

"Is that all?"

"Yes, sir."

"And, so, then you went and got in the car?"

"Yes, sir."

"And what did y'all do then?"

"Just pulled out of the driveway and started back down the road."

"And then what happened?"

"We drove, and we came to a little grocery store-filling station thing. And we pulled in, he said, 'This is a good place to rob, cause they wasn't, ain't nobody there.' So, we went in."

"First, now, when you pulled up there, did you pull the car right on the front?"

"Yes, sir."

"And when you got out and went in, both of you went in?"

"Yes, sir."

"What weapon did you have when you went in?"

"I had the .32 pistol."

"And what weapon did Gene have?"

"He didn't have none until after he – we got inside the place."

"All right. After you got inside, was there any customers in there?"

"No, sir."

"How many people was in the store when you first went in?"

"Just the man and woman that runs the place."

"All right. Tell me exactly what happened after you got

in the store?"

"We – I – he told the girl to open the cash register, and I walked behind the thing with the girl and opened the cash register."

"Now, did you have the gun on her then?"

"No, sir. I had it in my belt."

"Did she see the gun?"

"Yes, sir."

"And who told her to open the cash register?"

"Gene told her to open the cash register, and then he asked them if they had any more money any place in the place, and she told me that they had some, you know, in a wooden drawer. It was in a bag."

"And who got the money out of the cash register?"

"I did."

"And what was Gene doing then?"

"He was holding a gun on that man over in the last aisle."

"Now, which gun?"

"The shotgun."

"Well, now, you say when you first went in the store, you had the .32 pistol?"

"Yes, sir."

"Now, how did Gene get the shotgun?"

"After we got in the door. He went back out and got the shotgun, cause he said that they could see it if he tried to carry it in."

"Now, so after you got the money, tell me what happened."

"While we was getting the money, a man walked in the door, and we pulled the gun, pointed the guns at him and told him just to walk on over there with the other man and act like he was looking at stuff on the shelf. And I don't know how many people came in there. About five or six people came in there."

"Now, you still had the .32?"

"Yes, sir."

"And Gene had the shotgun?"

"I had the .32, yes, sir, cause a car pulled up and a woman come in. I think it was that one woman that we took with us. And her husband and her kid was in the car, and Gene told me to just walk out to the car real natural. And I opened the door up and put the pistol on them and made them come inside with us, too. And then a car pulled up and he brought somebody in."

"So, when you done that, do you know about how many people you had in the store at that time?"

"About six or eight people."

"And what did you make them do?"

"Lay on the floor over behind the cash registers."

"All of them?"

"Yes, sir."

"And tell me what happened after that."

"Well, we had the money stuck in our pockets, and we took everybody's billfolds. And Gene told me to bring the two girls with us, cause they wouldn't know if we pulled the line out of the thing, out of the phone cord. And he said, as long as we had the women with us, they wouldn't bother us or try to call the police or nothing like that. And I told them not for nobody to try to get up and they wouldn't nobody get hurt. And we left."

"Now, when you left, did you have to force the women in the car or – "

"No, sir."

"Did you have the guns on them while they was going out to the car?"

"No, sir. I had the gun in my belt. I never ever had no gun pulled on them while all the time we was inside the car."

"Now, let me ask you this. While the people was on the floor – "

"Yes, sir."

" – which gun did you have?"

"I had the shotgun then."

"And Gene had the .32?"

"Yes, sir."

"And who got the billfolds out of the people's pockets?"

"Both of us."

"And you know how many billfolds you got?"

"No, sir. I got all the billfolds out of the people's – no, he got two billfolds."

"And you got some out?"

"Yes, sir."

"And then, after you got the billfolds, you say you took the two girls with you?"

"Yes, sir."

"Now, where did they get in the car?"

"At the store."

"I know, but did they get in the front seat, the back seat, or – "

"In the back seat."

"Both of them?"

"Yes, sir."

"Were they screaming or hollering?"

"No, sir."

"And you and Gene got in the front seat?"

"Yes, sir."

"And who was driving?"

"Gene was."

"Tell me what happened after you left there."

"We left and started down the road. He told them we was just going to drive down and let them out away from any houses or anything so we could be gone before they got – he told them we was going to Georgetown. I told them that. And he said we was, you know, told them that we was going to let them out. I already knew that he was going to kill them because he told me."

"Who told you?"

"Gene did. He told me that we was going to kill everybody that we robbed and that way they couldn't nobody say who done it or not."

"When did he tell you that?"

"Before we ever left Huntington. He said if we're going to do it, that that's the way to do it and that way they don't nobody tell on you."

"Okay. So, you got the two women and you left the grocery store. Tell me what happened after you left."

"We was traveling back down the road that we'd been on, towards Myrtle Beach."

"Highway 17?"

"Yes, sir. And he asked them if they knew any roads, cause there was a bunch of houses down through there where we was at, and he asked them if they knew any roads that we could cut out where there wasn't no houses where we could let them out, and they told us to turn out a road. We turned left and I don't know the name of the road."

"Was it a paved road or a dirt road?"

"It was a paved road out for a while, and then it cut off to the right onto a dirt road. And we went out there, and on the way out there, I got in the back seat and one of the girls got up in the front seat, and I hadn't said – I never did say nothing. Well, I did after he told the girl in the front seat, he told her to take her clothes off."

"Wait a minute now. What did you do, climb over the front seat while he was still going?"

"I climbed, yes, sir."

"And when he told her to take her clothes off, had y'all already stopped then?"

"No, sir. We was driving."

"Still – and while you was – while the car was still moving, he told her to take her clothes off?"

"Yes, sir."

"What did she say?"

"She said she didn't want to, and he told her, you know, to take them off, and then she started taking them off."

"All right. Did she take all of her clothes off?"

"I don't know, sir. I know she took her pants off."

"And what about the girl in the back seat with you? Did you tell her to take her clothes off?"

"No. She just started taking her clothes off, and he told that girl to take hers off."

"So, both of them started taking their clothes off?"

"Yes, sir."

"All right. When they took their clothes off, did the one in the back seat take all of her clothes off or just take her panties off?"

"We drove down a road, and Gene said, 'This is a good place, cause they ain't no houses or nothing around.' And we cut down on a dirt road, and I went over in the weeds with the girl that I was in the back seat with, and he stayed inside the car and – "

"Now, when you and the girl you was with got out of the car, how much clothes did she have on at that time?"

"Pants and shoes."

"Did she have on long pants?"

"Blue jeans, I think."

"Now, she didn't have on any blouse or bra at that time?"

"No, sir."

"And, so, you and her went over there in the weeds. Tell me what happened when you went over in the weeds."

"We just had intercourse and we got back up and come to the car."

"Did she try to fight you any?"

"No, sir."

"What weapon did you have with you?"

"I had the .32 pistol."

"When you went out in the weeds with her?"

"Yes, sir."

"Now how far from the car were you and this one?"

"About 20 yards, 30 yards."

"Now, could you hear anything going on in the car?"

"We could hear them talking and we couldn't tell what they was saying."

"Did Gene have intercourse with the girl he was with?"

"I don't know sir. I didn't go over to the car."

"Did you hear her screaming or hollering or anything?"

"No, she wasn't screaming or nothing."

"Now when you had intercourse with the one you was with, you say she didn't fight you any?"

"No, sir."

"And when you got through, or let me ask you whenever you, before you had intercourse, did she take all of her clothes off?"

"Yes, sir."

"Did you take them off or did she take them off?"

"She took them off."

"When you got down in the weeds you told her to take them off?"

"Yes, sir."

"Did she say anything then?"

"No, sir, she just took her clothes off. All she had on was her shoes and her jeans and she took them off."

"In other words, she done what you said do?"

"Yes, sir."

"Was she very scared?"

"She wasn't crying or anything. The other girl was."

"The other girl was crying?"

"Yes, sir."

"The one you were with wasn't crying?"

"No, sir."

"About how old were these girls?"

"One of them – she told me – one of them was 24 and one of them was 31, I think."

"All right, so you were with the girl that – "

"I was with the youngest girl."

"Is that the one that came up with her husband at the store?"

"I don't know if she had a husband or not. She – there was – everybody started coming in all at once."

"Which one of the girls came up with her husband and left her husband and baby in the car?"

"I think it was her."

"The one you was with?"

"Yes, sir."

"So, after you got through having intercourse, what did you do then?"

"We walked back to the car."

"Did she put her clothes back on then?"

"Yes, sir, her pants and blouse and she left the rest of her clothes laying over there."

"Over where?"

"In the weeds."

"So, how long did you stay on top of her?"

"About 10 minutes."

"So, after you had intercourse with her, you say you and her – you and this girl – do you know what her name was?"

"No, sir."

"And you went back to the car?"

"Yes, sir."

"What was Gene and this other girl doing in the car?"

"When we got back to the car, they both had their clothes on and was sitting in the front seat."

"And tell me what happened then."

"He told them, you know, to get out and walk down the road a little piece, told me, said, 'Just walk them down the road a little piece and come back.' And when they got in front of me, he handed me the shotgun out of the car and told me when I got down the road to shoot them."

"All right. Now, when he – when you started walking them down the road, you say you took the shotgun?"

"Yes, sir, and the pistol."

"Did he stay in the car?"

"Yes, sir."

"At that time, did the girls know you was going to shoot them?"

"No, sir. I don't think so."

"And they walked ahead of you?"

"Yes, sir."

"And what did you tell them?"

"I told them to both stand together, cause he told me not to shoot two or three times, and I told them both to stand together. And I shot them. And one of the girls – "

"Which one did you shoot first?"

"The girl I was with, she was on this side."

"What weapon did you shoot her with?"

"A shotgun."

"Where did you shoot her?"

"In the head. I pointed it towards her head. I had to hold it down."

"Are you talking about the back of her head?"

"And the side."

"Did she turn around and look at you with the shotgun before you shot her?"

"I don't think so, sir."

"So you shot her?"

"Yes, sir."

"Did she fall right then?"

"They both fell down."

"When you shot the first time they both fell?"

"They both fell down. But the other girl turned around and looked at me and started to scream."

"What did you do then?"

"Shot her with the pistol."

"And when you left them, they both were still on the ground?"

"Yes, sir."

"And did you think both of them were dead at that time?"

"Yes, sir."

"And what did you do?"

"I just went back and got in the car, and we came back to the hotel in Myrtle Beach."

"About how far from the car were you when you shot the girls?"

"About 20 or 30 yards."

"So Gene saw you shoot both the girls?"

"Yes, sir."

"And when you come back and got in the car, you say you done what?"

"Got back in the car and drove back to the hotel in Myrtle Beach."

"And when you got back to the motel, about what time was it?"

"I don't even remember, sir. It was starting to get up in the evening."

"Was it after dark?"

"Oh, yes, sir."

"And you went back in your room?"

"While we was in the car, getting out of the car, while we was parking it, this girl, Beth is her name, I think. She lives upstairs. And her and another girl and two or three young dudes, young guys, was staying down there. And I hadn't met nobody yet, and I asked them if they liked to party, and they said, 'Yeah.' And I asked them if they wanted to smoke a joint, and they said, 'Yes.' So, I went down to the room and I drank a glass of water and a glass of milk, and then I left the room."

"All right. After you left the girl's room, where did you

go?"

"We went to Room 7, cause there was a bunch of people in her room, and one of the guys that was in there was in Room 7. And she – this girl Beth – the car belongs to this other girl. And she took this girl and a boy somewhere and came back, and she came to Number 7. Johnny, is that guy's name."

"All right. Let me ask you, Ronald, about how long were you at the motel, when you got back to the motel, about how long were you there before the police came up to the motel?"

"The first time that I knew they was out there, I didn't know it was the police. I walked out the door, and there was a man had a shotgun standing up on the steps up against that brick thing, and he told me, said, 'Young man, get back in your room.'"

"Now, at that time, that was Room 12 you was in with the other girl?"

"Yeah, I believe so."

"And Gene was in y'all's room. Is that correct?"

"Well, I went down to the room right before that to get cigarettes, and Gene wasn't there. The door was open, but he wasn't there."

"Okay. Let me ask you, Ronald, do you know a man by the name of Fisher?"

"Yes, sir."

"What's his full name?"

"John Fisher."

"And where is he from?"

"Huntington, West Virginia."

"And has he ever been to Myrtle Beach with Gene?"

"They told me that he had come down here about three weeks ago, him and Gene. They both told me that they was down here about three weeks ago."

"Did he say that they had done anything while they were down here?"

"No, sir."

"And he is about how old?"

"About 50."

"Okay. Now, do you know a fella by the name of Fred?"

"Yes, sir."

"Who is Fred?"

"I don't know who he is. He's a guy in Myrtle Beach that tells them where all the people's got old money and stuff."

"What kind of work does Fred do?"

"He owns a coin shop."

"Owns a coin shop?"

"Yes, sir."

"When did you first meet Fred?"

"The day we came to Myrtle Beach."

"Did you hear Fred say something to y'all about John Turner from Walterboro?"

"When we first walked through the door, the first thing he asked was, 'Where's John Fisher?' And Gene told him he wasn't there, and then he introduced me to Fred. And Gene asked him, he says, 'Things still pretty good?' He said, 'Yes, but the guy has a dog.'"

"What guy was Fred talking about?"

"John Turner."

"Now, is Fred the man that set up all your places? Is he the one that told you and Gene where John Turner lived and about him having all the old coins?"

"Yes, sir. Gene and John Fisher told me about it before we ever left Huntington. He told me that this guy named Fred knew where them was at, and a bunch more people had them."

"So, Fred knew that you and Gene was going to Walterboro to rob John Turner?"

"Yes, sir. He was buying all the coins. And, last night, when I opened the door up, or when I came downstairs, me and this girl came down the steps where she had some rum up there. We came down the steps to get some Coke, and Fred was coming into Gene and our room, mine and Gene's room then."

"After you had killed these people and got back to the motel, Fred came to the motel?"

"Yes, sir, cause Gene called him, cause he told me he was going to call him. I figured that's where he was at when I went down to get my cigarettes."

"All right. What did he tell Fred?"

"I don't know. I didn't – when I walked down the steps, I walked down the steps to get some change off of him, cause I didn't have no change, and he was walking out of the door, and I asked him for the change and Fred came around the door, around the corner."

"So, Fred knew that y'all killed these people?"

"I don't know if he – if he knew that we killed them."

"Well, whenever you left Myrtle Beach, or when you met Fred, did Fred know at that time that y'all was going to rob and kill them?"

"Yes, sir, because Gene called him on the phone, and he said, 'You know you won't be seeing them people no more after,' and Fred said, "That's okay.' That's what Gene told me he said on the phone."

"But you heard Fred tell you and Gene about John Turner, about he was supposed to have a dog and he had the old coins?"

"Yes, sir."

"And he knew y'all was going to rob him?"

"Yes, sir. He was – that's where we were selling all the coins is to him."

"Okay. Now is there anything else, Ronald, that you want to tell me that maybe I have failed to ask you?"

"I don't know, sir. Not right now I don't know nothing."

"All right. Now, is everything that you told me in our conversation here, is that the truth?"

"Yes, sir."

"And no one has threatened you or made you any promises. Is that correct?"

"Yes, sir."

"And you have been advised of your rights?"

"Yes, sir."

"And you understand your rights?"

"Yes, sir, I do."

"Now, is that about it?"

"Yes, sir.

"End of statement," Detective Causey said.

33

Prior to the testimony of Wanda Summers, Dunn presented to the court a letter from a Georgetown psychiatrist who had worked extensively with Wanda. Reading from the letter, Dunn told the court that Dr. James F. Hooper said, "I feel that it would be in Mrs. Summers' best interest from a psychiatric point of view that her testimony be given in front of the jury only and that the courtroom be cleared if possible during her testimony."

"Is there any objection?" Judge Harwell asked.

Stevens was on his feet immediately. "Yes, sir, Your Honor. We do not intend, and we have no desire, to do anything injurious to Mrs. Summers' health." Stevens hesitated, allowing himself to think about the psychiatrist's request.

"Just whom does the doctor suggest should be in the court?" Stevens then asked, and quickly added, "I do not believe that it is necessary or required, if the court so instructed the viewing public that they are to make no outbursts, that they are to remain absolutely quiet, that them sitting in this audience is going to do any more to her health than the very fact that we are sitting at this table, or the fact that she may be subject to cross examination. I don't know. Just based on that letter, Your Honor, I would have to oppose it."

"Have you seen the letter?" Harwell asked Stevens.

"No, sir," Stevens replied. "I haven't seen the letter."

The letter was handed to him. While the defense team examined the letter, Dunn approached the judge.

"Your Honor," Dunn said. "I'm advised by Mrs. Summers that she's prepared to testify in open court with whoever is here."

Judge Harwell considered the matter. "All right," he said. "Mrs. Summers, during your testimony, at any time if you need to stop or get a drink of water or just regain your composure, you just let me know, and we'll be glad to recess and do everything we possibly can not to cause you any more problems than you've already had. We're in no hurry. We'll stand at ease for about five minutes."

Following the brief recess, Harwell addressed the court. The jury was not present. "Ladies and Gentlemen, this is sort of out of the ordinary and unusual for me to make such a request as I'm about to do. I would appreciate it if you appreciate the situation that Mrs. Summers is in. This lady has been through a tremendous ordeal. Many of us could not live through the ordeal that she's been put through. I'm going to ask not only the press, but I'm going to ask the members of the public here in court to please realize your interest in this case, but please try to remember the interest of Mrs. Summers and refrain from any unnecessary commenting in your newspapers or in your conversation to other members of the public.

"I'm sure all of you are interested in her welfare as the court is interested in her welfare. She understands the rights of the defendant to a public trial, and she's willing to go forward with her testimony for which I admire her; but I am going to ask you – I can't make you do it – but I am going to ask that you all exercise a little mature responsibility and not to inadvertently or otherwise do Mrs. Summers any more damage or hurt than she has already incurred. With that admonition, we'll go forward with the case," Harwell concluded.

When the jury returned, Dunn said, "Mrs. Wanda Summers, come around, please." All eyes were on Wanda as she walked across the courtroom and took a seat in the witness box.

During Wanda's lengthy testimony, Dunn moved from his usual position to stand at the far end of the jury box. Wanda had been instructed by Dunn to turn her body slightly in her seat and look directly into his eyes as she spoke. Dunn hoped this would help Wanda keep her focus and avoid nervousness that could develop from looking at the large crowd. More importantly, he knew that the precise positioning of Wanda's body would allow the jurors to get a full frontal view of her face during her entire testimony.

Dunn led the courageous woman to the night of February 22. "I want you to tell the jury in your own words what happened on that day," Dunn said gently.

"I went to Jack's Mini-mall," Wanda began, "where I was employed, at approximately 6:30 p.m. I got out of my car . . . ."

The only sound in the courtroom was Wanda's voice, amplified by the public address system. She spoke hesitantly, at first, and then gained strength as she told the jurors of the robbery and the forced abduction from the store.

"Mr. Skaar took us out to the car," Wanda said, "Louise and I, and put us in the back seat. He got in the driver's seat and we sat there and waited on Mr. Woomer to come out. When he opened the door, he started to get in the back seat and he saw that both Louise and I were sitting in the back seat, and he said, 'That's okay. I guess we can change later.' So, he got in the car and we left. Mr. Woomer did have a pistol on both Louise and I in the back seat, and I asked him to put it away. There was no need for it. And he did as far as I know."

Wanda told the jury how she informed her captors as the Maverick pulled from the store that they were headed in the wrong direction. Wanda thought that she was helping and that Woomer and Skaar would be grateful.

Woomer asked Wanda and Louise if they knew of a deserted road, with no houses. When they reached an intersection at Highway 544, and Wanda thought Skaar might go down the wrong road, she tried to help again. "No, sir," she volunteered. "I know that road. There are houses. There are no deserted areas on that road that I know of."

Skaar chose another road. "We turned left on Highway 544, and we drove. I don't know how far. It was dark. I was scared. We came to a dirt road and we turned off. We drove to the end where there were lights and they got scared. So, they turned the car around and headed back towards the highway, and they parked. The highway was on – you could see it. I've left part of it out."

"Just take your time," Dunn said softly. The jury sat in stunned silence as Wanda dabbed saliva and told her story.

"Before we reached this dirt road, they made Louise get in the front seat, and Mr. Woomer got in the back seat with me. I heard Mr. Skaar tell her to remove her pants. Louise got hysterical and told him she was not going to do it. He told her if she did not, he would kill her. She was very upset. She was shaking. She was crying. She was hysterical.

"I reached over the seat, and I put my arms around her and I told her to do as they said or they'd kill us both. So, she removed her pants. Mr. Woomer had the pistol on me in the back seat. He told me to remove my blouse and bra, which I did.

"When the car stopped on the dirt road, Mr. Skaar got out and came around to the passenger side, opened the door and laid Louise down in the seat. Mr. Woomer made him move so that we could get out.

"We got out of the car and we walked to the right of the car, I think. It was across a ditch in a weeded, bushy area. I took my clothes with me that I had taken off in the car. I took those with me, not anticipating having to get back in the car. He made me remove the rest of my clothes and told me to lie down on the ground, which I did."

Wanda began to cry.

"Just take your time," Harwell said. "Take your time."

"Do you want a glass of water?" Dunn asked.

"Yes."

There was not one sound in the courtroom as Dunn helped Wanda with a glass of water. The jury watched as Wanda held tissues beneath where she held the glass to her mouth and dabbed away the water that spilled.

"I laid down on the ground," Wanda continued hesitantly. "Mr. Woomer did not remove any of his clothes."

Dunn's face appeared red and strained. Wanda had again begun to cry and had stopped talking. "I know it's difficult, ma'am. Just take your time," Dunn said.

Wanda continued her agonizing testimony describing for the court how she was raped at gunpoint by a man who insisted that she call him "Johnny." When she faltered, Dunn advised Wanda to use her best judgment and tell only those details that she was willing to tell. Certain that the jury needed to hear what she had to say, Wanda bravely continued for more than an hour.

"After he had completed his act," she continued, "he told me to put my clothes back on. I put on my pants and my shirt. I left my underclothes and I think my sweater there. He insisted that I hurry; I was taking too long.

"He walked me back to the car where Louise and Mr. Skaar were standing up outside of the car. Mr. Skaar and Mr. Woomer had a conversation then. I am not sure what it was about. I know they discussed how far back down the road they should walk us and leave us so that they could get away.

"Mr. Skaar walked around the car and got back in and cranked the engine. Mr. Woomer walked Louise and I back down the road away from the highway. He had two guns, a pistol and a shotgun. Louise and I walked very, very close together. It was raining that night. I remember her telling him that she had just recently gotten out of the hospital. She had had surgery, and that she was afraid that the weather – being out in the weather and rain was going to make her sick.

"He continued to walk us down the road. I don't know how far away from the car it was, because I never turned back to see. Then, we stopped. I don't know why we stopped or if he stopped us, but we stopped. And I didn't hear anything for a couple of seconds. So, I turned my head to the left, I think, to see if he was gone. The next thing I remember was an explosion in my face and seeing Louise fall to the ground. That's all I remember until I came to.

"I got up. They were gone. The car was gone. There was nobody there but me and Louise. Louise was laying on the ground, and I shook her, and I called her name. I said, 'Louise, get up. We've got to go get help.' And she wouldn't answer me. And I didn't know what to do. I didn't know whether to leave her there. I knew I had to go get help.

"I started running towards the highway. At that time, I realized that I had been shot. I looked down and I could see blood on my shirt. I looked at my hands. There was blood on my hands, and I could see parts of my face hanging.

"I started screaming.

"The one thing that was uppermost in my mind was my daughter. I knew I had to get home. This is on the twenty-second of February. I had to get home because her birthday was on the twenty-fifth. I had to get home to give her a birthday party.

"I ran into the highway and two cars passed me. I tried to stop them and they didn't stop. I ran across the highway. I saw lights coming from a mobile home. And I fell in the ditch. It had water in it. It was very cold. I got out of the ditch and I saw this man coming towards me, and I ran to him to try to get help. I heard him say, 'Oh, my God, she's been hurt.' And I heard him tell his wife to go get some towels and blankets.

"He laid me on the ground. I remember it very clearly. They wrapped my face in towels and put blankets over me. The ground was so wet. I tried to let them know that Louise was back down that road and that she was hurt and needed help. But I couldn't get them to understand.

"I remember some man. I didn't see him. I just heard him. He came there, and he said that he had heard on some type radio that there had been a robbery at Jack's Mini-mall at Pawley's Island and that two women were taken hostages. I let them know by trying to indicate that that was me, and that the other lady who was down the road – well, at that time, I discovered that somebody else had found Louise.

"The next thing I knew, the ambulance rescue squad was there. Somebody put me on a stretcher. They tried to lay me on my back and I started strangling. I did get across to them that I could not breathe, and they turned me over onto my stomach.

"They went down the dirt road. They picked up Louise. I know this because I turned my head and I saw Louise in the ambulance with me. And they took us to the Myrtle Beach Air Force Base Hospital where they looked at me.

"A man there gave me a pen and I wrote a note to him on the table, on the paper that was covering the examining table."

Dunn produced the paper and showed it to Wanda.

"I wrote my name, 'Wanda Summers,' and they asked

me the other lady's name, and I wrote 'Louise Sellers.'"

Dunn showed Wanda another piece of paper upon which she had written. "And what did you write on State's Exhibit 15?" Dunn asked.

"We were raped," Wanda answered.

"All right, Miss Wanda," Dunn said. "What happened after you left the Myrtle Beach Air Force Base?"

"They put me into another ambulance there, and they transported me to Grand Strand General Hospital. There was a man and a lady who rode with me in the ambulance. The lady held my head up, because I got so tired of holding it up, and I couldn't lay down.

"When we got to the emergency room, I saw a doctor and a policeman who were asking me questions, at which time I wrote another note. They asked me for a description of the two men in the car."

Dunn handed Wanda a third piece of paper. "And then you, in response to his questions, you wrote your answers on the paper. How did you describe the people?"

"I wrote 'White, over 25, two men.' They asked me what kind of car, and I wrote 'Brown, old,' and I didn't know whether it was a Maverick or Pinto."

"And what did you write?"

"I wrote 'Brown old Pinto or Maverick, one long and one brown hair.'"

"All right," Dunn said. "I show you State's Exhibit No. 3 and ask you if you've ever had an occasion to see that before?"

"Yes, sir. I wrote this. They asked me had I heard any names mentioned, and I told them these two names, Johnny or Jack. Johnny is what Mr. Woomer told me to call him, and Jack was what I heard Mr. Skaar call Mr. Woomer."

"Thank you, ma'am. Now, let me show you this brown paper bag. Please examine the contents and tell us if you've had an occasion to see those."

"This is the sweater that I was wearing that night, my bra and my panties."

"And these were the clothes that were left on the side of the road?" Dunn asked.

"Yes, sir."

"How long did you stay in the hospital, Mrs. Summers?"

"Approximately three and a half to four weeks."

"Are you under the care of any doctors other than regular medical doctors?"

"Yes, sir. An oral surgeon; an ear, nose and throat plastic surgeon; a psychiatrist; and a dentist."

Dunn picked up a picture that had been entered into evidence. "Have you ever seen that picture before?" he asked, handing the exhibit to Wanda.

"Yes, sir," she answered, looking at the photo. "That's me."

"And where was that picture, Wanda?"

"It was in my husband's wallet."

"Is this the way you looked before you were shot in the face?"

"Yes, sir."

"Do you see in court the man that called himself Johnny, that you later learned to be Ronald Woomer, that did all the things you've told us about here?"

"Yes, sir, I do."

"Would you point him out for me, please?" Dunn said and stepped aside.

"It's the blond-haired man seated next to Mr. Stevens."

Dunn turned to the defense table. "You might examine," he said, motioning to the defense attorneys.

"No questions," co-counsel Irby Walker said quickly.

Dunn turned back to Wanda. "Thank you, ma'am. Come down."

Dunn helped Wanda from the stand and led her across the courtroom to her seat, just a table length from where Woomer sat with his head down. Turning back toward the judge and jury, Dunn said, "State rests, Your Honor."

34

The defense rested without calling a single witness. After Wanda's testimony, Irby Walker looked to Stevens and mouthed, "Are you going to cross-examine her?"

"Hell, no," Stevens whispered emphatically.

"Didn't think so," Walker replied. "Just checking." Walker believed that if it were possible, the jury and perhaps others in the audience would have hauled Woomer outside and hanged him from the nearest tree. Indeed, when Harwell asked the defense if Woomer understood he could speak on his own behalf, Walker told the court that Woomer did understand. Despite the plan the defense had for the past ten days, Woomer suddenly chose not to take the stand in the guilt or innocence first phase of the trial.

The following morning the jury heard closing arguments. Dunn was confident that he need not address the court again until the second phase of the trial and instructed his co-counsel, John Breeden, to explain the technicalities of the State's case to the jurors.

"The burden of proof in any criminal matter," Breeden said, "is upon the State of South Carolina to prove the guilt of the accused beyond a reasonable doubt. We've proved this case to you in three different ways: the physical evidence, the statement of Mrs. Wanda Summers, and the confession. Can there by any doubt?

"I hope you sat here yesterday as I did and listened to the tape of Mr. Woomer, how he calmly abducted two ladies, raped Wanda Summers and snuffed out the life of Louise Sellers just like walking down Main Street.

"Did he sound concerned? Did he sound remorseful? Or did he sound like a cold-blooded murderer? Folks, this ain't television. This is not a novel. This, folks, is reality. This happened in our county."

Stevens began the closing for the defense by reminding the jury that he said in his opening statement that he wasn't going to "offer Woomer as a shining star with the brightest of armor." What he did instead was commend Wanda for her courage in getting on the stand.

"Wasn't she gallant?" Stevens asked. "Wasn't she brave? Wasn't she courageous to the last hour? But, not one time did I hear bitterness emanating from her heart. So, I ask you, when you leave us to talk about the crimes, do it, if you can, without emotion. Do it, if you can, as this lovely lady did, without bitterness, without anger. Think about it."

The jury did think about it. It took only an hour and fifteen minutes before the jury returned verdicts of guilty on all charges.

Following Judge Harwell's charge, the jury was released to begin their deliberations. At 11:20 a.m., and immediately upon entering the jury room, a call for a vote arose from the jurors. Raymond Finch, the jury foreman, reluctantly agreed to the vote though he was worried how the judge would respond if they returned too soon with five separate verdicts. As he distributed paper to be used for the secret ballots, Finch reminded his fellow jurors of their charge to review the evidence. That was ridiculous, was the reply, considering the open and shut nature of the case. After having already been sequestered for ten days, the jurors were eager to proceed with their task; there was no telling how long the second phase of the trial would take. Besides, it wasn't getting any cooler in their small room. When Finch collected and totaled the ballots for the first count, for the kidnapping of Wanda Summers, the vote was eleven for guilty and one for innocent. Scowls appeared on the faces of the jurors as they glanced about. Someone wasn't ready to make a final determination. Finch seized the opportunity and suggested pieces of evidence for consideration. One by one, the jurors began to speak. Not ten minutes elapsed, however, before the group called for a second vote. The vote was again eleven to one to convict. Frustrations mounted. After more deliberation and several more minutes, a third vote was taken with the same result. Individual jurors began to get surly and looked about accusingly. Keeping his eye on his wristwatch, Finch urged juror discussions. The testimony of various witnesses was discussed and a recommendation was made that the tape of the confession be played. When it became known, though, that the tape machine hadn't been released into evidence, and the jury would have to return to the courtroom to hear the tape, the recommendation was withdrawn. Again a vote came in at eleven to one and again jurors sat back with their arms crossed defensively and glared at one another. Following a fifth and then a sixth vote, a middle-aged male juror said in frustration, "I'd just like to know who the bastard is that keeps voting not guilty." After a respectable one hour of deliberations, Finch decided another hold out wasn't necessary. Upon his suggestion, ballots were distributed and the jurors again voted. When the count that time tallied twelve to none to convict, additional ballots were quickly distributed. The jury soon had guilty verdicts on each of the five charges against Woomer and returned to the courtroom at 12:39 p.m.

"Mr. Foreman, have you reached a verdict?" the clerk of court, Billie Richardson, asked.

"Yes, ma'am," Finch said with relief.

Richardson then published the verdicts.

"The verdict is as to count one, kidnapping of Wanda Summers: Guilty. Verdict as to count two, kidnapping of Della Louise Sellers: Guilty. Verdict as to count number three, criminal sexual conduct in the first degree upon Wanda Summers: Guilty. Verdict as to count number four, assault and battery with intent to kill upon Wanda Summers: Guilty. Verdict as to count number five, murder of Della Louise Sellers: Guilty. Is this your verdict, so say you all?"

All jurors answered in the affirmative.

35

The real trial, the fight to save Woomer's life, was about to begin. Under the South Carolina Code of Laws, a guilty verdict for murder is punished by either life in prison or death in the electric chair. A jury can spare a convicted murderer for any reason, even if aggravating circumstances are shown, but cannot sentence a murderer to die. in the electric chair if aggravating circumstances are not shown.

Woomer waived the 24-hour waiting period and court resumed at ten o'clock the next morning. A change in security was evident after Woomer's conviction. During the first phase of the trial, Woomer was typically led into the courthouse handcuffed by one wrist to one of two officers. Now, he was hustled in and out with four or five flanking officers and with his hands cuffed tightly behind his back.

The defense knew it had to pull out all of the stops to convince the jury that Woomer didn't deserve to die for his crimes. The mitigating circumstances Stevens hoped would sway the jury in his client's favor were Woomer's age, that Woomer had no significant criminal record of crimes of violence, and that when the crimes were committed, Woomer was under the influence of alcohol and drugs, the influence or domination of another person, and that his behavior was affected by a mental or emotional disturbance.

Dunn announced that the prosecution would offer no further testimony to show aggravating circumstances. He was confident the evidence already provided would show that Louise's murder occurred while in the commission of kidnapping and while in the commission of rape. Dunn would, of course, cross examine anyone the defense put on the stand.

The defense offered two psychiatrists, plus Woomer, and Woomer's mother for the jurors' consideration.

The first witness, Dr. Wayne Lockhart, testified as a forensic psychiatrist. The technique employed by Lockhart to examine Woomer was simple. Information about Woomer and his life was obtained by psychological tests and extensive clinical interviews; an attempt was then made to validate the information by conducting additional interviews with family members and persons close to Woomer. Lockhart spent three and a half hours with Woomer in one session and then attempted to verify as much of the information as possible with Woomer's mother.

Woomer was portrayed through Lockhart's direct testimony as a person from a poor background who lacked a real father figure. The oldest of five children, Rusty began running away at an early age to escape his father's brutality. Rusty failed to adjust to a succession of foster homes and began using drugs at the age of sixteen. He was an impulsive person who craved attention and was thereby easily led or influenced. Rusty's drug use accelerated and he began to employ different means to secure drugs and money to obtain drugs. A relationship with Eugene Skaar offered Rusty a friendship and a steady supply of drugs and money. When offered the opportunity by Mr. Skaar to make some money in South Carolina, Rusty accepted.

"As far as a diagnosis," Lockhart continued in response to Walker's questions, "it was my opinion that Mr. Woomer was certainly not insane. He does have a diagnosis of drug dependence, numerous types of drugs, and he also has a diagnosis of a personality disorder. A personality disorder is a mental disorder. It's not insanity, but is defined as a lifelong period of maladjustment, individuals that just don't get along well in the community."

Dunn's cross-examination of Lockhart provided some additional insights into Woomer's past.

"Now, Doctor, you say that he told you he had various difficulties with the law?" Dunn asked.

"Yes," said Lockhart. "He told me what he had been involved in."

"What did he tell you?"

"First of all, at an early age, running away from home. Juvenile type things whereby he didn't go to school or felt like he couldn't go to school because of his family situation. There were no clothes, and his mother verified this."

"All right. Answer my question, Doctor," Dunn said. "What types of difficulties did he say he had with the law?"

"OK," Lockhart replied. "That was the first. He was later involved in an armed robbery, and later a charge of statutory rape, and indicated he had been in the West Virginia Penitentiary several times."

"Now, did you inquire about how his other four brothers and sisters had conformed their conduct to the requirements of the law?"

"Yes," Lockhart continued. "I asked Mrs. Woomer to tell me how he differed from the other four children. I gathered that there has not been anything with the other four children regarding violations."

"So, in the home environment that Ronald Woomer was raised in, four of the children turned out all right, didn't they, evidently?" Dunn asked.

"Yes, but I've seen this in other situations where even people who come from the worst of families turn out quite good; and I've seen a number of cases where individuals who come from the best of families, the best of everything, education, background, turn out to be violators."

"So," Dunn followed, "assuming for the sake of discussion, if he had been raised with a silver spoon in his mouth, he still might have turned out just as he has, he might very well be the same Ronald Woomer that's here in this courtroom?"

"That's correct."

"All right," Dunn said. "No question but that Woomer is not insane?"

"No, sir. I did not find him to be insane."

"No question but that at the time and place that he committed the acts and deeds that he's charged with and having been found guilty of, he clearly knew the difference between right and wrong?"

"That's my impression that he did."

"And criminality means of a criminal nature?"

"That's my understanding."

"And there's no question, Doctor, but at the time he committed these crimes, he could appreciate that they were criminal acts?"

"That's my impression."

"Now, you say that you found that he was suffering from a drug disorder?"

"By history, he has a diagnosis of a drug dependence."

"You prefaced that remark by saying, 'by history,' did you not?"

"Well, a physician, whether he's a psychiatrist or otherwise, usually has to go by history."

"Oh, yes, sir. I'm not criticizing that," Dunn said. "But, you saw no evidence of withdrawal symptoms on your part?"

"No, sir. I did not."

"Which personality disorder does he have, Doctor?"

"Well, as I said, a personality disorder is a lifelong involvement in maladaptive behavior, poorly adaptive behavior, and his personality disorder is characterized by emotional immaturity. He is an impulsive individual who just doesn't think things out. He sees something; he does it without really thinking or coming up with a plan to see the consequences of it. He seems to be a very easily influenced individual and doesn't seem to profit a lot from previous mistakes in his life. Medically, we would refer to this as consistent with an anti-social personality."

"And that means anti-society?" Dunn asked.

"Well, it could mean that, but there are a lot of anti-social people who never become involved in crime."

"Yes, sir. There are a lot of people who have an anti-social personality, and they don't get involved in crime. Let me ask you this, doctor. You say he is impulsive."

"That's correct."

"Could I sum it up, Doctor, that when he decides to do something, he's going to do what he wants to, anytime he wants to, no matter how much it hurts anyone else? Is that a fair statement, Doctor?"

"Some anti-social people are like that. On the other hand, one that's easily influenced might not do what he wants to, but rather what somebody else wanted him to."

"All right. If the facts in this case and the evidence presented to this jury show and establish that Eugene Skaar called him on the telephone and asked him if he wanted to come to South Carolina and make some money; if he thereafter made the decision to come, and sometime later got in an automobile and came, and states by his own confession that they planned to leave no eyewitnesses when they left West Virginia, came down here and spent another day in a motel before he went on this killing spree, would that indicate to you impulsivity or would that indicate to you a planned scheme and design before he got here to do exactly what he did?"

"It would seem to be the latter, although I understand that it was Skaar's idea rather than his."

"Who do you understand that from, Doctor?"

"From the patient."

"Did he indicate to you that Skaar did all of it, and he was just doing what Skaar was saying?" Dunn asked.

"He was on drugs at the time, and Skaar was, by what Mr. Woomer told me, supplying him with drugs."

"Did he have a knowledge of right and wrong to enable him to say, 'No, Skaar, I'm not going to Horry County with you!'"

"Yes, he had that knowledge."

"Could he have said, 'No, Skaar, I'm not going to kill everybody!'"

"He could have, but as I said, he was on drugs at the time, and a person under the influence of drugs will have impaired judgment. He could have impaired judgment and still know right from wrong."

"Doctor, if he told in the most detail how he killed not only the lady for whom he's on trial, but three other people the same day, and attempted to kill two more the same day, told you the color of the car that was down in Colleton County, and where the schoolhouse was, and the person backing out, and the details of how he did this, that and the other, would you say he knew what he was doing at the time he was doing it?"

"Yes, sir. I would have to say that."

"Doctor, do I understand from what you've said – does he care what's going on right now?"

"He's certainly aware of what's going on."

"Does he care?"

"I assume he does."

"You assume he does. When he wants something, does he take it how he wants it without regard to how the other person may be affected?" Dunn asked.

"Yes, sir," Lockhart concluded.

36

The next witness for the defense was Woomer. Stevens reminded the sometimes soft-spoken Rusty to speak up so that the farthest juror, located approximately 15 feet away, could hear.

Stevens carefully led Woomer through a description of his relationship with his father, whom he hadn't seen in years. Woomer's father was apparently a jack-of-all-trades, but only worked sporadically.

"Let me ask you," Stevens said, "what kind of life you had growing up at home."

"I never had much of a life really," Woomer said. "I didn't get along with my father. He wouldn't take care of the family, and I guess because I was the oldest, I looked after the smaller kids a whole lot. I wouldn't put up with him mistreating them to the extent where it was unnecessary. I've seen him knock them across the room. Very seldom was we allowed to leave. If he was upset at us for anything, we wasn't even permitted to go to school."

"What was your relationship, Rusty, with your mother?"

Woomer began to cry. "I love my mother. I don't guess she could have been any better to me that what she had."

"Are your father and mother living together now?"

"No, sir."

"What happened to your father?"

"He remarried." Rusty's father remarried a woman younger than Rusty, making it difficult for Rusty and the woman to establish a relationship. She was too young to assume a mother role, and she didn't act toward Rusty like a sister.

"What type of relationship have you had with your

father since then?"

"I've seen him, I think, [in the last six years] once or twice."

"Do you know whether he knew the date of the trial?"

"Yes, sir."

"Did he come?"

"No, sir."

"Who came?"

"My mother and my brother."

"Let me take you back a bit, Rusty. Were you ever convicted of grand larceny?" Stevens knew Dunn would go after Woomer's criminal history, given that the defense was using Woomer's lack of a history of violent crimes as a mitigating circumstance for the murder of Louise. Harwell had ruled that aspects of Woomer's criminal history that involved crimes of moral turpitude, namely the larceny convictions, were admissible. Harwell warned Dunn to stay away from the statutory rape conviction.

"Yes, sir," Woomer replied to Stevens' question.

"Tell us about it," Stevens said.

"It was for breaking in a store."

"For what?"

"Money," Woomer said. "I was living on the street."

"Why were you living on the street?"

"Because my father was there at the house, and I wasn't going to live there while he was present. At the time, I didn't love my father, I don't guess."

"Did he indicate that he loved you?"

"No, sir."

"How much time did you serve?"

"Three years."

"After then, were you in any more trouble?"

"Yes, sir."

"What kind?"

"I was picked up a couple of times for trespassing and stuff like that."

"Can't hear you, Rusty," Stevens prompted.

"I was picked up for trespassing, petit larceny."

"Any more?"

"I don't know."

Stevens then took Woomer through the preparations for and the trip to South Carolina with Skaar, focusing on the drugs reportedly ingested by Woomer during the day of the crime spree.

"What time did you get up that morning?" Stevens asked.

"I guess around 10:30 or 11 o'clock."

"What did you do that morning?"

"The manager of the hotel was down there, and he was checking on the air conditioning or something. I got up and went in the bathroom and rolled some joints while he was in there talking. Until he left, we never smoked any reefer or anything. When he left, Gene had four Quaaludes left, and we split them, and we had half a bottle of whiskey left from the night before, and went over and got another bottle of whiskey around the corner."

"What did you do then?"

"Went back to the hotel and smoked some reefer and ate some Valiums, and we left the hotel."

"Did you smoke any en route?"

"Yes, sir. That's the reason we went around and got the other bottle of whiskey before we left so we wouldn't have to stop."

"And when you came back to Georgetown from Walterboro, were you still smoking and drinking?"

"Yes, sir."

"By the time you had gotten to Georgetown," Stevens probed, "that is, from the time you left Myrtle Beach and gone up 17 to Walterboro, and the time you got back to Georgetown at the mini-mall, do you have any idea of how many joints you had smoked or pills you had taken or liquor you had drank?"

"We had an ounce of reefer when we left, and I had three or four joints left when we got back to the hotel, because someone went and bought me another bag after we got back. So, I guess an ounce."

"When you got to the mini-mall, do you recall that?"

"Yes, sir. I remember, but I don't know how to explain it to you. I remember all of it, but it's like I was reading or something. I don't know."

"Could you explain that?" Stevens asked.

"I knew where I was at. I mean, I could stand and walk, talk, but I just didn't, I don't know, register, I guess, maybe. I just didn't have no feelings at the time. I was just doing things. I wasn't thinking about them."

"Can you tell us anything about how you felt about that? Do you recall it and what it meant to you?"

"I feel terrible about it now. A lot of people might think that sounds funny coming from me because of what I've done."

"When did you realize the full extent of what you were involved in?"

"I guess probably right before I gave the statement to Mr. Causey."

"How did you feel when you were giving the statement?"

"It just didn't seem real at the time. It still don't seem real."

"Was the statement true?"

"Yes, sir."

"Did you feel any different after you gave the statement than you felt before you gave it?"

"I guess I felt better by telling someone about it."

Jim Dunn moved quickly into his cross-examination.

"Were you sorry recently in jail when you said that you blew their shit away?" Dunn asked.

"I did not say that, sir."

"You deny that?"

"Yes, sir, I do."

"Now, you love your mother, right?"

"Yes, sir, I do."

"When is the last time you had gone to visit her before you got in this difficulty?"

"I guess I hadn't seen her in a year and a half."

"And when you got out of jail, who gave you a job, son?"

"My father did."

"Doing what?"

"He was self-contracting at the time."

"Who taught you a trade?"

"I picked it up on my own. Didn't nobody teach me nothing."

"From who?"

"My father and the people he worked with."

"Who took you hunting?"

"My father took me hunting."

"Your father gave you a job, taught you a trade, took you hunting. Is that right?"

"Yes, sir."

"Now, who was it that took care of the family when you say your father and mother split up? Was it you?"

"No, sir, I did not."

"Who was it?"

"My brother."

"Your younger brother. Is that right?"

"Yes, sir."

"He hadn't been in any trouble, had he?"

"No, sir."

"And you didn't want to go to school because you just didn't like to go to school. Is that right?"

"I don't know very many kids at 14 that does like school, sir."

"But, a lot of them go ahead and go, don't they?" Dunn asked.

"Yes, sir."

"All right. You had known Skaar for about a year. Is that right?"

"Yes, sir."

"And you say he called you one day. What was your line of work at that time?"

"I was self-contracting."

"Doing what?"

"Roofing, shingling."

"So, you could make a living, couldn't you?"

"Yes, sir."

"And you could make money at it, couldn't you?"

"Yes, sir. I could."

"And you could provide for your family that way, couldn't you?"

"Yes, sir."

"No question about you knew a trade?"

"I knew a trade."

"And no question about it that work was available?"

"Yes, sir. There was available work."

"All right. But, didn't you say old bad Eugene Skaar called you?"

"Eugene Skaar called me."

"And asked you what?"

"He asked me if I wanted to make money."

"Two weeks prior to coming to South Carolina, you knew full well what you were coming here to do, didn't you?"

"I knew we was coming down here to steal coins, yes, sir."

"And you knew you weren't going to leave one eyewitness, didn't you?"

"Gene said that we wasn't going to."

"And that was before you left West Virginia. So, how long was it before you left West Virginia to come down here that you knew full well that you weren't going to leave any eyewitnesses?"

"Two weeks."

"Two weeks! Is that right?"

"Yes, sir."

"And you lived up to it, didn't you?"

Woomer didn't respond.

"And you lived up to that commitment in West Virginia, didn't you?" Dunn asked again.

"I don't know," Woomer said.

"No, you didn't kill them all, did you? Where did you shoot Mr. Turner?"

"In the head."

"Where did you shoot Arnie Richardson?"

"In the head."

"Where did you shoot Earl Dean Wright?"

"In the head."

"Where did you shoot Wanda Summers?"

"In the head."

"Where did you shoot Della Louise Sellers?"

"In the head."

"Have you ever seen this gun before?" Dunn held out the sawed-off shotgun.

"Yes, sir, I have."

"Whose gun is it?"

"It belonged to Gene Skaar?"

"Look at it and make sure you can recognize it."

"I've seen it before," Woomer said.

"How did you shoot Mrs. Summers?"

Woomer again failed to respond.

"Show me how you held the gun?" Dunn insisted.

Woomer, clearly agitated, turned to Harwell. "Do I have to do that, Your Honor?"

Stevens spoke. "I object to that, Your Honor."

"Very well," Dunn said, putting the shotgun down. He then picked up the .32 pistol. "State's Exhibit No. 37. Now, where did that gun come from?" He again held the weapon out in Woomer's direction.

"West Virginia," Woomer answered.

"And where did it come from in West Virginia?"

"It belongs to Gene Skaar."

"Where did Gene Skaar get it?"

"From someone that we robbed."

"Gene Skaar's gun, and he got it 'from someone that we robbed.' Right?"

"Yes, sir."

"And who did you rob it from?"

Woomer sat without answering.

"Where did you get the gun?" Dunn repeated.

"Do I have to answer that, Your Honor?" Woomer asked Harwell.

"Yes, sir," replied Harwell.

"From my grandmother's house."

"And how did you get it?"

"I took it when we went there."

"In what manner did you take it?"

"I went upstairs and took it out of the drawer."

When Woomer and Skaar needed guns for the South Carolina trip, Woomer volunteered that he knew where they could get a couple. Woomer then concocted a scheme to rob his grandmother, with whom he was angry. While Woomer waited outside, Skaar entered the old woman's home and blindfolded her at gunpoint. Woomer then quietly entered and took the .32, some money, and the shotgun used during the crime spree. It was never made clear through interviews, detective's notes, or the trial transcript how the grip came to be replaced or when the barrel was sawed off of the shotgun.

"And, in your statement that you gave when you said you were telling the truth, whose gun did you say this was?"

"Gene Skaar's."

"And that was not the truth, was it?"

"It is Gene Skaar's."

"It is Gene Skaar's?" Dunn asked, his voice rising.

"It was when we took it," Woomer said. "It belonged to someone else before he took it."

"It belonged to someone else before he took it." Dunn paused and looked at the jury. "And there's just as much truth in that as about everything else you said."

"I've not lied about nothing," Woomer said.

Dunn continued his attack for the next hour, relentlessly testing Woomer's memory. Woomer's recollections of what happened on February 22 differed significantly from the testimony of several other witnesses who had previously testified. Woomer found himself trapped in inconsistencies again and again as Dunn stood close to the witness stand and fired questions. Woomer eventually crossed a line with his testimony that Dunn knew the jurors would not forgive.

"One final question," Dunn said, stepping to the jury box. Dunn paused to look at his notes. "When you raped Wanda Summers, you don't deny doing that, do you?"

"No, sir."

"Do you deny trying to have anal intercourse with her?" This was an old trick. While criminals will often admit to crimes they consider acceptable, given their twisted logic, they just as often won't admit to other acts they have committed that they consider unacceptable.

"Yes, sir, I do."

"You deny that?" Dunn asked.

"Yes, sir."

"She was not telling the truth about that, when she said that, was she?"

"No, sir."

"She lied about it. Right?" Dunn moved in.

"Yes, sir."

Dunn ended his cross-examination on a dramatic note.

"Have you ever seen John Holland before?" John was at the impromptu party at the Komo-Mai the night of February 22, when Woomer and Skaar returned from their killing spree.

"Yes, sir, I believe I have."

"Do you deny telling him that you had to kill somebody to know whether you were going to like it or not?" Dunn asked.

"I don't remember," Woomer said.

"You could have said it?" Dunn continued.

"I could have said it," Woomer confirmed.

"You could have said it. Do you deny telling him that it don't cost but eighteen cents to get a shotgun shell; when you kill someone, everything over that is profit?"

"No, sir. I don't remember that."

The third witness for the defense added little to assuage the damage Dunn had inflicted in his cross-examination of Woomer. In fact, Irby Walker later recalled that putting Dr. Edmond Camp on the stand had been a mistake. Although the defense expected Camp to be their best witness, his lengthy testimony was cumbersome and appeared to confuse and frustrate jurors.

Camp, then a psychiatrist from Darlington, testified that his examination of Woomer included various psychological tests in addition to a clinical interview where he ascertained family history information. And, again, the history showed that Woomer had an impoverished background and had been subjected to abuse as a child.

Camp agreed with Lockhart that Woomer had an anti-social personality disorder and added that, in his opinion, Woomer completely lacked a conscience. Camp wasn't able to conclude whether Woomer never developed a conscience or whether Woomer's conscience was destroyed during his pubertal years by his father's brutality. In either case, Camp concluded that although Woomer knew right from wrong, Woomer just didn't care.

"He does what he wants to do," Camp said of Woomer, "when he wants to do it, because he wants to do it; and if it's an illegal act and there are witnesses, then he simply kills them."

Dunn, in his cross-examination, picked up on this, of course, and took it to the next level.

"Doctor, does he profit from his mistakes?" Dunn asked.

"No, sir, he does not, not unless it's to his benefit," Camp replied.

"Does he profit from what he has done here? Has he learned anything?"

"I'm sure if he were to be let free, he would not leave a witness should he do it again, and he would do it again."

"When you talked with him, you say he was not remorseful?" Dunn continued.

"That's correct."

"Was he resentful?"

"Yes, sir. He has a lot of anger stored up; just like some people save money in a bank, he saves up anger."

"So, in regard to his coming to South Carolina, he was angry?"

"Yes. He was very angry with his family for not including him in the care and concern of a 14-year-old sister. This was just another incident to make him angry. Instead of repressing this anger, he displaced it onto the citizens of South Carolina."

"Doctor, of course Skaar was the leader in this matter, in your judgment. Right?"

"As he tells me," Camp said.

"As he tells you," Dunn repeated. "Well, in your opinion as a psychiatrist, was he under the domination of Skaar when he was doing that killing, or was he simply mad at his family?"

"As far as I can tell, he was angry at his family."

"Thank you, Doctor," Dunn said.

37

When Rusty Woomer's mother, Barbara, had gotten the news that her oldest boy had been arrested again, this time for murder, she had cried. Barbara had not recently seen her son but thought about him often. She remembered Rusty as a cute little boy who worried about things too much and always did as he was told. But that had been a long time ago, she admitted.

In the months leading up to the trial, Cleveland Stevens had grown fond of Rusty and began to understand the young man's feelings for his mother. She was one of the few people in the world with whom Rusty had ever had a close relationship. Stevens knew that her presence at the trial was good strategy, but he also felt that she and Rusty should spend time together. After the trial, no matter how it turned out, they wouldn't get to see one another, except on visiting days, and probably not then, considering that Barbara had other children to care for in rural West Virginia. If Rusty ended up on death row, visiting him would be nearly impossible.

When contacted by Stevens, Barbara said she didn't know how she could work out the details of an extended trip to South Carolina. Stevens assured her that if she could take care of things on her end, he would handle the rest. Spending his own money, Stevens secured for Barbara a bus ticket to Conway and a motel room just down the street from the courthouse. At the end of the long, hot trip, when Barbara disembarked from the bus in Conway with her worn suitcase, Stevens was there to provide a friendly face.

When a break came in the long trial, Stevens and his wife sat for several hours on their porch one afternoon with Barbara. Stevens assured Barbara that her son was being treated as fairly as possible. She had no illusions of anything else, she said; Rusty would have to pay the price for what he had done.

Mrs. Stevens sensed the pressures of the courtroom were overwhelming for the timid West Virginia woman. "I had followed the case," Mrs. Stevens said, "and I was glad that Steve brought her to the house to meet me. We talked about life in general. She was appreciative of what Steve was doing for her son."

After remarking several times about the scent of the freshly cut lawn, Barbara finally slipped off her shoes and walked barefooted around the yard.

Each morning of the trial, Barbara pulled on a plain dress with sleeves that hid a tattoo on her upper arm, flipped her hair in an attempt to look stylish, and set out on her lonely walk to the courthouse. No one she passed on the sidewalk recognized her connection to the trial that had garnered more public attention than anyone could remember in the history of the county. No one suspected that the unassuming-looking woman was going to the courthouse to try and save the life of her son.

"Would you state your full name, please?" Stevens asked, and smiled. It was clear that the small woman was nervous. Her eyes were red and swollen. The tissue she held was crumpled and damp.

"Barbara Ann Woomer," she replied. Rusty looked at his mother as she began her testimony.

"Are you the mother of Ronald Rusty Woomer?" Stevens asked.

"Yes, sir." She looked back at Rusty.

"Could you tell us, Mrs. Woomer, when you married Rusty's father, Jimmy?"

"In 1953."

"How old were you?" Stevens asked. His voice reflected the gentle concern he had for his client's mother.

"Seventeen," she replied.

"And Jimmy?"

"Eighteen."

"Where were you living?"

"With his mother."

"Was Rusty born at your husband's mother's house?"

"No. We lived there, but he was born in a clinic."

"Did you and your husband experience some marital difficulties shortly after Ronald was born?" Stevens asked.

"Yes, sir," Barbara said, nodding her head. "He drank and run around, wouldn't work."

"How old was Ronald when you and your husband separated?

"Approximately one and a half to two."

"Could you tell us what brought about this separation, Mrs. Woomer?"

"He didn't do anything but drink and run around and hunt."

"What kind of hunting did he do?"

"Coon hunting."

"How long did you separate from him at that time?"

"Approximately four years."

"And, thereafter, did you have an occasion to go back to live with Mr. Woomer?"

"Yes, sir. We met again and he said if we would go back together, he'd work and have a home for us."

Both Barbara Woomer and her son began to cry. Up to this point in the trial, Rusty's only display of emotion was out of concern for his mother.

"What did you say, Mrs. Woomer?"

"I told him I didn't know right at the time, and we seen each other again, and we decided to try."

"Did you remarry him?"

"Yes. I took care of the children, took care of the house."

"What was he doing? Did he work?"

"He had a job when we first got married, yes."

"How long before you noticed that there wasn't any substantial change in Rusty's father?"

"Very shortly. He got to where he wouldn't work anymore. He always found excuses. He didn't feel like going to work, but he could hunt at night."

"And was he having any difficult problems in relating to the children?"

"Yes. The children were just there. As long as the boys did exactly what Jimmy told them to do."

"Was anything wrong with that?"

"No, within reason, but when – like, for instance, his dogs. The boys had to care for those dogs. Jimmy hunted 'em, but the boys took care of them. If they missed a watering or they would forget to feed them or forget anything, it didn't have to be a big thing, he put them in their room as long as two weeks at a time and didn't allow them to come out."

"The second time that you were reunited," Stevens continued, "what kind of work were you doing?"

"The second time, I didn't go to work. The children was on welfare and I'm on disability."

"How was Jimmy's relationship with you in the presence of the children?"

"I was treated approximately like Bill and Rusty except that he didn't lock me in the room, because I had three little ones to take care of. Nothing us three did ever pleased him, regardless of what it was."

"How old was Ronald when he left home from you and Jimmy?"

"Around 14."

"Would you tell us why he left?"

"Because he couldn't get along with his daddy."

"Was it because he was disobedient?"

"No," she stated. "Rusty was not a disobedient child when he was home."

"Was it because he didn't want to subject himself to parental discipline?"

"No, I don't think it was that either. It was the cruelty. He never got praised for anything. Jimmy never could see any good in either of those boys."

"Did he take Ronald coon hunting with him?"

"When Rusty got bigger, yes, but it was Rusty's idea. Jimmy didn't ask the boys to go."

"Any particular reason for Ronald asking to go with his father?"

"Other than just wanting to go somewhere, maybe if he could go hunting with his daddy, he could get closer to him."

"What about family outings?"

"The only family outings we ever had was going to the grocery store, the laundromat, and visiting with one of Jimmy's sisters."

"What about church?"

"No, sir. I went with the boys sometimes, when Jimmy would let them go."

"Describe if you will what your life was like insofar as your living conditions."

"I sat down last night and figured up the different homes we'd lived in from the time we were married the second time, and it was nine."

"How many?" Stevens asked.

"Nine. The first place we lived in was the only place that I can recall that we did not get put out of."

"For what reason were you put out of the others?"

"Because the rent wasn't paid."

"You were living how far from town?"

"Different times, we've lived as far as 10, 15 miles from town. At one time we lived so far out I couldn't have screamed and had a neighbor hear me."

"I assume that you had all the necessary conveniences of an inside toilet and those conveniences."

"No, sir, we didn't. There was two that had the outside convenience, and there was two where I had to carry water."

"What about utilities? Did you have those in the house?"

"Yes, when the bill was paid. They were shut off quite a few times."

"I believe Ronald had some problems with school. Tell us about it."

"Well, he wasn't mean in school. He just didn't like school."

"And can you give us any information why?"

"Well, the boys didn't have clothes like the other children had to wear and, part of the time, they didn't have lunch money."

Mrs. Woomer began to cry again.

"Take your time, Mrs. Woomer." Stevens hesitated before continuing. "Was he disrespectful?"

"Rusty was never disrespectful to me," Mrs. Woomer

responded, shaking her head. "He never sassed me, not once. He was not a bad child."

"The jury ought to know whether or not there was physical encounters between you and Jimmy in the presence of the children," Stevens said.

"Yes, sir. I tried to stop him from using the belt on Rusty one time, and he threw me through the hall. It was over the dogs again. Rusty hadn't watered them when he was told to do it right at the time. I've seen marks he's left on the boys before when he whipped them with a belt."

"As a result of these disciplinary measures by the father on the son, did you have to take him to a physician?"

"No, sir."

"Did you ever administer any medication yourself?"

"No, sir, other than putting cold rags on their little legs."

The defense ended their attempts to show mitigation with Mrs. Woomer's testimony. When she stepped down, Rusty and his mother embraced and both cried in their seats.

Dunn chose not to cross-examine Woomer's mother, but introduced a forensic psychiatrist as a reply witness. Dr. Mario Galvarino was called to rebut the testimonies of Lockhart and Camp, the forensic experts for the defense.

In Galvarino's opinion, Woomer had a criminal personality, and not a personality disorder as earlier described by the defense experts. Woomer had a need to see people suffer, the doctor said.

When asked by Dunn why Woomer shot Louise Sellers in the head, Galvarino explained that there were three reasons why one person would shoot another in the head. It's the most effective type of injury if the aim is to kill someone; the shot disfigures the head, which gives the criminal personality type pleasure as they witness the head coming apart; and the head is the bloodiest part of the body. "Woomer is very, very mean," Galvarino concluded, "and thrives on hurting others. There is no question in my mind that he would perform the same acts again if given the opportunity."

38

Prosecution and defense attorneys made their final arguments Friday morning. There was no question among the lawyers concerning who would deliver the messages to the jurors. Stevens would speak eloquently for the defense, though Irby Walker was expected to shine in his moment. Still quite young, Walker had distinguished himself in the trial as a bright and perceptive adversary. Spectators who had attended the whole trial watched the jurors' expressions closely as Walker delicately constructed his argument for why Woomer should be spared.

Carroll Padgett went first for the State to warm the crowd for Dunn, though after Dunn's incisive cross-examinations, he hardly needed prepping. Dunn had demonstrated to the crowd that he possessed that rare quality that made him an individual others want to watch. The whole trial had clearly been Dunn's show.

As if anticipating that the jury would tire of the long closings, Padgett explained why the deliberations were necessarily long, on that day in particular. The Woomer death penalty case was one of the first in South Carolina and the first in Horry County to employ the format of two separate trials for guilt/innocence and sentencing. The two-phase format was not used for any other type of charge besides capital murder. The new death penalty law in the state was still experimental to some extent and prompted Padgett to ensure the jurors that justice would not suffer in the transition to the new system. Padgett painstakingly explained that the rights of a defendant included the right to two attorneys. Because of financial need if attorneys had to be appointed by the court, one would be public and one would be private. Further, the attorneys could be released from all other trial obligations for ten days prior to the trial. The defendant was entitled to discovery. In other words, the prosecution had to make known to the defense all evidence for the first and second phases, which included knowing ahead of time what aggravating evidence to expect if the second phase was needed. In addition, the defendant could directly address the petit jury panel during jury selection, the defendant could argue directly to the jury by making a statement in the second phase, and the defendant could have the last argument.

Padgett also cautioned the jury from being influenced by Woomer's youthful appearance and soft-spoken manner in the courtroom. "Did you listen carefully to the tape of his voice, his statement given some 12 to 15 hours after he was arrested? Was there any difference? Was there any difference from when he spoke to you during [jury selection] the first week, when he made his statement that, 'I'm Ronald Woomer. Please pay close attention because this case is important to me. I'm on trial for my life.' Was there any difference? Was it the same cold, calculated voice that you heard on that tape?"

Perhaps in an attempt to lighten the jurors' burden, Padgett also explained what would happen if the jury made a recommendation of death to the court. "All of you must sign. What then? Does it end there? No, it doesn't. His Honor, before he can impose the death penalty based on your recommendation, must make some affirmative findings: one, that the recommendation of the jury is justified under the evidence presented; two, it was not the result of passion; three, it was not the result of any prejudice against the defendant; four, it was not the result of any other arbitrary factor whatsoever. Then, he is obligated and must impose the death penalty.

"Wanda Summers has to get up every day of her life and look in the mirror and see her face. Jimmy Summers can't kiss the same face he used to kiss. Don Sellers can no longer clasp the hand of his wife. Did they do anything in the world to deserve such treatment? No.

"You know, ladies and gentlemen, the trouble with our country is not in Washington. It's in the unbuttoned minds of a few misfits like Ronald Woomer who deserve nothing more than what they have decreed for everybody else in society. On February 22, 1979, Ronald Woomer declared war on all of us. Ladies and gentlemen, rid our society of this prophet of terror."

Dunn began his closing by speaking quietly to the jury and anticipating what the defense would say. "Woomer will have an opportunity to come up here, and he'll ask you to be merciful," he said. Suddenly, Dunn turned toward the door that witnesses used when entering the courtroom and said in a loud voice, "Della Louise Sellers, come around!" Dunn paused and continued to face the door. Startled persons in the audience turned their heads and looked at the door. Dunn spoke again loudly, his voice booming, "Come around, Della Louise Sellers! And tell us what mercy he extended to you when you lay there on the ground screaming!" Turning back to the jury, Dunn continued earnestly, "When Don Sellers said, 'That's my wife and I love her! Please don't hurt her!,' what mercy did he extend? When he took this shotgun that he stole from his grandmother and blew Wanda Summers' face all to smithereens, what mercy has he shown? Mercy? Those who seek mercy should do mercy."

Dunn took another opportunity to call down the dead for the jury. "Let's talk a minute about the trial of Della Louise Sellers." Pointing out to the jury that Woomer in his trial had procedural safeguards that his victims didn't, Dunn carried on an imaginary conversation. "Della Louise," Dunn said, looking to the empty witness stand, "what crime did you commit?" Dunn turned slightly and answered in a soft voice, "I got in the way of Ronald Woomer." Turning again, Dunn continued. "What else did you do?" Again turning, Dunn answered, "That's all I'm indicted for."

"How were you tried? By God and country as this defendant has been?" Dunn walked quickly across the courtroom. Turning to face the witness box, he rested his hand on Woomer's shoulder. "Here was the foreman of the grand jury that indicted Della Louise Sellers!" Woomer shrugged. "Here is the solicitor that decided to seek her death penalty! Here is the foreman of her jury! Here is the judge that resided in her trial on an old wet dirt road in

Horry County." Dunn paused for emphasis, then continued. "And her just out of the hospital! Bless her heart. Who sentenced her to death? Ronald Woomer! And who was her executioner? Ronald Woomer! Fair and impartial trial?" Dunn walked to the witness stand. "Mrs. Sellers, you have the right to remain silent. Anything you say may be used against you in a court of law. You've got the right to an attorney. If you can't afford an attorney, Mrs. Sellers, I'll have one appointed to you at no cost to you."

Dunn paused. His reddened face appeared tense and tired. "Where are we going in this country, ladies and gentlemen?" he said softly.

"What arises out of a death sentence for Ronald Woomer? It has two functions. Number one, it punishes Ronald Woomer. Number two, it is a message to society: Don't come to Horry County and rape and kill our women!

"Ladies and gentlemen, where you sit, you hold the peace and good order of your county in your hands. What are you going to have in Horry County? Send the message. It's time for you folks to get the brush and discharge your sworn duties and responsibilities. It's in your hands. Thank you very much."

During the recess that preceded closing arguments by the defense, Rusty's father and grandmother entered the courtroom for the first time since the trial began. Arriving during Dunn's closing, the relatives of Woomer were detained and searched before being allowed to enter the courtroom. Rusty and his father, whom he hadn't seen in several years, shook hands and spoke briefly.

Stevens did about the only thing he could in his closing. His voice faltered as he resorted to religion and urged the jurors to allow God to be the ultimate arbiter of justice. When he finished his impassioned plea, having performed his duties in the first capital case of his long and productive career, with tears spilling from his eyes, Stevens sat down, folded his hands as if to pray and bowed his head.

Sniffling was heard through the courtroom.

Following the lengthy charges by Harwell, the jurors were finally allowed to begin their deliberations at 3:38 p.m. on Friday, July 20, 1979. Though the spectators were free to move about, problems with the air conditioning kept them close to their seats, since the courtroom was the only room in the building that was tolerable.

Just one hour into the deliberations, a sharp rap from the jurors' door caused a commotion as persons caught off guard quickly streamed into the courtroom in preparation of a verdict. Ripples of nervous laughter spread through the crowd when it was discovered that the jurors had simply requested that some cold drinks be sent to them.

Two knocks at 5:41 p.m. did finally signal that the jurors had reached a decision. The crowd quieted when Harwell issued the usual warnings that no outbursts would be tolerated. Wanda closed her eyes in anticipation and said a prayer.

Suddenly, persons close to the front of the courtroom looked toward the door to the jurors' room. Irby Walker froze in his position and turned his head. *That sound*, he thought, *Can it be?*

Shushing sounds rippled through the courtroom as persons leaned in, straining to hear. The sound of a song, softly, at first, and then more strongly, wafted through the courtroom.

It really is, Walker thought. *It's a hymn.* Walker smiled, closed his eyes and listened. The jurors were singing.

Wanda also smiled as the faint sound assumed a familiar rhythm.

"On-ward Christ-ian so-l-diers, marching as to war . . ."

Woomer and his mother emerged from the prisoner's room holding hands and took their positions. Woomer then placed his hand over his eyes and bowed his head. At 5:55 p.m. the jurors entered.

"Mr. Foreman," the clerk of court asked, "have you reached a verdict?"

"Yes, ma'am," Finch replied. "We have."

A slip of paper was handed to the clerk, who read aloud. "We, the jury, having found beyond a reasonable doubt the existence of the following statutory aggravating circumstances to wit: rape and kidnapping, and now recommend to the court that the defendant, Ronald R. Woomer, be sentenced to death."

Woomer stood emotionless, with his head slightly bowed, as he listened to his fate. Behind him his mother wept quietly.

"Would you please present the defendant," Harwell requested.

Woomer looked frail and began nervously wringing his hands behind his back as he stood with Stevens and Walker before Harwell.

"Mr. Woomer, is there anything that you, your lawyers, or anyone on your behalf would like to say?" Harwell asked.

"Yes, sir," Woomer answered, his voice cracking. "I'm just sorry that I come down here and caused the people of South Carolina the trouble that I have. I figured I'd be scared if this happened and I am in a way, but I know I have Christ with me now. That took a whole lot off of me because I don't worry so much because I know he's going to take care of me.

"I just want to apologize to the people here that I just caused them trouble. I'd like to apologize to Jimmy and Wanda Summers and hope they can put their lives back together."

Woomer began to sob. His chest heaved and tears streamed down his cheeks as he continued. "Mr. Sellers," he said in a shaky voice, "I know that his wife won't ever come back to him. I'm just sorry that I was the cause of that. That's all, Your Honor."

"Anything further, Mr. Stevens, as the chief counsel in this case?" Harwell asked.

"Your Honor," Stevens said in a quiet voice, "I know better than to quarrel with the jury's verdict, but I want this court to know and I want this family to know that the words spoken by this young man are from his heart and they are true. Please believe him. Thank you."

Wanda sat quietly holding hands with Jimmy and Assistant Solicitor Breeden as Woomer and then Stevens spoke. The hollow words proved meaningless for Wanda. Jimmy also dismissed the apology as just more words, but took the moment to experience the first relief he'd felt during the trial. The anger he'd felt for Stevens for possibly doing too good of a job began to subside. Don Sellers' chest swelled as he listened to Woomer's pitiful apology. Sellers held the ring he gave Louise on the day they wed in his clenched fist as he stared at the back of Woomer's head.

"Mr. Woomer," Harwell began the sentencing, "I think you perhaps at this time do appreciate the horrible consequences that you have brought upon the citizens of this state. I have defended and prosecuted cases and, as a trial judge, I have had to try some of the most horrible cases in this state, but the horror, the tragedy that you brought about as a result of your actions really defy my imagination. How a human being can be so callous and so thoughtless and so reckless toward his fellow man is beyond my belief. If I didn't impose the death sentence in this case, I don't believe that I could ever again impose it in another case. I personally think it would seriously jeopardize the constitutionality of our death penalty statute here in South Carolina. But I want you to know that I don't do it lightly. It's not something I volunteered for, but it's a part of my responsibility as the presiding judge of this court and, as long as I wear this robe, I fully intend to discharge my responsibility and to uphold the laws of this state.

"If there's nothing further, the defendant, Ronald R. Woomer, was found by the jury herein to be guilty of the offense of murder. The jury has recommended that the defendant should be sentenced to death. He is now asked if he has anything further to say why the judgment of the law and the sentence of the court should not be pronounced against him. He gives no sufficient reason why the judgment and sentence should not now be pronounced.

"It is, therefore, the judgment of the law and the sentence of the court that you, Ronald Raymond Woomer, the prisoner at the bar, be taken to the county jail of Horry County and thence to the state penitentiary, henceforth to be kept in close and safe confinement until the twenty-eighth day of September, 1979, upon which day between the hour of six o'clock a.m. and the hour of six o'clock p.m., you shall suffer death by electrocution in the manner provided by law. May God have mercy on your soul."

Woomer was escorted from the courtroom but was brought back for further sentencing for his additional crimes. In addition to the death sentence for Louise's murder, Harwell sentenced Woomer to life in prison for kidnapping, thirty years for rape, and twenty years for assault and battery with intent to kill, all to run consecutively.

When Woomer was once again escorted from the courtroom Harwell addressed the jury for a final time. Visibly overcome by the weight of his responsibility, Harwell began to choke and had to pause to wipe tears from his eyes.

"Mr. Foreman, ladies and gentlemen, I just want to take the opportunity to thank you on behalf of your court, your state and your county for your service. I know this has been an awful experience for you. I want you to know that I understand the problems that you have when you have to sit in judgment of your fellow man. It's an experience that I hope you don't ever have to share again.

"Without your help, being the good jurors that you were in this case, I don't know what would come to our society. And for whatever it's worth, I think you reached the only verdict that you could reach in this case. If I had been in your shoes, I would have done exactly the same thing. I realize it's difficult for all of you, but I did want to take a few minutes to let you know that I understand, and the Lord understands. I appreciate your work, the pains of your conscience, and I hope that somewhere, somehow, such tragedies that have been inflicted on these innocent people will come to an end. Thank you very much."

The jury, as it turned out, had reached the only decision possible for them. When asked whether their decision was a difficult one, the foreman, Raymond Finch, declared, "We felt we could not allow that man to continue to breathe the same air that we breathe."

39

The person who wrote the headline of the *Georgetown Times* article one month after the conclusion of the trial, "Worst over for Crime Victim," had no way of knowing what actually lay in store for Wanda and her family. "Things are returning to normal," the journalist wrote. Unfortunately, in hindsight, "normal" ended for Wanda the moment she walked into the door of Jack's Minimall the night of the robbery. The "worst" was anything but over.

Wanda was alarmed and upset when Eckert and Cunningham outlined a treatment plan that would include hospitalization for eight months. She insisted that she be allowed to have a family life, and she eventually got to go home. However, her initial hospital stay was still nearly a month. Her weight continued to drop, finally reaching ninety-eight pounds, and the doctors threatened to put her back in the hospital to control her intake of calories for the duration of the expected treatment plan.

"How am I supposed to keep my weight up?" Wanda had argued with the doctors. "I can't eat."

"Put some butterbeans in the blender," Eckert responded as he warned her. "You have to keep your strength."

Five months after the accident, during the trial, Wanda was visibly thinner to those who knew her.

Wanda did eventually manage to keep down soft foods, but only with effort and the help of her family and friends. In addition to mashed potatoes and lots of grits and eggs, Wanda had a steady supply of homemade potato soup, brought to the house after each surgery in quart-size Mason jars by the daughter of her hairdresser. As the surgeries gradually reshaped her mouth, she was able to eat better and she regained some of the thirty pounds she had lost.

The four major surgeries that Wanda had in the five months prior to the trial revolved around a schedule that allowed her to participate in the preparations for the trial and to be present in the courtroom. After the trial, however, the schedule for the surgeries became particularly grueling, and for several years dominated every aspect of life for the Summers' family.

The typical routine for Wanda included regular visits to see Eckert in his Myrtle Beach office, some 35-five miles from her home in Pawley's Island. Eckert, and sometimes Cunningham, examined the work previously done on her mouth and throat and then planned for the next hospitalization and surgical procedure. For each surgical procedure Wanda entered the hospital on a Sunday night, had surgery the following morning and recuperated in the hospital for one to two weeks before going home. Once at home, Wanda was usually confined to bed for an additional week or two, and required around the clock assistance before she was well enough to get up and be "normal." Normalcy was short-lived, however, usually lasting for only one to two weeks. Once Wanda had healed enough for medical procedures to move ahead, the whole process began again. During the period of time between 1979 and 1985, not including the four medical procedures prior to the trial, Wanda underwent more than a dozen repetitions of this cycle. Some of the procedures were more extensive than described above, such as procedures involving bone and skin grafting, and some were less involved. All of the procedures, however, taxed Wanda's physical and emotional capabilities to her limit.

"My doctors said that I should dwell upon how much is being gained even though it is very painful," Wanda told a newspaper reporter.

The routine was also very difficult for Wanda's family and varied slightly, depending on whether school for Traci was in session. Jimmy took Wanda to the hospital on Sunday evening and stayed for the night and the following day of the surgery. He left in time to get to work on Tuesday, but every evening he made the long drive back to the hospital when he got off from his job in Georgetown. In the summer traffic, the 40-mile drive sometimes required two hours.

Wanda's mother and father provided invaluable help in taking care of Traci during those years, but the little girl was gradually forced to become more and more self-sufficient. Wanda's mother, Betty, went to the hospital to stay with Wanda during the day. Betty got up at 4:00 a.m. and made breakfast for her husband Reggie and Traci. Following breakfast, Betty prepared lunch so that it was cooked and ready. Then, either Traci and Reggie took Betty to the hospital in the morning and drove back to Pawley's Island to eat lunch and do chores, or they took Betty to the hospital after lunch and then went back home to take care of chores. When Reggie got back in the car and drove to Myrtle Beach in the evenings to pick up Betty, Traci sometimes chose to stay at the hospital overnight with her mother and with Jimmy, who was just arriving from work. In those instances, Traci then rode back the following morning with Jimmy in time for her to get to school. When Wanda was in the hospital, the only opportunities that Traci had to spend with her daddy were at the hospital in the evenings and on the ride back to Pawley's Island the next morning.

Traci became more and more distant from her classmates, many of whom knew something was going on in her life, but they lacked the maturity to understand what. "I went from one day being a six-year-old child to the next day being a six-year-old adult," Traci recalled. "God love everyone that helped me, but to hear 'You have to be strong,' 'You have to be good,' and 'Your momma can't worry about you right now, we have to get her better,' is a lot of pressure. Nobody knew that puts in the mind of a six-year-old that, 'If I'm not those things, then what happens? Does my momma get worse? Does she go away again? If I don't do these things that I'm supposed to, then am I not good?' I began to feel that it was up to me to make everything better. Better for my family, better for my mother."

Traci began to assume responsibilities for the household and helped by doing chores, such as laundry and washing dishes. In addition, Traci began to worry when Wanda wasn't in her sight. "If I leave to go somewhere, will she go away again?" Traci said, recalling the questions she had as a little girl. "A lot of times I thought I shouldn't go somewhere to spend the night or play, because what if momma needed me?" Traci said she never felt resentment, though. "I just simply didn't want to be somewhere where she was not."

Traci gradually assumed a protector role and became sensitive to the reactions of others as they first saw her mother. Wanda had stopped making eye contact with persons she encountered, and Traci began to witness how people would often stare at Wanda if they were not prompted to look away. In response, Traci stepped behind Wanda and stared back or made faces at the offending persons until they looked away in embarrassment. "I felt like I had to control what everyone did," Traci said, "for Momma's sake. I loved my mother," she added. "I was going to do whatever I thought in my six-year-old mind was right to do for her."

Wanda experienced guilt that others had to assume responsibility for what she thought a mother should be doing for her child. "I had to have help come in to cook, clean, and get Traci off to school." Wanda still expresses regret that she had to miss a lot of the normal activities that a mother enjoys with her child.

Gradually during the years that the stressful routine lasted, Wanda had to adjust to being in the hospital more and more by herself. Though her mother still made the trip to stay with her during the days, Jimmy had started a new business and had to devote extra time to make it grow. As Jimmy found it more and more difficult to keep up with the financially and emotionally draining medical procedures, he put into practice the remedy he knew best. He just worked even harder.

On more than one occasion, Wanda was delirious following surgery and called Jimmy. "Please," she whispered frantically into the phone by her hospital bed, "I need you. The nurses are trying to beat me up."

Jimmy got out of bed and drove 35 miles to the hospital, only to find Wanda sedated and sleeping.

Jimmy began to relieve stress with alcohol. Consumed by the need to provide for his family, he drank during the only available time he had, which was late at night. He soon experienced a lack of sleep but didn't miss work or shirk a family responsibility.

Eckert, who was also the recipient of Wanda's middle of the night distress calls, noticed that Jimmy's behavior was becoming erratic. Eckert correctly determined that the beleaguered husband and father would not be able to sustain the hectic pace he set for himself, and Eckert began to call Jimmy. At the concerned doctor's insistence, Jimmy began to meet with Eckert occasionally, in the evenings and on Saturdays. Eckert listened patiently as Jimmy vented his frustrations. It was clear to the Summers' family that Eckert was not only working tirelessly to fix Wanda's face, he was also tending to the broken heart of the family.

One day, about a year and a half after the accident, Jimmy was with a friend in a grocery store in Pawley's Island. Jimmy had gotten the beer he wanted to purchase out of the cooler when he saw a slim-built, shaggy-haired man standing in the cashier's line.

"I don't know what happened," Jimmy remembered, "but thank God a friend of mine was with me or I'd probably be in prison."

The unfortunate man standing in the line felt Jimmy's stare and turned to ask if there was a problem. In an instant, Jimmy had his knife out, opened and pointed at the man.

"For some reason, and I knew it didn't make sense," Jimmy said, shaking his head, "the man looked to me just like Woomer. When he smarted off, I lost it. I didn't know how he got out of jail, but I was going to rid the world of him once and for all." Laughing the type of nervous laugh that expresses relief, Jimmy added, "My friend grabbed me just in time."

The startled man quickly changed his attitude and hurried out. The store manager decided not to call the police when Jimmy's friend explained the situation. Everyone in the small community of Pawley's Island in 1981 knew what had happened to Wanda.

"It's funny how things work," Jimmy said recently. "Everything revolved around my family, and there I was, about to do the very thing that would have made everything worse. Looking back on it, you'd think I would have learned something from it. I should have seen that incident as a warning sign for what was to come."

He didn't.

Jimmy continued to drink. His life had taken an abrupt turn and the more he fought to hang on to the last threads of normalcy available to him, the more futile his efforts became. Within six months after the incident at the store, Jimmy's health had deteriorated to the point where he collapsed at work and had to be rushed to the emergency room. When he awoke several days later he was strapped to a bed in the intensive care unit of the Georgetown Hospital. Blood clots in his lungs had almost killed him. The situation worsened when Jimmy became psychotic, necessitating the use of restraints. If Jimmy was to get better, the doctors said, he must have absolute rest; even incidental movements posed extreme risk in his weakened condition. Jimmy's delirious behavior continued, however, and two weeks later, he was sent by ambulance to the psychiatric wing of the medical university in Charleston.

Jimmy's stay in the institution proved to be the stimulus he needed to make a life-change. Day after day, as he rambled around the ward, he gradually regained his focus. One day, in a moment as he was throwing an empty soda can in the trash, Jimmy realized he had almost lost himself. If that had happened, he would have lost everything for which he had worked so hard. Knowing that Wanda and Traci depended on him, and with the resolute determination he had shown many times before, Jimmy made a decision. As it happened, the next day the psychiatrist responsible for Jimmy's treatment provided just the opportunity he needed to put his decision into play.

The psychiatrist had become more suspicious of each new addition to Jimmy's story. She had listened patiently as he told stories of his childhood that indicated a desire for a normal family life. There was nothing particularly unusual about that, she had told Jimmy. But when she tried to probe deeply into his adult life, Jimmy had become angry and defensive. He resented any further intrusions into the intimate details of his family life. The only information

Jimmy had revealed was that his wife had been through a terrible ordeal that left her without a whole face.

"Mr. Summers," the psychiatrist told Jimmy, "I'm not saying I don't believe your story. But you've got to admit, it has some remarkable elements. It's time for me to meet your wife," the psychiatrist said and slid the phone across the desk. "I want you to call her right now. Tell her I want to meet her. I think then we may be able to move ahead, when we see together that she is all right."

"What do you mean 'all right'?" Jimmy asked.

"That her face isn't missing."

The psychiatrist working with Jimmy was dumbfounded when Wanda arrived at the hospital to take Jimmy home. The necessary paperwork was completed and Jimmy was discharged from the hospital. With Wanda hurrying after him, Jimmy ran across the parking lot to the car.

Once in the car, he said, "Wanda, thanks for coming to get me."

Wanda was more than glad to be with Jimmy again. The two weeks he was in the institution had been very difficult for her, and she hadn't been able to visit him during that time. Jimmy knew that his phone call had caused his wife to suffer. Wanda hadn't been able to be home alone, even during the day, in the two years since the assault. Driving a car out of town had been unthinkable.

"I don't know how I made it here," Wanda replied. "But I know I don't ever want us to be apart again."

"That sounds about right to me," Jimmy said.

On the way home from Charleston, Jimmy told Wanda of his decision. He was through drinking, he said, and added that he knew he needed help. Wanda agreed to do whatever was necessary to help the man who had done so much for her.

During the two years of surgeries and doctor's visits, Wanda's life had become a series of mad dashes from one moment to the next, with her never being able to catch her breath. Though the surgeries would continue for over three more years, Wanda rejoiced in her quiet way on the ride home from Charleston with Jimmy. Through everything that had happened, they still had each other.

When they arrived at home, Jimmy and Wanda were greeted by Traci and by the newest addition to the family. The Summers had finally gotten a pet; they now had a large brindle bull guard dog. Wanda and Jimmy never found out what happened to the puppies they had gotten for Traci for her sixth birthday.

40

Just several hours after the trial ended, Woomer's soon-to-be new friends in prison watched quietly from their cells as Rusty was ushered in shackles down the walkway of his new home – Death Row at Columbia Correctional Institute. In his cell were the few possessions he was allowed to have; among them was a Bible he'd received as a gift from Cleveland Stevens.

Though the date of Woomer's execution was set for September 28, 1979, just two months after the sentencing, an automatic stay was granted when the case was appealed to the South Carolina Supreme Court. When Stevens notified the State Attorney General's office of the "substantial errors" in the trial that made the appeal necessary, the newspaper headline reflected what Stevens had said: "Woomer's Appeal May Take Three Years."

Though Wanda thought that three years sounded like a long time to wait to see justice carried out, she had plenty to do. Just after the removal of the wires holding together her shattered jaw, Wanda checked into the hospital on Mother's Day to begin the slow and painful process of having the inside of her mouth reshaped using skin the doctors had removed from her hip.

When the surgeries resumed following Woomer's July trial, Eckert told Wanda that the scars on her face would require a year or more to fade following the last of the surgeries.

"I won't worry about the scars if he can renew my chin," Wanda said, optimistic that she would soon or at least eventually resume a normal life.

By August, the newspaper reported of Wanda, "Although her chin and jaw line are still missing, her appearance has improved markedly. Her speech is clear and she seems to have regained much of her confidence."

Meanwhile, Woomer began settling into his new life on Death Row and waited to hear of his appeal. Dunn announced that he intended to wait until the outcome of the appeal before pursuing the murder charges pending against Woomer in Georgetown County. "If the Horry County decision holds up, there is no reason to make the taxpayer in Georgetown pay for another trial." Dunn also stated, though, that he intended to talk with the families of the victims and that he would pursue the charges if they felt it was necessary.

The "substantial errors" to which Stevens had referred included: the court did not grant the requested change of venue, the defense was provided only two thousand dollars for psychological testing and expert witnesses, the continuous mention of crimes Woomer committed in other locales – the murders in Georgetown and Colleton Counties – and the reference to Woomer's West Virginia parole officer during the testimony of Sheriff Brown.

Interestingly, the appeal also challenged the 1977 South Carolina Death Penalty Statute for its constitutionality. In effect, the question was, "Does the death penalty constitute cruel and unusual punishment?" The first points of the appeal being examined, and thereby costing the taxpayers more money, were considered by some who had watched the proceedings as a tolerable safeguard of the legal system, providing that the process didn't stretch out indefinitely. On the other hand, questioning whether electrocuting a man responsible for the heinous crimes for which Woomer had been convicted was in any way cruel or unusual seemed ludicrous. It was noted that while Wanda had to use a straw to eat, Woomer was eating three meals a day and gaining weight. While Wanda suffered at night with nightmares of the assault to the point that she had to be medicated to rest, Woomer slept without threat in a clean cell under the watchful eyes of men paid to protect him. While Wanda attended sessions with psychiatrists, a practice she would continue for many years, Woomer attended meetings with his court-appointed lawyers to plan strategy for his upcoming trials. In addition, Woomer began forming relationships with others through his interest in Bible study.

Don Sellers was not at all satisfied that Woomer was in any way suffering for the death of his wife, Louise, and was again seen sitting behind Woomer with clenched fists when the Colleton trial began in June of 1980, 11 months after the Horry conviction. Similarly, friends and family of John Turner were in attendance for the weeklong trial in Walterboro, a town near Cottageville, and were not disappointed when Woomer received a second death sentence for his crimes. The Walterboro *Press and Standard* reported that Woomer showed no emotion when the verdict was announced, and when he stood before the court, Woomer said, "I know it sounds phony, but I have found Christ since my arrest." Dressed in street clothes and with his hair longer and shaggier than for the trial in Horry County, Woomer looked to the conservative citizens of Cottageville like "a turd in a punch bowl" as he again asked for mercy for his misdeeds.

Colleton County Solicitor Randolph "Buster" Murdaugh dismissed Woomer's statement as jailhouse Christianity. "They just repent and say they're sorry," Murdaugh said. "Of course they'll cry and beg."

Woomer was returned to his cell at CCI, but within two weeks he was back on the road to Horry County for the trial of John Fisher and Fred Whitehead. Woomer's testimony was largely responsible for the convictions of both of the accomplices in the crime spree, but how that testimony was secured became a point of controversy and threatened to disrupt the status quo for a community still trying to regroup after the mayhem of February 22, 1979.

In exchange for his testimony against Fisher and Whitehead, Woomer was offered a two-fold deal: Colleton County officials agreed to ask Governor Richard Riley for a commutation of Woomer's death sentence in Colleton County, and Dunn agreed not to seek the death penalty for the Georgetown murders. The deal provided some interesting moments in the trial of Fisher and Whitehead.

John Fisher, labeled the "kingpin" by Dunn, was charged with criminal conspiracy. Fred Whitehead was also charged with criminal conspiracy, but additional charges of accessory after the fact and receiving stolen goods were filed against him. Both men were defended by Myrtle Beach Attorney, J.M. "Bud" Long, Jr. Neither of the men testified, either on his own behalf or to blame the other. Woomer testified, however, and told of Fisher's involvement in the planning of the initial robbery and of meeting with Whitehead before and after the robberies and murders. Whitehead was aware, Woomer said, that Turner was to be murdered, but expressed concern only for the coins.

Bud Long's cross-examination first established Woomer's and Skaar's roles in the crimes. Then, specifically addressing the deal Woomer had received for his testimony, Long said, "You've got a new lease on life by testifying here today."

"Yes, sir," Woomer replied, "But I wouldn't lie."

Long questioned this statement in his closing argument asserting that if a man will lie, he will lie to avoid the electric chair. "Would you trust him with your daughter?" Long asked the jurors and then turned to look at Woomer. "Would you trust him with your wife? Would you trust him with a five-dollar bill? Yet the solicitor stands here and tells you to trust him enough to send two men to the penitentiary."

The jury must have believed Woomer, at least, in part, for after three and a half hours of deliberation, Fisher and Whitehead were found guilty on all charges and given the maximum sentences allowed by the court. For their parts in the crime spree in which five people died and Wanda was critically wounded, Fisher received five years and Whitehead received a total of twenty-five years.

An editorial piece in *The Sun News*, entitled "Plea Bargain Danger Too Easy to Detect," printed after the trial, pointed out a problem posed by the agreement that Dunn made with Woomer. The death sentence for Woomer in Horry County was under automatic appeal. If Governor Riley granted the commutation for the death sentence in Colleton County, then not seeking an additional death sentence in Georgetown before knowing the outcome of the appeal in Horry County presented the possibility of Woomer skating by on a life sentence, if the Horry death sentence was overturned and not reinstated. "What concerns us, obviously," the editor said, "is that Woomer might escape the sentence that he was given. Equally possible, it seems, is that he might yet be executed. Nonetheless, the very fact that there is doubt on that point gives rise to wonder about plea-bargaining in the first place. The issue is – as they say in legal circles – whether the state used a little fish to catch a big one, or a big fish to catch a little one. The first is acceptable; the second isn't."

Jim Dunn felt obliged to defend the agreement with Woomer and called a press conference in front of Jack's Mini-mall in Pawley's Island. On hand with Dunn were Wanda and Jimmy, Don Sellers, and a contingent of family members and witnesses to the robberies and abductions.

"I want to respond," Dunn began as the television cameras rolled. *"The Sun News* editor apparently misconstrued my intentions. Although the editor might not have approved of my handling of that case, I have victims and families of victims here tonight, and they approve of my actions."

Dunn compared the Horry and Georgetown cases against Woomer. In Georgetown County, Dunn said, the only witness to the murders was a five-year-old who had been under the care of a psychiatrist since witnessing her father's murder. In Horry County, there were five eyewitnesses. "The case in Horry was much easier to prove than the one in Georgetown. When you've got the death penalty against a fella one time, it doesn't matter how many other times you get it. You can only execute a man one time."

Responding to the big fish, little fish analogy, Dunn said, "If the editor feels [that Woomer] is a little fish, then he ought to quit editing and go to fishing. I used a barracuda to catch two sharks."

The prediction of *The Sun News* editor turned out to be prophetic, however. When the Supreme Court response to the appeal was finally issued, it became clear that Horry County had not seen the last of Rusty Woomer.

41

The factory stores appeared on the left side of the road just as the Summers' car rounded the top of the bridge crossing the Intracoastal Waterway and headed west out of Myrtle Beach. Wanda looked across the divide and saw with dismay that the parking lot was almost full.

Jimmy glanced at Wanda's expression as he maneuvered the car into the other lane and prepared to turn. "We can probably get what we want somewhere else, without getting in that crowd," he offered. Traci sat in the middle of the front as she always did and looked up at her mother. From that angle, the difference in the curves of Wanda's face as it was framed against the window was particularly noticeable, but it more intrigued than scared Traci.

"No, we couldn't either, Jimmy," Wanda said slowly. "Not for the price." She crossed her arms, and then added, "Thanks, anyway." Wanda sat quietly as Jimmy smoothly turned the car into the first entrance of the front lot.

"Which side do you want to go in?" he asked. Jimmy glanced at Wanda again. The factory stores were spread over several acres and resembled a mall, with some stores opening off inside halls and some stores opening to the outside.

"Just right around here is good. We have to go in the pottery." Wanda began wringing her hands in her lap.

The Waccamaw Pottery had grown in a few short years from a large store specializing in glassware and linens to an assortment of stores under one roof offering factory seconds on brand name clothes and much more. The large Christmas section in the original building drew shoppers interested in year-round bargains on decorations of every description.

Jimmy eased into a parking spot, switched off the

ignition and waited for Wanda to make the first move. Coming had been her idea. Since the accident a little less than two years earlier, Wanda had begun spending more and more time alone, working with ceramics and tending to her African violets. The first of the flowers had been purple in color and a gift from Jack and Connie Clemmons. When Jimmy put up shelves and grow lights in the extra bedroom, Wanda spent more time with her flowers and blossoms of other colors began to appear.

Wanda took a deep breath and opened her door. *Getting out of the house is a good thing,* she thought to herself. Though Wanda had always been outgoing, and possessed a friendly nature that drew people to her for company and conversation, she was also somewhat reserved and, on occasion, needed solitude to regroup. As such, it had become too easy following the accident for the introverted side of her personality to become dominant. Wanda retreated into herself further than ever, until even she realized that she had to grab on to the outside world as it passed by her, before it was too late.

Besides attending Woomer's trials, visits to Eckert's office, where she was always allowed to bypass the waiting room and, of course, her trips to the hospital, Wanda had not ventured far from her home community. In Pawley's Island, if she had to visit any of the small shops or the grocery store, she encountered familiar persons who would politely nod and then go about their business. She knew traveling to the neighboring community of Myrtle Beach posed a different level of risk. As a well-known resort community, with hundreds of motels and restaurants, the population was more transient. Wanda knew that the possibility of an encounter with a stranger was much more likely and even probable. She and Jimmy had discussed the matter on several occasions. That the first encounter would prove so disastrous was a possibility she hadn't expected.

Just as Wanda got out and stood by her door, a couple of women passed the front of the car on their way into the store. As Traci reached for her mother's hand and scrambled out of the car, one of the women happened to look in Wanda's direction. Wanda smiled timidly, but immediately became tense as surprise registered on the woman's face. Wanda watched as the woman grabbed her friend's arm and said something. The other woman then turned to look and said something back to her companion that Wanda couldn't quite hear. When both women turned again to stare, Wanda felt herself becoming angry. Her face instantly flushed. *When does this end?* she thought. The months of struggle were turning into years of struggle, with Wanda thinking all the while that her appearance would someday be normal.

Pulling away from Traci's small hand, Wanda suddenly ran across the parking lot in the direction of the women.

"You want to look?" Wanda shouted. Stopping short of the closest woman, Wanda leaned forward, putting her face just inches from the startled woman. "Is that it?" she yelled again. "You want to look? Well, then, have a good look." Wanda began backing the woman across the blacktop by advancing in step with the woman's retreat. "This is what you wanted to see, isn't it?"

"Wanda," Jimmy yelled. Quickly stepping up, he reached to grab Wanda's arm. She turned her shoulder, pulled out of his grasp and continued toward the startled woman.

"No, she wants to look." Wanda stretched her neck so that her face continued to jut forward. "Here it is!" Wanda shouted. "Look at me!"

Jimmy reached for her arm again, this time grabbing her tightly and stopping her advance. Stepping in between Wanda and the women, Jimmy pulled Wanda to him and wrapped his large arms around her shoulders. "Wanda, no," Jimmy said, and his eyes began to mist.

Wanda struggled for a moment, but then folded her body into his embrace and began sobbing.

"I'm sorry," Jimmy said in the direction of the women, who had huddled and were moving away quickly. "She's been through a lot."

Still crying, Wanda pushed away from Jimmy, leaving him standing with his arms outstretched. After staring in frustration at Jimmy for several seconds, Wanda turned away. Her sobs as she gasped for air were heard across the parking lot.

Traci watched from where she stood by the car as her father slowly lowered his arms. Jimmy walked back to the car and got in. Traci waited until her mother returned a couple of minutes later before getting in the car.

The Summers' family then rode back home without having visited the shops to get what they had intended. No one spoke during the long ride. It was many years later before Jimmy went shopping with Wanda again.

42

When the response to Woomer's appeal finally came in April of 1981, Jim Dunn was disappointed. Although the conviction of Woomer for the kidnap and murder of Louise was upheld, the South Carolina Supreme Court overturned the death sentence; the second phase of the trial would have to be retried. Dunn again asked Wanda to summon her strength and courage to appear in public and once more face the person responsible for her suffering.

In a four-to-one opinion, with former Circuit Judge David Harwell, now South Carolina Supreme Court Justice Harwell, excusing himself, the court ruled that Dunn and Harwell had each made a procedural error, due, as it turned out, in both cases, to the newness of the South Carolina Death Penalty Statute of 1977.

In his dramatic and sometimes emotional closing during the sentencing phase, Dunn apparently overstepped his bounds as a prosecuting attorney when he told the jury that ultimate justice would be determined not by their collective voice but by the judge who would consider their recommendation.

"Now, what is His Honor's role?" Dunn had asked at the trial as he summed up his remarks. "Ladies and gentlemen, I think you should clearly understand that if you make a recommendation for the death penalty that you should expect that that should be carried out. I'm not trying to spread your responsibility thin. But His Honor cannot, he shall not, he must not, and I submit will not follow your recommendation until he has found that your recommendation is supported by the evidence. He must find it was not done arbitrarily, it was not done with prejudice, not done capriciously. And he must, as his duty as the trial judge in this case, make that finding affirmatively on the record."

Though Dunn was correct in stating that the judge would make the final decision, and he was correct in inferring that the judge could override the jury's decision if necessary, the Supreme Court ruling stated that "the solicitor's argument lessened the jury's responsibility." Dunn's statements, similar to statements he had made in closings before, were not allowed under the new law.

The majority opinion further stated that "No principle of law is more firmly established than the solemn duty of the court to determine the law of the case and declare it to the jury."

In his lengthy charge to the jury, Judge Harwell did make it clear that the new South Carolina law only allowed a recommendation of death by the jury if one or more of the aggravating circumstances presented by the prosecution were proved. He did not make it clear, however, that the jury could disregard evidence of aggravation, if they so chose, and make a recommendation of life in prison. This recommendation for mercy could be made, according to the new law, for any reason that the jury might have. The judge, in that instance, could follow the jury's recommendation, or could override the jury and sentence the convicted individual to death, given, as stated above, that aggravation had been shown.

The resentencing of Woomer took place three months later in July of 1981, two full years after the original conviction and sentence. Wanda was again present in the courtroom to face Woomer, the evidence of her long struggle readily apparent.

Woomer appeared to have matured. His face was more full, and dressed in the suit provided for him by Stevens, and with his hair cut short and combed, he looked more like one of the lawyers than the rag-a-muffin defendant of two years earlier. All pretense to be more than he was disappeared, though, when Woomer opened his mouth. He again asked for mercy because of his poor upbringing, and this time he played the religion card for all it was worth.

The jury was clearly more interested in what Wanda had to say, however, and watched through squinted eyes as she struggled to the witness stand on crutches. The surgeries to rebuild Wanda's chin from hip material had progressed. Wanda had a titanium jaw-piece in place to allow the skin and muscles of her face to adapt as the contours of her mouth and throat were reshaped. The effect appeared macabre as the skin from her cheeks had been stretched down around the metal jaw and appeared transparent; underlying work involving screws and wires was obvious. The ends of wires holding the jaw-piece in place protruded through the skin and stuck out as points, giving Wanda a prickly look.

A terrible moment for Wanda came when Agent Michael Carter was testifying about evidence gathered at the Komo-Mai the night of the arrest. When Carter held up and described a picture of Traci that was found at the motel, Wanda was overwhelmed by a sense of being powerless to protect her child.

"I thought to myself, 'My God, here I am sitting in a courtroom in Conway, South Carolina, and they are talking about my baby, my beautiful, innocent daughter.' I felt helpless to protect her, to somehow keep her out of all this. They had her picture, and there they were talking about her."

When Wanda recalled during an interview for this book how she felt in the courtroom that day, she became upset, and paused. She quickly wiped tears from her cheeks as she strained to find the words to describe the feeling of contamination, of being dirty, that she had felt. Woomer's appearance in court in his suit was certainly not an accurate portrayal of him as he was on the night of the assault. The repulsive smells of Woomer on the night of the robbery and rape were not available in court — his hair had been stringy and greasy; his body odor had been close and rank; his breath was smoky and tasted of stale liquor; his dirty blue jeans had a dark, slick appearance down the thighs and on the back where he had repeatedly wiped his nasty, sweaty hands.

"When I heard Traci's name, and I had the realization that she was being associated with the filth of the whole thing, I became hysterical, and started to scream and cry. Jimmy and I had done all we could to keep her out of it. And here she was anyway, being discussed by strangers. Court had to stop because of my crying. Then, to my disbelief, the judge told me that I either had to control myself or I couldn't remain in the courtroom."

● ❖ ●

When Wanda began to cry in court, Dunn made an exaggerated show of standing behind her and placing his hands protectively on her shoulders. Judge Finney became agitated and quickly excused the jurors. Dunn led Wanda out of the courtroom to an office where Eckert attended to her needs.

Just over an hour later, Stevens stuck his head in the office and asked Wanda if she could speak with Barbara Woomer. When Wanda reluctantly agreed to the meeting, Barbara entered and stood nervously clasping her hands. "I appreciate you seeing me," Barbara said, avoiding eye contact with Wanda. "And I wouldn't blame you if you didn't. But I just wanted you to know how sorry I am all this has happened."

Wanda didn't respond, being unsure of what would be an appropriate response.

"That's all, I guess," Barbara said quietly. "I'm just so ashamed and . . . well . . . I'm sorry." Barbara turned and quickly left.

● ❖ ●

In the end, the jury's deliberations ended in another death sentence. Woomer's personal plea to the jury had included several references to his new beliefs. Speaking softly, he said, "I've never seen God, but I know he's there and that he's been with me up there in prison. I've prayed for the victims. The only way I can describe how I feel is terrible. Mr. Dunn calls it jailhouse religion. I think it's great that God can come to you wherever you are. I don't know if

I could have lived the last two and one half years without Christ.

"If y'all sign that paper, you will put me in the electric chair. Mr. Dunn told you the Ten Commandments say, 'Thou shall not kill.' But that also means thou shall not kill me."

Wanda said she breathed a sigh of relief after the death sentence was handed down again. Though she knew the new sentence would be appealed, she felt more confident that Woomer might actually get what had been twice determined for him. "There had been talk that he might get off with a life sentence and that worried me," she said. "I felt at that point that I wasn't going to be able to move ahead until he died for what he had done. And not for just what he had done to me, but to Louise and Don, too, and all the others." An embarrassed look crossed Wanda's face as she said, "I worried about whether that made me a terrible person. Wanting him to die."

43

Wanda felt she was learning how the system worked to attend to the needs of criminals. The needs of victims were secondary, if victims received any attention at all. After the flare of publicity that rose and fell each time Woomer was required to show his face in public, Wanda was simply left on her own to do the best she could.

The next three years came and went and the world continued to turn, largely unaware of the struggle of Wanda Summers and her family. The titanium jaw-piece had to be removed after a year and reset because of an infection in the bone. Doctors Eckert and Cunningham continued working diligently with their admittedly difficult case involving complete reconstruction of a lower face. A dozen additional major surgeries kept Wanda in and out of the hospital and shuttling back and forth between Pawley's Island and Myrtle Beach. When the issue of teeth came up, Wanda realized how tired she was of the whole process.

"Jimmy, I just can't bear the thought of leaving home anymore," Wanda said.

Jimmy had learned to remain quiet and let Wanda take her thoughts wherever she needed.

"It doesn't seem like it's worth it," she added. Wanda and Jimmy had discussed with Eckert that the process seemed to have reached a plateau, with little visible progress being made. The inside of Wanda's mouth and her throat had long since healed and she was able to eat pretty normally, albeit without teeth. An experiment with false teeth hadn't worked. With only enough room in her mouth for either an upper or lower plate, an upper plate was chosen and made. When fitted, though, it proved unsatisfactory and made

Wanda leery of the irreversibility of surgically implanted teeth. She decided that she had adjusted well enough to not having teeth and worried that artificial teeth would cause additional problems.

The problem that was forcing a reevaluation of the surgical process, however, was of a different sort.

"I'm getting nervous right now, as I think about it," she said, looking at her hands shake as she referred to her impending surgery. "And I don't have to go again for several weeks."

"All right," Jimmy said. "Let's talk about it."

"I feel like Traci is 12, going on 22," Wanda said. "She's so grown up now. I hate that I've missed so much. She needs me, despite how she thinks about it."

Traci and her mother, and perhaps especially Traci and Jimmy, as Traci was becoming so much like her daddy, were starting to have communication problems. Traci felt that since the accident she had been forced to look after herself, and she had done just that, without resentment. She had always wanted to help in any way possible and had been supportive of the family effort. Now that her mother was doing much better, though, Traci felt her mother and father were trying to make up for lost time by exerting control over her, which she did resent.

"Traci's hard-headed like I am," Jimmy said, "but she'll be all right. What is it really, Wanda?" Jimmy knew of two issues.

"I feel as if I'm out of control the second I walk into the hospital," Wanda said, her voice reflecting urgency. "I don't know how much longer I can stand to feel that way." Her efforts to regain control of her life had gone reasonably well through her hobbies and her interest in her artwork, a newly discovered talent. Relinquishing all control at the hospital, however, was becoming frightening to her. Just thinking of having additional surgeries was enough to produce feelings of extreme anxiety. "I want to feel normal."

"That makes sense to me," Jimmy said. It did, of course. Jimmy was sympathetic to any ideas of taking charge and making things happen.

"I'm going to ask Dr. Eckert again about having a

baby," Wanda blurted, watching Jimmy's expression.

Here it is, thought Jimmy. "You know what he's going to say, Wanda, the drugs and all."

"Then I'll stop the surgeries," Wanda suggested, as she had before.

Jimmy took a deep breath. "Wanda, we've been through this," he said, the frustration becoming evident in his voice.

"I know, I know," she replied. "Not in a long time, though. It's different now."

"What's different? You tell me what's different." Jimmy shook his head.

"Jimmy," Wanda said, stepping in front of her husband. "Jimmy, look at me. Look right in my eyes."

Jimmy did as she asked.

"I'm ready to stop," she said. "I don't have to tell you what this has been like. I couldn't have made it without you. You know that. That's not what this is about. I just believe I'm ready, Jimmy."

Jimmy continued to look at his wife.

"I need to know, though," Wanda continued. "You tell me how you'd be, really, if I told Dr. Eckert that I'm going to stop the surgeries. We've all discussed this anyway. We knew this was coming. I'm tired of pretending that things are just going to be as they were before. It's been six years, Jimmy. Six years! I feel sometimes I hardly know my daughter. I barely leave the house. I've worn out everybody I love. I just can't keep doing this."

"I feel the same as I always have," Jimmy said. "You're the one who has to be all right with this."

"Well, I'm saying I am all right with it now," Wanda said quickly.

"Wanda, you've needed so badly to look normal again," Jimmy said. "What about that? If you stop now; where does that leave you?"

"The hope has been gone, Jimmy." Wanda wiped at her eyes with a tissue. "For you, too," she added in a soft voice. "We're just going through the motions."

"How do you want me to tell you I'm all right with what you decide?" Jimmy asked and sighed. "I'm here, Wanda. I've always been here."

Wanda nodded, and smiled self-consciously. A tear ran down her cheek before she caught it.

She had always felt Jimmy was with her. Many men might not have been able to hang on through the worst of it, but Jimmy had.

"I can continue with the surgeries, Jimmy," she said slowly. "I really can." She wrapped her arms around Jimmy's neck. "Just tell me that you want me to, if you do."

"Wanda, I love you just as you are," he said, returning her embrace. "If you want to, we'll call the doctor right now."

A little over a year later, Wanda, Jimmy and Traci welcomed to their family James Arnold Summers, Jr., a healthy baby boy. Sharing the happiness with Reggie, Betty and other family members and friends at the hospital were Jim Dunn and Buddy Causey. In addition, Drs. Eckert and Cunningham and many of the persons who participated in Wanda's care over the years stopped by her hospital room to say hello and wish her well.

Though no one imagined it at the time, the new baby was more than just an addition to the Summers' family. Jamie became for Jimmy, Wanda and Traci a symbol of the family's future, untainted by the past struggles of Wanda's care forced on them by Woomer's vicious behavior. Each family member suddenly had an opportunity to try to find in Jamie's birth what was most needed to move the healing process forward. Jimmy had the son he always wanted and would subsequently be a mentor and coach and all of the other things he believed that fathers are supposed to be. Traci became a young mother for Jamie, virtually adopting him as her own. Wanda had another chance to raise a child and poured her energy into the new life of the family. Jimmy's business was expanding and doing well. Traci was happier and not nearly as angry as she had been over the years. Wanda felt, as did Jimmy and Traci, that the sun had finally broken through the dark clouds.

Unfortunately, the sun would quickly disappear again and the storm would rage on for the Summers' family.

44

Woomer's name and crimes were generally no longer news to anyone outside of the tight circle of his victims' families and friends until *The State* ran an article in December of 1987, entitled "Love Bug Finds Killer Set to Die." Apparently, in between eating, lying around, and the Bible studies available on Death Row, Woomer had managed to find love. He and his betrothed had already applied for and been issued a marriage license by the Richland County licensing bureau.

"He has evidently expressed an interest and told the chaplain he wants to be married," a department of corrections spokesperson told a reporter. "We have told him to give us a request in writing."

Woomer didn't have to ask permission to get married. His request was for assistance with the details of arranging the ceremony and for help in finding witnesses.

The marriage, which did take place, was Woomer's second. A marriage when he was in his early twenties in Owensboro, Kentucky, near the West Virginia border, had ended in a bitter divorce. The house of his ex-wife's father burned down shortly after the split "under mysterious circumstances," but the Owensboro police said charges were never filed in connection with the fire. Woomer wound up in a Kentucky penitentiary shortly afterwards, anyway, on a rape charge.

Woomer's new bride-to-be when the "love-bug" article appeared was unavailable for comment. Perhaps she hadn't realized that his celebrity status wouldn't allow privacy for their proposed union. Perhaps she wasn't certain about his future.

Woomer's case had wended its way through the lengthy appeals process but was finally nearing an end. The week just before the article appeared in the newspaper, the U.S. Supreme Court had once again rejected his request for a new trial.

• ❖ •

The appeals process in South Carolina is apparently lengthy by design. Following the temporary halt to executions by the U.S. Supreme Court in 1962, South Carolina did what all of the other states with capital punishment laws did: Legislators began a long and often contentious examination of the use of the death penalty in the state.

No accurate records for the state are available before 1912, when public hangings were allowed but, from that point until 1962, 241 persons were electrocuted in South Carolina. The last two persons, executed on Good Friday, April 20, 1962, (one for rape, the other for murder) were strapped into the chair within five minutes of each other in the Death House at the Central Correctional Institute. Prior to the final adjustment of the black leather death mask, each man had looked out through the recently installed glass partition, which was part of the renovations made to the chamber the year before in response to an outburst during an execution. Just as the switch was about to be thrown for the convicted murderer, a witness had yelled, "You're going to hell! You know that?"

South Carolina was one of 39 states in 1972 to have its death penalty law nullified by a U.S. Supreme Court decision that found that capital punishment as used in a Georgia case was unconstitutional. In Georgia and, ultimately, the other 38 states with similar laws, the high court ruling specified that jurors must no longer be given discretion over who lived or died; the death penalty must be applied uniformly for specific crimes.

The debate over the use of the death penalty accelerated in the S.C. General Assembly and included among the arguments for why the state did or did not need a death penalty, suggestions for a more "humane way" to carry out the penalty than the electric chair. Recommendations for lethal injection and the gas chamber notwithstanding, the state senators produced in 1974 a bill that "attached a mandatory death sentence (by electrocution) to the crime of murder committed with such aggravating circumstances as rape, kidnapping, or armed robbery." After overriding the veto of then-Governor John C. West, the General Assembly put the law on the books.

The backslapping was short-lived, though, for in 1976 the U.S. Supreme Court struck down a similar mandatory provision in the law of other states and added that aggravating and mitigating circumstances had to be evaluated whenever a death sentence was considered. South Carolina modified its law once more and in 1977 the law that is presently in place, calling for a two-phase capital-case process — the first phase for guilt or innocence, the second for sentencing — was finally passed. The debate over the current version of the law wasn't without its share of exciting moments, though.

The Black Legislative Caucus had argued for years that the capital punishment law of South Carolina had in the history of the state been used to discriminate against black and poor individuals. With statistics in hand showing that 81 percent of the 241 persons executed between 1912 and 1962 were black, with most being laborers or farmers, the caucus launched a four-day filibuster in the House to make sure that if a new law was passed it would at least contain stringent safeguards to ensure due process for all citizens.

Then-Representative Jean Toal told *The Columbia Record* that the filibuster didn't prevent important debate from occurring. '"No one was under any illusions about what the issues were, she said, and adequate time was allowed for opinions to be expressed," the journalist wrote, quoting Toal.

Toal was further quoted as saying, "One thing the opponents did accomplish was to 'introduce a good many safeguards into the bill. Our statute has more protections than almost any other in the country. In fact, some think our process is too lengthy.'"

• ❖ •

Though Rusty Woomer had been on Death Row for nine years at that point, it's doubtful he thought the process was "too lengthy." He began to worry the following year when the electric chair was moved from its home at CCI to the new Capital Punishment Facility at the Broad River Correctional Institute. The newspapers were on the scent when hearing of the move which then prompted prison officials to say, "Nothing should be read into the chair's relocation. We're just following the work schedule; we have received no orders." It seemed highly likely, however, that the timing of the chair's move was more than coincidental.

Woomer completed the eighth step of his appeal process the previous September (1988) when the Fourth U.S. Circuit Court of Appeals in Richmond, Virginia, upheld his death sentence for Louise's murder. The appeal process consists of nine steps broken into three's: Following a conviction and a death sentence, a case is automatically appealed to the S. C. Supreme Court and then to the U.S. Supreme Court. A civil lawsuit can then be filed in the state circuit court, with subsequent appeals to the S.C. and U.S. Supreme Courts, and then suit is filed in U.S. District Court (in Columbia), with subsequent appeals to the Fourth U.S. Circuit Court of Appeals in Richmond, Virginia, and then the Supreme Court for a third time.

Mark Dillard, spokesperson for then-state Attorney General Travis Medlock, said, "Of the capital cases that have reached the U.S. Supreme Court a third time, only about five percent of them are accepted by the court. The idea is that the lower courts can take and apply the principles set forth by the Supreme Court. They are one court for the whole nation, and they usually take cases only if they feel some legal principle that they need to look at is involved."

One might assume, then, that following the circuit court denial in Richmond, and the denial for a new trial by the U.S. Supreme Court two weeks earlier, the only steps left for Woomer would be steps 10 through 13 – the S. C. Supreme Court verifies that all appeals are exhausted, the court notifies the commissioner at the Department of Corrections, the date is set, and the execution is carried out.

As it turned out, however, there was a lot more legal maneuvering on Woomer's behalf. In fact, by the time Woomer was executed in April of 1990, his case had been before the U.S. Supreme Court four times and before the S.C. Supreme Court eight times.

When Christmas rolled around in 1988 and Woomer asked for his lawyer's thoughts on whether he would still be alive the next Christmas, instead of hesitating, the attorney might just as well have said what Beth said to Woomer the night of the party at the Komo Mai. "Sure," Beth had said, shrugging her shoulders, when asked if she wanted to smoke some pot. "Why not?"

45

Every time Jimmy thought about Wanda's situation, he came to the same conclusion. She needed to get out of the house and find something to do that would lift her spirits. Wanda now sat for hours at a time in a chair by a window in the den, getting up only when she had to. The period of excitement following Jamie's birth had passed, and Wanda was left to confront the psychological reality of never looking completely normal again. Eckert and Cunningham had done a wonderful job reconstructing Wanda's damaged face and she looked remarkably improved. However, discontinuing the surgeries meant she no longer had any hope of looking into a mirror without remembering that cruel night. In addition, when leaving her home, she was unable to keep her struggle for recovery a completely private affair, free of the inquisitive stares of others.

Wanda's depression made it difficult for her to devote full attention to Jamie. Fortunately, Traci welcomed the opportunity to tend to her new brother and felt very much the little mother as she fed and dressed Jamie, once taking him to the mall to get his picture taken. Traci knew as she stood in line waiting for the photographer with the other mothers that she had found what she needed. The strength she felt when protecting and nurturing Jamie negated the helpless feelings she had experienced through her childhood as she watched from the sidelines while her mother slowly healed. Jamie became Traci's proof that she was needed in the family.

Wanda's primary need was to feel connected to the world in a way that allowed her to once again feel productive and useful. For Jimmy, that meant Wanda needed a job.

"Hey, McNeal," Jimmy said as he stepped through the door of the small veterinary clinic. A pleasant-looking man with glasses and brown hair spilling down his forehead stood behind the counter looking over the shoulder of a receptionist.

"Hello, Jimmy," Dr. McNeal replied. "What can I do for you?"

"I was wondering if I could ask you something," Jimmy said.

"Sure," McNeal said. "Ask."

Jimmy glanced at the receptionist and hesitated. McNeal noticed and said, "I tell you what. Why don't you come on back and we can talk while I clean up a mess I just made."

Anyone living near Pawley's Island in 1986 knew good springer spaniel or Boston terrier puppies could be obtained at Jimmy's and Wanda's. The Summers had initially gotten into the dog-breeding business a couple of years earlier for the extra income. There were usually a couple of litters growing in the large pen Jimmy constructed by their house and the purebred pups fetched a handsome price. An additional benefit, however, was that Wanda loved the animals, particularly the puppies, and she found that spending time taking care of the details of breeding was therapeutic. When Jimmy thought about Wanda getting a job, he thought about McNeal.

Dr. Dennis McNeal, known as McNeal, Mac or just Doc to the locals, was a long time resident of Pawley's Island and had treated all of Wanda's and Jimmy's dogs. McNeal had been friends with Wanda and Jimmy since before the accident and, like so many others around Pawley's Island, knew of Wanda's bubbling, effervescent personality before the crimes and felt protective of her.

"Mac," Jimmy said, faltering as he looked down, "I need to ask a favor." Though Jimmy was normally able to speak his mind without hesitation, he found it difficult to ask for help.

McNeal again saw Jimmy's discomfort. "Whatever I can do," the veterinarian said reassuringly.

"Wanda needs a job," Jimmy said. "She's been looking in the paper, but nothing seems to come up that she wants.

When she started looking she found some things she thought would be good and even applied for a few of 'em. She called up the places – one was a secretary job, you know, something she feels she can do and be good at — and everything seemed good when she spoke with them over the phone." Jimmy felt his anger begin to flare. "But then when she went in to interview, she was told the jobs had been filled. She could tell by the expressions of the people that wasn't true."

McNeal nodded his head, but remained quiet.

"I was thinking maybe Wanda could work here with you," Jimmy said. "You know she loves animals. She's good with 'em, too. But most important is that they love her in a way that people can't. People have hurt her so much. Those dogs of ours, though, they make her feel good about herself. Ever since her mom died . . . ." Jimmy wasn't sure how much to say and hesitated.

"Well," McNeal said quickly. "I guess that's something I wasn't expecting to hear this morning. Let's think about this a minute."

Jimmy recounted for McNeal the unexpected death of Wanda's mother a year after the birth of Jamie. Betty was a main source of emotional support for her daughter and the profound grief Wanda experienced by her mother's death was compounded by Reggie's death thirteen months later. The psychiatrist whom Wanda still saw on a regular basis thought it best that Wanda be hospitalized until she pulled through the crisis phase of the reaction to the losses. Following a stay of several weeks in the hospital, Wanda's depression had lifted somewhat but she still sat by the den window for hours on end, seemingly lost in her thoughts and simply staring.

"Man, Jimmy," McNeal said and sighed. "You know I'd like to help. The problem is I'm over-employed now. I've got two girls working who both want to be full time, and I don't have enough work for them. The second office I just opened in Garden City has got me financially strapped. Maybe if things pick up there."

"She could just help out somehow, McNeal," Jimmy suggested. "She's got to do something. She's just had such a damn tough time of it." Jimmy felt he was imposing on his friend and found it difficult to look into McNeal's eyes.

"I wish I could help," McNeal said. "I'm just not sure what I can do."

"If it's the money, don't worry about that. I'll pay her salary," Jimmy said.

"What?" McNeal asked, crossing his arms.

"I'll give you the money to pay her," Jimmy said again.

"No, that's not . . . I don't like that idea," McNeal said, shaking his head.

"Why wouldn't that work? I could give you the money and you could give it to her."

"What? Man, I don't know about that. You mean, without her knowing about it? Oh, no."

Jimmy looked at McNeal, aware of the implied deception, and shrugged. "Mac, I don't know what else to do."

The two men stood awkwardly, avoiding the other's gaze. McNeal broke the silence.

"Jimmy, I can't afford anybody else right now. Payroll is my biggest expense. Maybe I can soon. You know I'd help Wanda if I could."

"She's a good worker, McNeal," Jimmy said, raising his eyebrows. "You know you can use the help."

"I know, it's just . . . ." McNeal began to pace. "All right," he said a few moments later. "Look, one of the girls is going on vacation for a week, so Wanda could fill in. But I'll pay her something."

"No," Jimmy insisted. "What day do you write checks? Friday?"

McNeal nodded reluctantly.

"OK," Jimmy said. "On Friday morning, I'll bring you the money, cash, and maybe you can give Wanda a check. Would that work?"

McNeal took his glasses off and rubbed the bridge of his nose with his wrist. "Jimmy, I'm not sure about that."

"No, it has to be, McNeal. I can't ask you to pay Wanda. I just want her to have something she can do that'll make her feel better."

McNeal and Jimmy stood in silence as the seconds ticked by. McNeal finally said, "I'll split it with you, Jimmy.

She'll be providing a service for me so I can't let you pay her everything. I wish I could do more."

"McNeal, I don't want my coming here to cost you money. Let me – "

"No," McNeal said decisively, "And don't try to talk me into it. I can use the help, Jimmy, at least for a week. And then let's see."

Jimmy heard the agreement in McNeal's voice and began to think practically. "How can we do this?" he said, then looked in McNeal's eyes. "Can you call her? Make her think it's your idea?"

"Call her and ask her to work for me?" McNeal asked.

"Yeah."

"What do I tell her?"

"Tell her your girl's going on vacation and you need somebody."

McNeal smiled. "I guess I could."

Jimmy smiled back. "One suggestion? Whatever you do, don't let her know I talked to you about this."

"Aw, man," McNeal said. "Jimmy, are you sure about that?"

"I am definitely sure about that," Jimmy said, nodding vigorously. "She has to think she's doing this by herself. Otherwise, she'll think it's a handout and she's really gotten to hate that — people doing everything for her. Can you do that for me – for her – McNeal?"

McNeal shook his head and laughed. "You're a good man, Jimmy Summers."

"No, Mac," Jimmy said, sighing. "I'm a desperate man."

The following day, McNeal called Wanda and asked if she would come to work for him. He explained that one of his employees was going on vacation, and he needed someone to fill in. He wasn't sure beyond that, but with his new office he felt sure that he could use the additional help, at least on a part-time basis. Wanda replied that she didn't know anything about the vet business. McNeal assured her that he could give her initial instructions, and then she could learn additional duties as time passed.

Wanda was overjoyed and couldn't wait until that evening to tell Jimmy the good news. The following day she went to work at the veterinary clinic in Pawley's Island. As it happened, the employee on vacation called from Key West and asked for an additional week off. Wanda was glad to continue to fill in. After the second week, McNeal kept Wanda on, rotating her between the offices in Pawley's Island and Garden City as she learned the business. As agreed upon, each Friday morning Jimmy stopped by the clinic. He waited until Wanda went to the bathroom or stepped out of sight for a moment and then slipped McNeal a one-hundred dollar bill. McNeal reluctantly took the money. Both men felt guilty about the secrecy of their actions.

Several months later, when another employee quit, McNeal contacted Jimmy about changing the arrangement to add Wanda to the payroll. The business had grown as predicted, and he did need Wanda. Wanda had proved herself to be a quick learner and she fit in well with the customers, many of whom were most particular about the care their pets received. In addition, her cheerful attitude was contagious and it was clear to McNeal that Wanda had forged her own identity within the business. Thirteen years later, Wanda still works part-time for McNeal.

Jimmy was as relieved as McNeal when the deception was discontinued. Both men believed that Wanda was emotionally healthier and agreed that she should probably not be told of the original arrangement.

However, two years later, Jimmy let the secret slip. Wanda was particularly tired one day following work and complained that she didn't want to come home and clean up after animals, having done just that all day at the clinic. During the ensuing argument, Jimmy remarked that she wouldn't be cleaning up at the clinic if it weren't for him. Immediately realizing his error, Jimmy tried to redirect the exchange. Wanda zeroed in on the remark, however, and made Jimmy explain himself. When he admitted to his and McNeal's actions, Wanda drove immediately to McNeal's house and asked him if what Jimmy said was true. When McNeal admitted it was, Wanda unleashed her fury on him and then went home and continued her tirade with Jimmy. Both men worried that their deception would end up being more harmful than beneficial, as they had intended. Wanda returned to work a couple of days later, still upset, but reassured that the now pitiful-acting men had been motivated by love. She realized the job was very good for her self-esteem and later admitted, "It literally saved my life."

46

The end of May 1989 saw a flurry of activity related to Woomer's case, and it really appeared that the long wait for his death would soon be over. Following a request from Attorney General Travis Medlock, the Supreme Court notified Corrections Commissioner Parker Evatt that all of Woomer's appeals had been exhausted. That same day Evatt notified Woomer that he had until June 16 to get his final affairs in order. Interestingly, the review of Medlock's petition included only three of the five justices for the State Supreme Court. Justices David W. Harwell and Ernest A. Finney, Jr., excused themselves because both had been involved with Woomer's case as Circuit Court judges. Harwell presided over Woomer's 1979 trial and Finney was the judge at Woomer's resentencing in 1981.

Don Sellers had his characteristic way of responding to the execution date. "I think the son-of-a-bitch should have been dead ten years ago," he said. "It's been ten years and four months, and I just want to see him dead." Buddy Causey felt the same way. "If anyone deserves the death penalty," Causey said, reflecting on Woomer's pending execution, "he is the best candidate I know of."

In setting the execution date, the State Supreme Court turned down a 60-day delay request by Woomer's attorneys. John H. Blume of the nonprofit South Carolina Death Penalty Resource Center and Gaston Fairey, a private attorney from Columbia, wanted time to review the case and to draft a petition requesting that Governor Carroll Campbell commute Woomer's death sentence to life in prison. Blume said that Campbell could commute for a legal issue that hadn't been adequately addressed and even for mercy or some other reason unrelated to the legality of the conviction or sentence.

Medlock was incensed and quickly responded. "The defendant has had the opportunity for review of his case through nine different steps of the judicial process. It has been eight years since he was resentenced for his crimes. Throughout that time, the courts have consistently and repeatedly upheld his conviction and sentence."

Nonetheless, Blume and Fairey continued their fact-finding activities with a fervor that is apparently common preceding executions. "The actions taken are likely to be repeated several times during the coming week as Woomer's attorneys search for a way to save him from becoming the 244th person to die in the state's electric chair," wrote a reporter for *The State*. In a sworn affidavit, Fairey told the courts that the last minute efforts to save Woomer weren't because he and Blume had been saving some of their ammunition until the eleventh hour. Rather, he professed his own inexperience with death cases and admitted that he hadn't recognized the validity of some of the issues involved. When Blume, the more experienced lawyer in death cases, was brought on board, the activity on Woomer's behalf intensified.

Indeed, Woomer's last-minute "volley of appeals" included activity on three fronts.

Additional appeals for a stay of execution while new issues were being considered were submitted to the S.C. Supreme Court, and then, on denial, to the U.S. Supreme Court. The new issues were included in a lengthy post conviction relief (PCR) appeal filed in Horry County. The 650-page PCR package included an issue that came out of a ruling the week of the scheduled execution. On the Monday before the Thursday night/early Friday morning scheduled execution, the U.S. Supreme Court ruled that, "Juries deciding between life and death shouldn't have their passions swayed by praise for the victim. Such arguments may overshadow evidence." In anticipation of the ruling, which resulted in the high court granting Demetrius Gathers, a S.C. Death Row inmate, another sentencing trial, Blume and Fairey included the argument in the PCR. The 125-page motion stated that Jim Dunn had been guilty on numerous occasions of "overly impassioned comments" to juries and that he "played on the passions and sympathies of Woomer's sentencing jury by exalting the victims of the February 22, 1979, crime spree."

The "new" evidence available in the PCR included examinations determining that Woomer was hypoglycemic and suffered from brain damage, and that Woomer was under the influence of drugs when he and Skaar went on their crime spree. "For one day in 1979, 24-year-old Rusty Woomer acted completely uncharacteristically. Theretofore, he had been nonviolent. Any hope of explaining that one day rested upon proper evaluation and testing," the motion explained. "Prosecutors hid evidence about Woomer's drug abuse, causing psychiatric examiners to think he was just mean." A supporting affidavit by Cleveland Stevens made the claim that Stevens hadn't been made aware by the solicitor or police of any drug involvement in the case. Jim Dunn scoffed at that and suggested that Stevens reread the transcript of the trial and his own examination of Woomer's drug use on February 22. "We had an ironclad, open-and-shut case on Woomer," Dunn said. "There was no reason for us to hide any files."

An additional supportive affidavit included in the PCR was by John Fisher, who at that time was in prison in West Virginia under a mandatory, three-strikes life sentence for another crime besides his involvement with Woomer's crimes. Fisher claimed that he knew of extensive drug use by Woomer and Skaar during the days just prior to February 22. The statement further claimed that Skaar was a pervert who enjoyed hurting women, and that Woomer was Skaar's pawn on the day in question and surely acted under his domination.

An additional issue uncovered in the review of the case that would prove to be a sticky point arose from Woomer's resentencing trial in 1981. The appeal to the U.S. Supreme Court claimed that then-Circuit Judge Ernest Finney led the sentencing jury to think that sympathy for Woomer could not be considered in their deliberations; their decision had to be for death unless the evidence didn't support it. The so-called "no sympathy instructions" were being contested as a violation of the Eight Amendment barring "cruel and unusual punishment." The high court had agreed a month earlier to hear Saffle vs. Parks, an Oklahoma death penalty case that raised the same issue. Fairey said he was optimistic that the Oklahoma decision would have a bearing on Woomer's case.

Meanwhile, the days slipped by and Woomer got closer to his appointed hour. On Tuesday, just as preparations were being made to move Woomer from his cell on Death Row to a cell at the Capital Punishment Facility, Governor Campbell rejected his bid for clemency with a one-sentence statement: "The Governor will not intervene in the workings of the judicial process in the case of Ronald 'Rusty' Woomer." Woomer expressed disappointment but was buoyed by Fairey and Bloom to remain confident and continue praying. Though only five percent of cases are set aside by the high court and most of those then result in an eventual death sentence, he was told that last-minute reprieves are sometimes granted. In 1985, Joseph Carl Shaw, the first person to be executed in South Carolina under the new death penalty statute of 1977, received a stay 18 hours prior to his scheduled electrocution. In 1945, Timothy Parler had already been strapped in the chair when he received word of his stay. Though his sentence was subsequently commuted to life in prison, Parler reportedly never stopped trembling and spent the rest of his days at CCI known as "Shaking Timothy."

Just as soon as Woomer got settled into his cell at the new death house, Corrections Commissioner Parker Evatt stopped by for a visit. "If I'm going to kill somebody, I've got to know who I'm killing," Evatt said. As the top prison official in the state, Evatt was responsible for all of the preparations for an execution, and Woomer's was the first to occur since Evatt took office. "I couldn't do this if I didn't meet him first," he added.

Evatt admitted that the responsibilities of his job posed for him a personal dilemma. His religious beliefs and his involvement for 40 years with his church in Columbia had shaped his view that capital punishment was wrong. He knew when he took the post as commissioner, however, what the job included. "I have to uphold the laws of this state,"

Evatt said, "and I will."

Another state official for whom the execution was reportedly difficult was Governor Campbell's Deputy Chief of Staff Robert McAlister. McAlister had met and become friends with Woomer and Cleveland Stevens through a Death Row ministry that included Bible reading and praying with the condemned. The Governor's press aide, Tucker Eskew, said Campbell knew of McAlister's religious beliefs when he appointed him to the top staff position and that there hadn't been any resulting problems. McAlister kept his ministry activities private and had removed himself from any discussions surrounding Woomer's request for clemency. Eskew added that McAlister's view of the death penalty put McAlister in a distinct minority among senior staffers in Campbell's administration.

The religious beliefs of Evatt and McAlister received newspaper coverage as part of the bigger battle being waged between supporters and opponents of capital punishment in South Carolina. As the scheduled execution neared, a news conference was planned at the State House so that religious leaders from across the state could voice their opposition directly to Campbell and urge his reconsideration of the issue. In addition, plans for a candlelight vigil the evening of the execution were announced. Members of the S.C. Coalition against the Death Penalty planned to meet at a downtown Columbia church to offer prayers for the lawmakers who wrote the death statute and the Supreme Court justices responsible for imposing it. The marchers then planned to go to the Governor's mansion where a vigil would be held until the execution. "It is not too late to commute Rusty's sentence to life without parole," the head of the coalition said. "Where there is life, there is hope."

Jim Dunn anticipated the broad coverage and announced plans for a memorial service at the Horry County Courthouse honoring the victims of Woomer's and Skaar's day of carnage. Referring to large pictures of the murder victims he had made for display at the service, Dunn said in his press conference, "Here are four people who received capital punishment on the same day. I want the emphasis to be on the people who were murdered. I think that too often the attention and sympathy go to the murderer and the victims are forgotten."

Close to three dozen articles appeared in newspapers across the state in the week leading up to the June 16 execution date. Seven of the only ten articles that mentioned the victims of Woomer's crimes did so in the context of the memorial Dunn planned. Dunn also correctly predicted that visual images would play a big part in the coverage of the media event and prepared for the memorial by having a large tombstone constructed that identified the victims by name in large bold letters. The striking reminder appeared in pictures alongside several of the newspaper articles and was featured several times on television.

Preparations for Woomer's death moved forward. The Friday morning execution was to be the first in the new Capital Punishment Facility. The only other two executions since the 1977 death law came into effect had taken place in an old building called the Death House at CCI. When Woomer was placed on execution status early Tuesday morning, after having his identity determined from fingerprints and his belongings inventoried and placed in storage, the newly painted walls of the Capital Punishment Facility still had a fresh smell and look. As the first occupant, Woomer would take his dead man's walk under bright lights past empty cells. He did get the movie version of a last walk as he left CCI Monday night. Prior to the walk down the worn corridor of the CCI Death House, Woomer was allowed to exchange goodbyes with the other cons, and shook the hand of Pee Wee Gaskins, who took his own last walk in 1991. Woomer wrote a letter to be distributed to his prison friends after his death in which he promised to do reconnaissance work to find fishing holes in heaven. He also encouraged doubters to accept Jesus as their personal savior as he had done.

During the three days prior to the scheduled execution, details of funeral arrangements and witnesses for the execution were taken care of while prison officials ran through daily training drills, testing equipment just around the corner from where Woomer occupied a cell under constant vigil through a glass partition. With the opportunity to order his first nonprison food in over ten years, Woomer chose a pizza without anchovies for his last meal.

Woomer was allowed visitation by lawyers, family and friends and had around-the-clock access to the prison chaplain. Woomer's visitors included his father, a brother, two sisters and a brother-in-law. Rusty's mother had died two years earlier. At the advice of Fairey, Woomer declined interviews with reporters, though he knew a couple would be present at the execution. Woomer also knew his friend, Bob McAlister, would be there, as would Don Sellers, who reportedly couldn't wait to watch Woomer die.

The Sun News ran an Associated Press article that highlighted the religious views of a brother of Louise Sellers. "I don't want it to end this way," the brother said. "I wanted the killing to stop in 1979." Based on a personal conversion he experienced, the man felt strongly about the sincerity of Woomer's Christian beliefs and withstood strong family opposition to his speaking favorably of Woomer. "To me," the brother said, "he is not the same guy who killed my sister." Following a visit to Death Row to meet with Woomer, the man said, "God can change a person and I believe he has changed."

Don Sellers let it be known that he wasn't interested in whether Woomer had changed his life or not. "I don't have anything to say to him," Sellers said disgustedly. The only time he wanted to see Woomer was when he got to watch through the glass partition as prison officials strapped Woomer into the chair. "I'm just ready for it to be over."

47

Wanda had decided to treat the days preceding the execution as any other and go to work. She did attend the memorial service on Wednesday as part of the crowd but, otherwise, she recognized that her normal routine helped her keep her mind off the fact that another human being was about to die. The long wait, though, had taken its toll on her struggle to regain her emotional health.

Both Wanda and Traci had experienced conflict over their involvement in Woomer's upcoming execution. Had Wanda somehow contributed to his impending death through her testimony? Had Traci, through her hate for Woomer and her wishes that he was dead, become a part of a loathsome anomie that she was still too young to fully grasp?

"That man hurt my momma and almost took her away from me," Traci said. "I still hate him for that."

After all of the years, neither Wanda nor Traci could say the name "Woomer" aloud.

Jim Dunn's work as solicitor placed him squarely on the dark road where evil had cracked sharply in the night and then sped away without a second thought for the life that spilled into the tire ruts. Dunn had felt many times as if he were there that night, leaning forward, hands on his knees, whispering, "Get up, get up, you can do it." Wanda had gotten up, her reason to live too strong to be extinguished.

Dunn knew, however, that Wanda's struggle as a survivor wasn't without continuing problems. Recurring nightmares and the self-blame that accompanied being victimized still threatened to overwhelm her. "I can't get over that Louise saw me get shot and knew she was next. I had told her to cooperate and that everything would be all right."

Dunn knew that the saying, "Anything that doesn't kill you makes you stronger," was sometimes a lie. "Anything that doesn't kill you," sometimes left you beside the road, wounded and maimed, partially destroyed, a remnant of what you once were and might have been. Dunn knew that, "Anything that doesn't kill you," could be the cruelest fate of all. He was determined that wasn't going to happen to Wanda and the families that Woomer had left beside the road.

Close to 200 persons attended the Murder Victims' Memorial Service at the Horry County Courthouse, where Woomer had received his death sentence. Standing behind a granite tombstone on the porch of the courthouse, Dunn eulogized the deceased by holding up their pictures and telling what each had done the day before their lives ended so tragically. Just underneath the tombstone bearing the victims' names was a wall where the large pictures of Woomer's victims were placed, side by side. In a blank space in the middle of the wall, instead of a picture, were the words, "A beautiful five-year-old girl." Large bouquets of yellow and white flowers surrounded the display.

Dunn had tried to never use the familiar name, "Rusty," when referring to Woomer and on that day didn't mention Woomer's name at all. "How Great Thou Art" rang from an acoustic guitar as audience members, some crying and holding hands, stood with their heads bowed.

"There is a mountain of tragedy here today," Dunn said solemnly, "But from the top of that mountain, let sympathy roll down." Gesturing to the pictures, he added, "Let it roll down for the families and friends of these people. They were decent human beings. If compassion is with us, then let it roll down and caress these people."

Following the hymn and the final prayer of the service, friends wiped moist eyes and hugged and lingered to talk softly to each other. Reporters moved through the crowd.

"I want everybody to remember the victims, the people who suffered," Wanda said to Chrysti Edge of *The Sun News*. "I'm a survivor, not a victim," she added. "I'm glad Jim has done this because I don't think the victims should be forgotten." Though Dunn made reference to Wanda as she stood in the crowd, Dunn didn't use her name or single her out to those who might not have known about her part in the tragedy.

Don Sellers was in attendance and expressed his appreciation for the service. "I'm glad to see it," he said. "It's been real long for the victims."

Don's stepdaughter, Jenny Chisholm, also expressed relief that their wait was about to come to an end. "It will soon be over," she said with a sigh of relief, "and all of us can stop our nightmares."

48

Wanda remembers she was at work washing a poodle when the call came. When she picked up the phone and a voice identified the caller as a representative from the Attorney General's office, her heart dropped. "Wanda, I'm sorry to tell you this," Mary Ann Morris said, "but the United States Supreme Court has granted Rusty Woomer a stay. He won't be executed tonight as planned."

After listening quietly to the explanation of why the stay had been granted, Wanda politely thanked Morris, hung up the phone and collapsed.

"I felt like I'd been struck by a Mack truck," Wanda later said. "I was stunned."

The high court had granted the stay just 13 hours before Woomer was to have been electrocuted. Morris told Wanda that the reprieve was in effect until at least October, the first chance that the court would have to address Woomer's petition asking for consideration of his appeal. Also in October, Morris said, the justices would hear the Oklahoma case of Saffle vs. Parks and deliberate the "no sympathy instructions" issue that Woomer's attorneys raised as an appeal point. If the court denied the point in the Oklahoma case, Woomer's petition to have his appeal evaluated would most likely be denied.

"Speaking of sympathy," Jim Dunn said angrily when he heard the disappointing news, "here we go again. The families and friends of the victims will have to go through one more legal maneuver and relive this tragedy one more time. Carrying out the death penalty in this case has thus far inflicted much more punishment on the victims' families than it has on Woomer."

Following up on a statement made earlier in the week, when he said he would retire as solicitor if Woomer got out of his date with the chair, Dunn said, "I've had several calls from people such as Wanda Summers and Don Sellers. I've got a commitment to them and to Mrs. Turner, and I'm going to stick with it. I will continue to pursue this case and leave no stone unturned until we run out of stones."

Attorney General Travis Medlock spoke to the press, expressing sorrow for the victims and their families, and noted that the delay did not speak well for the criminal justice system in the state. The case had been reviewed by the S.C. Supreme Court eight times, and the stay would place the case before the U.S. Supreme Court for a fourth time.

Not everyone was unhappy. "We're just absolutely ecstatic," said the director of the S.C. Coalition to Abolish the Death Penalty. "It is impossible to show respect for human life by killing human beings." Expressing grief for the murder victims and their families, the director further said, "Rusty's death would only ravage another family with anguish."

The stay was announced just as religious leaders from across the state were scheduled to hold a news conference on the Statehouse steps to protest the execution. The announcement allowed a shift of focus, and the protest and the prayer service scheduled for later that day became a "celebration of life" instead of the expected candlelight vigil at the Governor's mansion.

Late Thursday morning, on their way in to tell Woomer about the stay of execution, Fairey and Blume quickly gathered together Woomer's available friends and family members for an impromptu celebration. When Woomer heard the news, the relief was overwhelming and he began to cry. A former prison counselor who had traveled from Virginia to visit with Woomer in his "final" hour was there. "I sort of think he was in shock," she said. "He was crying and thanking God for us."

Corrections Commissioner Evatt spoke to a reporter of his two-hour visit with Woomer the day before, when the execution was still scheduled. "He had peace in his heart," Evatt said. "I think he was ready to go and, of course, now

I'm sure he's ready to live a little while longer."

Woomer reportedly had developed his faith to the point where he was able to minister to others on Death Row. Woomer said he thought the stay would demonstrate the strength of his faith to the other convicts.

In Woomer's letter to Governor Campbell submitted as part of his appeal, he spoke freely of his faith and how it changed his life. He was no longer the person who took the drugs that led him to follow Skaar's orders and do the things he had done, he said. He finally had something that he had never had – a reason to live. "Even on Death Row I have so much more to live for than ever in my entire life," Woomer wrote. "For the first time in my life I have friends that truly care for me and that I truly love."

Corrections officials, pleased with the turn of events, stopped all preparations being made for the execution. The order for the hearse to carry Woomer's body from the prison was canceled. Just several hours after he had been scheduled to die, Woomer was moved back to his old cell on Death Row.

Back at CCI, Woomer was permitted to join other inmates in the chapel for a service that was already in progress. When Woomer entered, he reportedly stood at the back and sobbed as the chorus of male voices launched into a favorite hymn. "Amazing grace, how sweet the sound, that saved a wretch like me . . . ."

49

After making a statement to the press concerning the stay, Dunn spent the afternoon on the telephone trying to explain to the families of Woomer's victims the complicated legal issues and provide assurances that his efforts would continue to be directed toward the case. No one doubted his loyalties, but emotions ran high and Dunn understood the need for the families involved to vent their frustrations. The headline in *The Sun News* the next day said it all: "Woomer Stay Stirs Cascade of Victim Rage."

"We were patient and quiet for ten years," said Jenny Chisholm, one of Louise's daughters. "We had confidence in the judicial system, and it has let us down. Now it's time for us to fight with them." It appeared that the collective sigh of relief that she and many others experienced 24 hours earlier at the victims' memorial service was premature.

"It's just a damn disgrace," Michael Carter said. Since the crime spree Carter had left SLED and become sheriff of Georgetown County. "It's just ridiculous that our system is so easily manipulated for an individual who's had well over his due consideration."

Wanda had also been confident that the execution would allow her to shift a gear. "I thought surely this was the end," she said angrily, "but it would appear not. I don't understand why we have trials by jury if [cases are] going to get hung up for 10 years in the courts. I don't know how much the victims' families are supposed to go through."

Wanda had avoided the press as much as possible and had given relatively few interviews over the years. Most of her time had been spent recovering with her family. The unexpected stay had suddenly left her in the lurch. She was again struggling, but this time for answers.

"I had always wondered why God let me survive that night," she said. "I knew there had to be a reason. I know, now, that I'm not going to be quiet any longer. I will spend the rest of my life fighting for victims' rights. I just want people to know how unfair this is. We're human beings, too."

Wanda wanted desperately to once and for all put the memories of Woomer behind her. Testifying at the trial and then again at the resentencing had been excruciating. As long as an appeal for Woomer was outstanding, Wanda had no assurance that she wouldn't be forced back into court to again provide her testimony against Woomer, to listen again to the sordid details while Woomer sat several feet away smugly holding his Bible. The thought that the U.S. Supreme Court might grant Woomer another resentencing trial, ten years after his crimes was infuriating.

The day after the stay was announced, while the press began to dig into the details of the PCR and publish background stories for the resurrected case, Wanda sat down to put her thoughts onto paper. "Dear Mr. President," she began the letter to President George Bush. "I realize that I am only one very small and insignificant part of our great nation and it may be presumptuous of me to be writing you, but you are my last hope . . . ."

When she finished, satisfied with her effort, Wanda mailed the letter and felt better. She had spoken out and expressed what had been brewing inside of her for a long time; she knew that taking action was an important step in her recovery as a survivor. What she didn't know was that her action would cause such a stir.

Wanda wrote additional letters to other leaders and politicians and, within a couple of weeks, replies started to arrive. A U.S. Department of Justice official responded for President Bush with a three-page personal letter acknowledging the tragedy and outlining actions taken by the President's Task Force on Victims of Crime. Included with the letter were copies of the published final report of the task force for 1982 and a four-year update indicating what federal, state, and local changes had followed the report. In addition, the letter indicated how Wanda might contact organizations in South Carolina for information concerning victims' assistance and compensation. Enclosures indicating the letter had been forwarded to appropriate persons at the state level allowed Wanda to follow up and pursue a course of action.

Governor Campbell passed his letter on to the Executive Assistant for Research and Special Projects for S.C. who also acknowledged the tragedy but explained that the Governor could not intervene in decisions of the Supreme Court.

Congressman Robin Tallon personally responded and acknowledged his inability to provide much in the way of assistance. He did, however, forward the letter to Travis Medlock and to the Clerk of the U.S. Supreme Court. Wanda heard from the Congressman once more in a follow-up that included a letter he had received back from the clerk. In addition, Medlock, with whom Wanda was now acquainted, acknowledged the contact.

The replies were all beginning to sound the same, but Wanda kept up her hope that something positive would happen.

Following the stay of execution, Jenny Chisholm had begun her own letter writing campaign on behalf of Louise, her mother. "I just cried and cried," Jenny said, recalling how she felt on June 15 when she heard about the stay. "There was nothing else to do."

Jenny's attitude of resignation quickly changed to anger, however, and within a few days she and her sisters, Dorothy Brock and Tina White, and her brother, Ray Hewitt, had begun circulating petitions to take to the U.S. Supreme Court when it reconvened in October. The petitions, which would eventually garner thousands of names, began reaching out across South Carolina.

"I was glad to think that it was finally going to be over," Jenny said. "It's been 10 years, but it's still not over yet for us. We want the public to know just how stinking this system is."

Jenny and her family quickly connected with Sherie Carney, the Director of the South Carolina Victim Assistance Network. Formed in 1984 following the passage of the Victim's and Witness's Bill of Rights Act, the nonprofit organization provided support for victims by providing interagency communication for state victim-witness programs, monitoring legislation affecting victims of crime, and providing referral and public education services. Carney assisted the family by writing letters to television talk show hosts Oprah and Geraldo Rivera in hopes of getting national attention for the story.

Meanwhile, on August 3, Wanda received a personal note from Strom Thurmond with a copy of a speech that the U.S. Senator had delivered that day on the floor of the U. S. Senate. "The purpose of the statement," Thurmond wrote of the speech in the letter to Wanda, "was to illustrate the critical need for reform of habeas corpus law which allows endless appeals, especially in death penalty cases. The numerous years of delay surrounding the execution of Ronald Woomer as punishment for the heinous acts he perpetrated against you and other victims serves as a prime example of the obstruction of justice surrounding habeas corpus cases." (Habeas corpus law is the federal term for what in South Carolina is called the post-conviction relief procedure.)

There, Wanda thought. *Something has really happened.* Wanda felt proud of her actions as she thought of the legendary orator, with his thick drawl, delivering an impassioned speech before a packed Senate.

Several days later, Wanda received a call from a staff person in Senator Thurmond's office. The Senator, it was explained, was a member of a Senate Judiciary Committee that was convening in Washington in September for a hearing on the death penalty. Senator Thurmond hoped Wanda would accompany him to Washington to appear before the committee. Since the Woomer case illustrated the suffering that delays cause victims and their families, her presence would emphasize the point more dramatically than a thousand speeches.

It suddenly appeared to Wanda that the moment of truth had arrived. *Uh-oh*, she thought. *What have I gotten myself into?*

She sat down to discuss the opportunity with Jimmy. On the positive side, the trip was scheduled to last only a couple of days, and it offered Wanda the possibility of telling her story to decision-makers, people who made things happen. Wanda felt a real need to try to be part of the solution. She also felt good about her interactions with members of Louise's family. Though she didn't have a deep history with any of them other than Don, they had established a bond; her presence in Washington would serve their memories of Louise as well as her own.

On the other hand, going with the Senator required that Wanda speak in public. Who knew what that meant? Would there be reporters? Would there be television cameras? Senator Thurmond was a very important person, third in line for the Presidency. She had not actually met the man himself. What hidden agendas might he or other members of the committee have? Would she be used for someone else's purpose? Wanda wasn't so naïve as to imagine that the show was about her. Just what did the big dogs do when they gathered to eat? She had seen many times how her situation had drawn to her people with a hungry look.

Wanda made a decision that was cinched when a representative for the victim assistance network volunteered to go with her to Washington. Wanda knew the woman and thought she possessed a level of sophistication, a worldliness that would smooth out some of the wrinkles and would help her blend. There now remained only one problem. Going with Senator Thurmond meant that Wanda had to take her first flight in an airplane.

Jimmy and Wanda shared their first experience of walking into an airport with the television viewing audience of WECT in Wilmington, N.C. Wanda's companion was already there and within minutes she and Wanda boarded the plane. Following a quick flight to Charlotte, where Senator Thurmond boarded, the plane lifted off again for a hop to Washington National Airport. Wanda watched from the window as the plane passed over the Potomac River.

Wanda was amused as Senator Thurmond got off of the plane carrying a diaper bag, another bag, and holding a briefcase under his arm. Ever the gentleman, Thurmond made sure before taking care of persons he knew were going with him that a woman he had been seated beside in the rear of the plane made her connection. Within a few short minutes, and after telling the limo driver to ignore red lights and stop signs, Thurmond whisked Wanda through the streets of Washington and to her hotel. Thurmond disappeared for the evening, leaving Wanda to see the sights with a first-class tour guide.

The following morning Wanda realized during the cab ride to the Dirkson building where the hearing was to be held, that she was terrified. The tour of the city the evening before had been a pleasant distraction, but the moment of her testimony rapidly approached. Sure enough, her fears heightened when she stepped into the hearing room and saw the Judiciary Committee panel seated on a raised platform in an angular arc surrounding the seat where she would speak following the lunch break. An important-looking man she was told was a "representative from the administration" was answering questions posed by various committee members. Other well-dressed, impressive-looking people sitting throughout the gallery watched calmly. Some, who wrote on pads, she assumed were reporters. Large mounted cameras, overhead spotlights and persons with hand-held cameras sitting on the floor before the senators addressed her question concerning whether her testimony would be witnessed by persons other than the committee. It looked to Wanda as if the whole world might watch her speak.

Some of the faces of the senators were recognizable to Wanda – Edward Kennedy and, of course, Strom Thurmond; she thought Joseph Biden, who was chair of the committee, looked familiar and very pleasant, comfortable somehow. Some of the senators were not familiar – Orrin Hatch, Howard Metzenbaum, Patrick Leahy, Paul Simon and Arlen Specter, though Wanda had heard of a few of them.

As Wanda took a seat off to the side to watch, she wondered if people looking in her direction knew why she was there. She remembers the rest of the morning as a blur of sensory impressions. When the noon break finally came, actually less than an hour later, Wanda stepped out into the hall and took several deep breaths. While her heart pounded in her chest, she asked herself again, *What have I gotten into?*

At lunch in the Senate Dining Room, Wanda sat with James C. Anders, a solicitor from Columbia, S.C., and one of

Thurmond's senior staff persons, who explained the schedule for the rest of the day. Anders was first up to address the committee immediately after lunch, then Wanda, and then two law enforcement officials to round out the pro-death penalty presentations. A question and answer period would follow. Not to worry, Wanda was assured. The audience was friendly. None of the questioning was designed to evaluate her or test the validity of her views.

Interestingly, at lunch as Wanda pushed her loosely-held spoon around in the bowl of "Senate-bean soup" sitting on the cloth mat, she overheard someone at the next table say that the hurricane coming up the coast – Hurricane Hugo – was going to hit South Carolina, perhaps in a place called Pawley's Island. At its current rate of speed and direction, it was expected to make landfall late the following night. Wanda had known a storm was brewing but had been preoccupied with the impending trip. She hadn't paid attention to news reports. Wanda suddenly experienced the surreal feeling she had on other occasions. Here she was in Washington, D.C., sitting with a bowl of bean soup across from senators and God-knows-who-else, preparing to testify before the world about her life, while a hurricane bore down on her home and family far away. She felt very alone.

After somehow making it back to the hearing room, Wanda took her assigned place at the front table. She placed her typed notes in front of her and decided to try and keep her shaking hands in her lap. *Should I read or try to talk through my notes?* she thought. The anticipation of her turn grew as Anders spoke and the minutes ticked by. Wanda's stomach churned. She steadied her hands on her legs and thought of when she would have to turn the page of her notes. *Maybe I should spread them out now.* Then the tone of Anders' voice abruptly changed and everyone seemed to turn in Wanda's direction. A hush fell over the room. Wanda felt light-headed as she leaned forward to the microphone and began talking.

"Hello, my name is Wanda Summers. First, I would like to thank all of you for having me here today." *So far, so good,* she thought, though she felt her voice quavering.

"I am certainly no expert on the death penalty so what I

would like to do is simply tell you about my own experience over the past ten years with a death penalty case and the impact it has had on my life."

The Senators watched in rapt attention as Wanda spoke deliberately of Woomer and Skaar and their killing spree through South Carolina. She told how she and Louise had begged for their lives and how Louise had died. She described how she had been shot in the face with a sawed-off shotgun. "Since that time," Wanda said, her voice smoothing and becoming stronger, "I have had many reconstructive procedures. What you see today is a major improvement over what I saw in the hospital." Pausing briefly, she glanced up and then cast her eyes back down.

Reporters wrote furiously as Wanda spoke of testifying and then waiting during the second phase of the trial for the sentence to be handed down. "Finally, the jury went out to deliberate," she said. "I wasn't even sure I knew what my feelings about the death penalty were at that point. I did know that in South Carolina, life without parole is not an·option and the possibility of parole was unacceptable to me. So, I prayed. I am a Christian and believe strongly in the will of God. In my prayer I told God that whatever the jury's decision was I would accept as His will. Shortly afterward, as we sat in the courtroom, we heard hymns being sung in the jury room. I suddenly felt at peace. Evidently, the jurors were asking for God's guidance, as well.

"Ronald Woomer was sentenced to death. Now, ten years later, he is still alive."

Wanda continued speaking, using one of her hands to emphasize her message. She described the interminable appeals process and how she was reminded, as the execution neared, of February 22, 1979. "Every time we picked up a newspaper, every time the telephone rang and another reporter asked, 'How do you feel?' we were forced to relive that night yet again.

"But it was all right," she said calmly. "It was finally going to be over." Leaning in to the microphone, she said, "Then 13 hours before the execution was to take place, WHAM! The United States Supreme Court granted a stay of execution."

Wanda told the senators that she had been victimized once by Woomer and then many times as a casualty of the judicial system. "The families of crime victims do not deserve to be treated so cruelly," she said.

"Ronald Woomer inflicted pain and suffering on many, many people." Wanda's voice cracked for the first time. She continued, the anguish apparent in each sentence. "He brutally took the lives of four innocent people. These people had families and friends who loved them. I know how my family has suffered and I am still alive: My parents, who have since passed away without ever seeing justice; my two brothers; my husband, who has been very strong and supportive; my daughter, now sixteen, who lives every day of her life with the memory of seeing her mommy taken away, who now doesn't want to grow up because she doesn't like this adult world we live in; my little four-year-old son, who asks, 'Mommy, what happened to your face?'" Wanda used the balled-up tissue in her lap to wipe her eyes.

"Do you know how you would feel if this had happened to your mother or wife or sister or daughter?"

Wanda quickly examined the panel of men, one-by-one. Senator Biden leaned forward in his chair, his eyes never wavering as Wanda looked back. Senator Kennedy's eyes were cast down at something in front of him. Senator Thurmond's eyes misted as he slowly nodded encouragement.

"And what impact has all of this had on my life? Well, the obvious, of course." Wanda's eyes reflexively looked down. Her face flushed.

"The disfigurement," she said meekly. "It's very hard to get up each morning and look at this face in the mirror. It's hard when children stare and adults try not to. It's hard to talk to somebody when they avoid looking you in the eye. I never smile and it's hard to laugh because I know it would look grotesque." The corners of her mouth turned up slightly in a well-practiced, embarrassed smile. Her lips were held tightly together. Wanda looked at her notes and continued.

"And emotionally, it has been an uphill battle. There was a time when I was almost an emotional cripple, afraid to leave my house. However, time and a good psychiatrist have helped a lot."

Wanda cleared her throat while blinking rapidly. "But, these are my own demons," she said matter-of-factly, "ones I have to conquer."

She looked up, her eyes meeting Senator Biden's soft gaze. "The problem with the death penalty, as I see it, is in the lengthy appeals process. I do believe in the death penalty, very strongly, but you have to use it in order for it to work. We can't have cold-blooded killers like Ronald Woomer living in our society if this is going to be a safe and secure country in which to live and raise our children." Wanda paused. As she slowly closed the folder on her notes, she realized her hands were no longer shaking.

"Thank you all very much for your time and attention. I appreciate having this opportunity to tell you how I feel."

Several seconds elapsed. Silence echoed off the ceiling.

Biden spoke first and broke the tension. "Ms. Summers, you bring to the table an incredible amount of character – an incredible amount of character," he said admiringly. "You've been through an awful lot," he paused, and then added awkwardly, shaking his head as if in disbelief, "and you're here, presenting your testimony and have comported yourself as well as anyone who has ever sat here."

Persons in the crowd shifted self-consciously in their seats. Previously suppressed coughs sounded sharply amid sighs as relief spread through the crowd.

Wanda and the other speakers answered several questions. Senator Biden, Wanda remembered, was very interested in what victim's assistance services had been available for her in South Carolina, and seemed genuinely concerned over her response that she had not received any compensation.

Biden sought Wanda after the panel broke for the afternoon and congratulated her for her courage to appear and to speak before the committee. When the powerful chair of the Senate Judiciary Committee told Wanda that he had been deeply moved and would take her remarks to heart, Wanda felt her effort was a success. She was more confident that something good had come from the trip when she later learned that the senator was not a supporter of capital punishment.

Wanda returned to South Carolina that evening in time to prepare for a mandatory evacuation the following morning for Hurricane Hugo. Though the eye of the storm made landfall south of Pawley's Island, actually hitting McClellanville, the counter-clockwise pattern of the swirling winds of the class-five storm subjected areas just north of the eye to the worst damage. Despite the widespread damage to the entire coastal area north and south of Pawley's Island, Jimmy and Wanda lost only a few trees to Hugo.

50

Buoyed by her success in Washington, Wanda continued her work for victim's rights throughout the fall of 1989.

When Woomer was first prosecuted in 1979 the concept of victim's rights was vague and unknown to the average citizen in South Carolina. In their attempts to navigate the legal system, victims quickly discovered there were no services specifically designed to help them through their ordeal. There was no timely notification of hearings or court dates; victims were often informed at the last minute that they were required to be present in court, sometimes far from home. There were no liaisons within solicitors' offices familiar with personal details of each case; victims often found themselves unprepared emotionally to be face-to-face with a perpetrator. Well-meaning but busy lawyers were known to rush into court, with files of unfamiliar cases in hand, and address victims in a crowd by loudly asking, for example, "Are you the rape victim?"

In addition, victims found that in many instances they were intentionally excluded from the justice system. Many persons working within solicitor's and defender's offices paid lip service to the concept but saw victim's rights as potentially slowing an overwhelmed system. With crime on the rise and court dockets already backed up, who had time to notify victims and adjust dates and times of hearings and trials around the schedules of victims? Victims were seen as witnesses, at best, and sometimes only as bystanders. The idea of constitutionally guaranteed rights for victims was unknown.

The first Victim's Bill of Rights in South Carolina was passed and enacted in 1984. Lacking state funding to assist jurisdictions, however, the bill had no comprehensive enforcement powers and individual circuits within the state were allowed to consider budgets and staffing when determining the nature and scope of services to offer. Horry County, largely because of Jim Dunn's personal interest in victim's rights, had more services than many circuits. Nonetheless, prior to 1989 and the establishment of the first Victim-Witness Assistance Program under the direction of Ralph Wilson, the Fifteenth Circuit offered only limited notification of court dates and some assistance for victims with respect to completing impact statements and compensation applications.

Ralph Wilson served under Dunn as an assistant solicitor and was then personally selected by Dunn as his successor. When Dunn eventually left office in 1991, after three terms, Wilson became the first African-American solicitor in South Carolina. Like Dunn, Wilson felt a special bond with average, hard-working people. Having grown up in modest surroundings with eight brothers and sisters, Wilson knew the value of a strong support system and brought his understanding of extended family relations to the solicitor's office. In Wilson's tenure, the Victim-Witness Assistance Program became "more than just a good idea," Patty Fine, the director of the program said. Several years would pass before an amendment to the South Carolina Constitution in 1996/1997 would outline the responsibilities of state agencies to victims and witnesses. But in his day, Wilson, building on the foundation laid by Jim Dunn, was recognized as a strong advocate of victim's rights and, as Dunn had before him, Wilson stood on the courthouse steps proclaiming the need to recognize the rights of victims as a moral responsibility of the state legislature.

Other forces were at work in 1989 to support the efforts of crime victims and their families and friends. Following the announcement of Woomer's stay of execution, a frustrated letter-writer complained to *The State* that the newspaper had dramatized the process of electrocution without a corresponding gory description of the original crimes for which Woomer was to be executed. "But why such detail in the defense of Woomer?" wrote the concerned citizen. "I quote from page 8A under the subtitle 'Schedule . . . his body will snap and pull against the leather restraints binding his arms, legs, chest, and lap. His flesh and internal organs will burn, his eyes could pop out of their sockets underneath the hood. He may defecate, urinate or vomit.' I don't recall the victims being written up in such detail," the writer protested. "My point is that nowhere in the article does it mention the utterly atrocious rape and killing that 'Rusty' Woomer took part in. Basically, it is just another case of us worrying about the convict's rights and forgetting that there ever was a victim. Or was it four?"

In December of 1989, Wanda, Traci, and Jenny flew to New York for a taping of a segment on the national show "Geraldo" featuring talk show host Geraldo Rivera. The well-done piece entitled "Waiting for Justice" featured a panel of persons frustrated by having to wait to see justice carried out for criminals responsible for the victimization of them and their families. The six-person panel included Wanda, Jenny and representatives of three other families.

Geraldo began the show by saying, "Wanda, the injury done to you by the shotgun blast is quite apparent." He then asked Wanda and Jenny to describe the events of February 22, 1979. As audience members shook their heads and frowned, Wanda fought back tears and told of Woomer's depraved behavior. In turn, Jenny sorrowfully described how her mother had been slain.

A New Jersey man whose daughter was murdered by a convicted murderer on parole described the horror of having to wait years after the trial and sentencing to see justice done. That his daughter's murderer had been released from prison after serving only a few years for a first murder almost drove him and his wife crazy, the distraught father said. He believed initially that the trial of his daughter's murderer would bring some satisfaction and allow his family to move ahead. It wasn't until later that he realized, "The criminal justice system duped us because we realized very shortly after the trial that it isn't over." He expected his family's wait for justice to include at least ten more years of appeals by the criminal. Another guest described how her wait for justice was on hold because the convicted murderer of her ten-year-old daughter was awarded another resentencing hearing, ten years after the original conviction. She and her family would once again be forced back into court to relive the details of the tragic murder. At the upcoming resentencing scheduled for the month after the taping of the show, her daughter would have been twenty years old. The last of the panelists were the parents of a teenage girl murdered by serial killer Ted Bundy in 1974. Their wait for justice finally ended on January 24, 1989, the day of the Bundy execution in Florida. The toll of the 15-year wait on their family was indescribable.

Similar video clips of Woomer and Bundy as they were led into court for one of their many appearances showed each man smirking, obviously enjoying the celebrity status, as they realized the crowds of people were there just for them.

Traci spoke several times from the audience where she sat by experts Geraldo had on hand to provide input for the controversial show. Lula Redmond, Executive Director of the Center for Crime Victims and Survivors, and Henry Schwarzschild, Director of the Capital Punishment Project for the ACLU, listened as 17-year-old Traci, still unable to say Woomer's name aloud, expressed her disillusionment with the constitutionally-guaranteed appeals process for criminals in America.

"He talks about his constitutional rights," Traci said, her voice cracking, "but I don't think that my mom's constitutional rights were what he was thinking about when he did that to her. We're taught about life, liberty and the pursuit of happiness. Her life – that cannot be given back. Her constitutional rights were denied." Traci was unable to hold back her tears as she asked, "What about the pursuit of happiness? Do you think my mom's been very happy? I just don't believe [in the process] anymore." Geraldo embraced and comforted Traci as the panelists and experts continued the rapid-fire and informative exchange.

Other facts about the costs of being victimized by crime were presented. When lawyer fees and medical bills are added, the dollar cost for a victim's family is usually in the six-figure range. In addition, citing the over 14 million dollars

dollars spent on Bundy by the state of Florida alone, one panel member related that the average cost in 1989 for taxpayers of each appeal in a death penalty case is between one million and one million, four hundred thousand dollars. The panelist suggested that this is almost a moot point since only one of every thousand convicted murderers faces a death sentence. Criminals know they are not likely to be put to death for their crimes. So confident of this was a murderer in Pennsylvania, the panelist said, that the murderer requested a death sentence because he knew the cells on death row where he would be incarcerated had individual televisions.

Perhaps the most poignant moment of the unsettling show came toward the end of the program when panelists were describing the effects of the crimes for families through multiple generations. Children and grandchildren not even born when the victimization occurred had grown up and learned of the horrible acts perpetrated against loved ones. "Tragedy," a brokenhearted father said, "is a part of your family heritage forever."

In March of 1990, the U.S. Supreme Court threw out the Oklahoma case of Saffle vs Parks, ruling against the "no-sympathy instructions" given to juries. The ruling was considered a plus for rights of victims since it shot down the claim that juries in deciding between life and death sentences should not be influenced by sympathy, passion, or prejudice for or against a defendant. In other words, prosecutors can present to the jurors in the sentencing phase of death-penalty trials information regarding personal characteristics of victims, such as whether the victim was civic-minded, or regularly attended church. Jim Dunn applauded the decision and noted that, once again, the decks were cleared for Woomer's execution.

On April 3, 1990, the S.C. Supreme Court again set an execution date for Woomer, this time a date that would be kept. Woomer's days were now numbered, though the expected flurry of last minute appeals went forward.

Although Dunn would not officially turn over the reins of the solicitor's position to Ralph Wilson until January 10, 1991, he made a public announcement in late 1989 concerning his intent to resign. Dunn began his first term as solicitor with Woomer's case and ended his third term twelve years later with the conclusion of the same case. Dunn spent over a decade of his life trying to clean up a horrible mess made in a single day by an unconscionable murderer. It's no wonder, as a reporter wrote, that Dunn's stock answer to questions about the possibility of his re-election for solicitor or whether he would run for Congress was, "A judge couldn't sentence me to a four-year term as solicitor or any other office."

Dunn clearly had things other than politics in mind when he encapsulated his plans to retire in a poem for a reporter:

"All I want is a pick-up truck,
a small shrimp boat and a little luck,
chewing tobacco and a baseball bat,
and a hat to tell me where I'm at.
I want a little dog, he can have some fleas,
I'm headed out for the Florida Keys."

51

Daylight had barely begun to trickle in through the opened window. Wanda sat up abruptly. *April 27, 1990, a day I'll remember,* she thought.

Jimmy rolled over and patted Wanda's back. "Can't sleep, honey?"

"I feel like I've been up all night," she replied. Wanda glanced at the clock. The alarm wasn't due to sound for several more minutes.

"I'll get some coffee going," Jimmy said, and started to sit up. Wanda's tossing and turning all night had kept him awake and he felt drained.

"I'll get it," Wanda said, moving quickly to her feet and starting across the room. "You stay here."

Jimmy's head fell back to his pillow, but his eyes remained open. He realized he hadn't slept well in a long time.

The long-awaited day of Woomer's execution had arrived. Again. Sleeping fitfully and awakening suddenly confirmed Wanda's fear that the day was going to be interminably long. Thank God, Thursdays were grooming days at the clinic and she could stay busy. Wanda wasn't at work long before pet owners began arriving with their dogs and cats.

As she washed and dipped animals, Wanda thought it very strange that people who entered the clinic were smiling as usual and seemed unaware that anything out of the ordinary was going to happen that day. *Perhaps they're just being polite,* she thought, and then frowned. *Maybe it's just me.* Though she began the morning trying to interact with customers as she normally did, Wanda quickly found she preferred to work in the back of the clinic where she could be alone with her troubled thoughts.

Wanda had spent the earlier part of the week in Columbia but didn't want to stay for the execution on Thursday and returned home late Wednesday afternoon. Governor Campbell had proclaimed the week of April 22-28 as Victim's Rights Week. Wanda and Jenny received a special invitation to be in attendance for the state-wide conference planned to examine and call attention to victimization by crime. During a ceremony on the steps of the Statehouse, Campbell presented Wanda and Jenny with a proclamation honoring their work on behalf of victim's rights. That same day, Wanda was featured in a big photo on the front of *The State* receiving a kiss from Lt. Governor Nick Theodore. Also, that week Wanda received a Silver Scales of Justice Award from the S.C. Victim's Assistance Network. The Public Sector Award, one of only a handful of honors awarded by the organization each year in the state, recognized Wanda's efforts "for increasing awareness of a victim's plight after surviving an assault."

Wanda learned a lot and appreciated the efforts of everyone associated with the conference, but the victim's rights sessions left her feeling uneasy. The crowds and the attention were more than she had anticipated. Wanda was aware that Buddy Causey and Don Sellers planned to join Jenny and Jim Dunn and go to the prison Thursday night. She had no plans to be there, however. The thought of an execution, even Woomer's execution, meant another human being was going to die.

Wanda watched the clearly visible second hand on the big wall clock and grew increasingly unsettled. She slipped the cordless phone into the pocket of her smock. As 11 a.m. approached, which was the hour of day she had received word of Woomer's stay of execution from the Attorney General's office nine months earlier, she found it more and more difficult to pay attention to what she was doing.

• ❖ •

Following the procedure of nine months earlier, with the execution scheduled for late Thursday night/early Friday morning, Woomer was moved on Tuesday from CCI to the Capital Punishment Facility to begin the deathwatch. He was again fingerprinted, inventoried, scrubbed, dressed and allowed extensive visitation with family and friends. He again ordered pizza with no anchovies for his last meal, but again he wouldn't be disappointed if he didn't get to eat it.

On Tuesday, Jim Dunn loaded his pick-up truck with the tombstone and all of his files on Woomer and drove to Columbia. Rather than keep watch in Conway as he had nine months earlier, Dunn checked into the Radisson Hotel across the street from the Attorney General's office so that he might be available, if necessary, to assist with arguments before the U.S. Supreme Court. Remembering the eleventh hour stay Woomer had received, Dunn had a wait-and-see attitude concerning the execution. "The thing about it is," he told a reporter, "we've already done this once before. The families have prepared themselves for an end to this horrible chapter in their lives. This time I'm proceeding with an abundance of precaution. I'm not going to believe that it's happened until it happens." When asked if he was frustrated that Woomer's lawyers were working night and day trying to find the loophole that would again spare Woomer, Dunn said, "Any frustration I have with the system is so far outweighed by the frustration of the families until mine doesn't count."

Wanda felt slightly better when 11 a.m. came and went, but she still jumped every time the phone rang. In addition to the regular calls coming in to the clinic, Jimmy had called every hour or so to see if there was any news. There wasn't, but no news was good news.

Woomer had again asked his friend and spiritual mentor, Robert McAlister, if he would attend the execution. McAlister declined to witness his friend's death but did promise Rusty he'd stay with him until the last moments. Woomer declined to designate someone else, so the corrections commissioner chose a witness for Woomer. Other witnesses, also determined by state law governing executions, included a witness chosen by the family of the victim, Don Sellers, and two witnesses chosen by drawing from among names of media persons who volunteered to witness the execution. Both the representative from the S.C. Press Association and the person chosen by the Radio-Television News Directors Association of the Carolinas would serve as pool reporters and immediately after the execution provide a report for distribution among the media outlets.

Woomer met during the day Thursday with friends and family members until 4 p.m. and then ate his pizza. In addition to his lawyers and corrections department personnel, Woomer visited during the deathwatch with his father, two sisters and one brother. Conspicuously absent during the deathwatch was Woomer's wife. The Rock Hill woman Woomer married three years earlier had quit visiting him.

Woomer also gave an interview to reporter John Monk of *The Charlotte Observer*. Monk spent a half-hour with Woomer in his cell during the late morning and reported, "Woomer said he was ready to die if that will bring peace to the families of his victims." Present during the interview was McAlister, who maintained that Woomer's conversion was real. "Rusty is a biblical example of how the Lord Jesus can make a new person. I stand on that," Monk wrote, quoting McAlister.

During the probing interview when Monk asked Woomer how he felt about Jim Dunn, Woomer said, "I don't have anything bad to say about Mr. Dunn. Mr. Dunn is doing what he thinks is right." Woomer added, "One of these days the Lord will talk to Mr. Dunn. It's not never too late for anyone. The Lord can get you anywhere, anytime."

When Dunn was later told of Woomer's remark, he responded, "If I find the Lord, it won't be Rusty Woomer that introduces him to me." Dunn was leery of what he and others had referred to as jailhouse religion and said, "There're three things you can depend on with a person like Ronald Woomer. They're going to be shaved, they're going to be saved, and they're going to be sorry."

• ❖ •

Wanda assumed that the more time passed, the less likely a stay of execution would be and she felt better as the afternoon wore on. Close to 5 p.m. when she began making preparations to go home, the phone sounded sharply. Wanda hesitated momentarily and then answered. When the caller identified herself as a representative of the Attorney General's office, Wanda froze. *Not again,* she said to herself, her heart sinking.

"Mrs. Summers," the caller said, "I'm just calling to let you know that we haven't heard yet from the U.S. Supreme Court. We'll let you know as soon as we hear anything."

Wanda thanked the caller and hung up, her head spinning. *I could have done without that,* she thought.

Wanda drove the short distance to her home and busied herself in the kitchen preparing dinner for her family.

• ❖ •

A contingent of persons from Horry and Georgetown Counties went to Columbia on Thursday to be part of the crowd that always gathers outside a prison when there is an execution. In anticipation of problems, corrections officials roped off separate areas outside of the gate to Broad River Correctional Institute in hopes that this would prevent death penalty supporters and opponents from clashing. Death penalty opponents were urged by the ACLU, Amnesty International, and area churches to avoid the prison gathering, which most did, and instead attend a scheduled service at a church in town. As it turned out, most of the 300 or so individuals who showed up at the prison were death penalty supporters. Though only half a dozen guards normally roamed the gates outside the prison, before the night was over more than 60 officers would be needed to control the crowd.

Despite an editorial in *The State* that morning that accused Jim Dunn of "grim grandstanding," Dunn moved the tombstone from where it had been on display at the State House to Broad River where it was decorated with flowers.

Dunn ignored the criticism that the tombstone display was "unprofessional, morbid, tasteless, and unbecoming of a public servant." Dunn was again correct in his prediction that the tombstone, as a reminder of Woomer's victims, would appear in newspaper and television coverage of the media event.

In addition to Wanda, Jimmy, Traci and Jamie, Wanda's two brothers, a family friend, and a reporter prepared to spend the long evening at the Summers' home awaiting the execution. The phone rang again and again throughout the night. In many ways, wrote Chrysti Edge in a special article for *The State*, the evening was "as normal as any middle-class family watching television on a Thursday night. Sometimes the only sounds were of crickets chirping outside the open window." For Wanda, however, the night was as long as the day had been as she impatiently waited for 1 a.m.

At 8:10 p.m., the phone rang. As she had earlier, the caller began by identifying herself as a representative of the Attorney General's office. Wanda again felt her heart leap. This time, however, the news was good. The U.S. Supreme Court had turned down the last two of Woomer's applications for a stay of execution. Woomer would keep the appointment with his destiny unless his lawyers successfully pulled some last minute strings. *There is still time for that to happen*, Wanda thought, looking at her watch. If Wanda had learned anything in 11 years, it was not to let down her guard.

A planned protest at a downtown Columbia church drew about 75 individuals for a service that was expected to culminate in a candlelight march to the Governor's mansion. Nine months earlier, a similar gathering had turned into a celebration because of the news of Woomer's stay. This time the service took place as planned and included a poem read by Woomer's sister-in-law, a recording of three death row inmates singing "Blowing in the Wind," and various speeches and quotes of scripture. Catholic Monsignor Thomas R. Duffy made a statement recorded by the newspaper, "I really don't think Rusty is going to die for what Rusty did. I think he's going to die because of our unwillingness to accept the idea of spiritual redemption for everyone." This sentiment was extended by the pastor of the church, Reverend William Bouknight, who was quoted in the newspaper as saying, "Let God bring peace to their [the victims and their families] souls that revenge cannot deliver. Help us stop the periodic burnt offerings to the pagan gods of vengeance and fear."

The Reverend's choice of words made reference, though no doubt unintentionally, to an execution in Florida two years earlier. According to an article in *The Charleston News & Courier* (May 9, 1988), Jessie Tafero was electrocuted fourteen years, two months and twelve days after he murdered two police officers at a rest stop on Interstate Highway 95. When the current was switched on, the saline-soaked sponge that rests on the head and conducts current into the body caught fire, igniting the headset. As the current was turned on and off, flames were seen for several minutes shooting out from underneath the leather mask covering Tafero's face. Apparently, someone had changed the procedure from using the "natural ocean sponge" used in the 21 electrocutions in Florida from 1979 to 1988 to a sponge of a different composition, perhaps a synthetic material. The gory detail-rich article, which was typical of the national coverage of the electrocution, identified the murdered officers only by name and rank. One sentence provided the only other reference to the victims of Tafero's crimes: "Tafero, like the officers, died a messy, violent death."

● ❖ ●

Wanda smoked and shifted uncomfortably in her easy chair beside the window. She felt jittery, but only in part because of the coffee she drank, and she continued to jump each time the phone rang. At 10:50 p.m., the Attorney General's office called once again. Don Zelenko, the Chief

Deputy Attorney General, told Wanda that Woomer's lawyers had not filed any additional motions and it looked doubtful that anything would change the scheduled execution. Wanda dutifully thanked Zelenko and hung up, relief apparent on her face.

Laying her head back on the headrest, Wanda realized that as the moment for which she had waited so long became near, she was again unsure how she felt about the death penalty. She had certainly heard all of the arguments. Is capital punishment retribution? Is it deterrence? Is it a lingering vestige of a brutal human nature? Perhaps, as she had heard opponents argue, capital punishment, no matter how it is defined, lessens a society by making the law a killer. She knew only that she was tired: tired of the pain, tired of the uncertainty, tired of picking up the pieces of Woomer's mess, still scattered after 11 years. Perhaps Woomer himself was tired, as the writing later found on the wall of his cell seemed to indicate. "Three life sentences, two death penalties. It wasn't worth it. God help me."

Outside the prison, Jim Dunn was upset, as was Jenny, by the party atmosphere that had developed. It was difficult to distinguish, among the university students and the persons who had driven in from all over the state, who was there in legitimate support of the death penalty and who was there for the party. As the beer-drinking crowd swelled, the noise level accelerated and pockets of revelry began to break out spontaneously.

Don Sellers felt certain he was going to witness Woomer die. Cleared by a SLED background check, Don had listened attentively the week before to the description of an execution at a briefing he was required to attend at state corrections headquarters. On Thursday, as Don waited with the other witnesses for the van to escort them to the death house, he nervously clutched in his hand the key chain with Louise's ring and told the reporters of the promise he had made to Louise 11 years and four months earlier. The promise to his beloved wife was about to come true.

Woomer was prepped for his electrocution by having his head and right leg shaved. The right leg, below the knee, had been cut out of the prison-issue pants he wore. Conducting gel was applied in a smear to his leg and in a glob to the top of his bare head. The sleeves of his blue shirt were rolled above the elbows. The shoes he wore lacked laces.

Wanda tuned in and out of the conversation. Traci had gotten a newspaper and was speculating about what was happening in Columbia at the prison. Jimmy sat and smoked and waited. The late news came on television, but the report on the pending execution didn't provide new information.

Don and the other witnesses were led into the small witness room and seated side by side less than ten feet from the electric chair. A glass partition separated the spaces. Two medical officials of the prison sat directly behind the witnesses.

Jim Dunn tried unsuccessfully to calm the crowd that had begun to chant. Less than 15 persons were there in opposition to the death penalty. The candles they held flickered feebly amid the jeers and excited cries of the mob as the seconds before 1 a.m. slowly ticked off.

Woomer was led into the death chamber at 12:57 a.m. and was seated in the electric chair. On the other side of the glass partition sat Don Sellers, still clutching his wife's ring and nervously tapping his foot. Don stared at Woomer as two men, one on either side of the prisoner, began strapping his legs, then his arms, lap and chest to the chair. Woomer clenched his fists and glanced at the witnesses. Even when he looked directly into Don's eyes, Woomer showed no apparent signs that he recognized him.

The warden leaned forward and asked Woomer if he had anything to say.

Woomer opened his eyes and said, "I'm sorry. I claim Jesus Christ as my savior, and my only wish is that everyone in the world can feel the love that I've felt from Him."

Woomer again closed his eyes as a strap around his mouth was tightened to hold his head to the back of the chair. Following the adjustment of the headpiece, a cloth hood was placed over Woomer's face.

Wanda looked at her watch and noted that 1 a.m. had passed. She still had a headache despite the medication she had taken. *What will happen now?* she began to wonder. *Has it already happened? How will I know?*

As 1 a.m. arrived, the noise level accelerated as persons in the crowd outside the prison gate began to howl and chant for Woomer's death. Jenny shook her head sadly as Jim Dunn continued to try and calm the crowd by attempting to make himself heard above the laughing and cheering. "This isn't appropriate," he said repeatedly.

After the cables were in place to send the surges of

electricity through Woomer's body, the warden ordered everyone out of the chamber except for another prison official and a physician sitting calmly in the corner. At 1:05 a.m., the warden picked up a telephone and gave the order to turn on the current.

Wanda remembers the 17 minutes between 1 a.m. and 1:17 a.m., when she received a final phone call from the Attorney General's office, as 17 of the longest minutes of her life. During that time, Wanda rehashed the thoughts that had plagued her since her life was turned upside down 11 years earlier. *What if Jimmy hadn't been the loving husband and father he has been?* she thought. *What if someone in my family was left without support to fend for himself? No! That doesn't excuse him! Woomer hurt me! He hurt my family! Only he is responsible for where he is right now.* Looking across the room, Wanda saw that Jimmy appeared calm, but Traci seemed nervous. Wanda shut her eyes tightly and clutched a balled-up tissue to her forehead.

Woomer slumped slightly when he was hit with a five-second, two-thousand-volts surge of electricity. He then remained motionless during a surge of one thousand volts, which lasted for eight seconds. Woomer's lifeless body slumped forward slightly again as the final surge of two hundred fifty volts was applied for two minutes.

As Don Sellers watched the life drain from Woomer, he thought of Louise's struggle and how she had begged for her life. When two doctors entered and began looking for remaining signs of life in Woomer's limp body, Don scowled and said, "That was too easy."

Outside the prison a cheer went up as the hearse carrying Woomer's body was sighted approaching the gate.

As the gate slowly opened and the hearse began to pass by on its way to Richland Memorial Hospital for an autopsy, chanting began again and assumed a familiar tune. "Na-na-na-na, na-na-na-na, hey-hey-hey, good-bye!"

When the phone rang, everyone in the room instantly quieted. Wanda hesitated as she picked up the phone. Taking a deep breath, she put the receiver to her ear.

"Wanda," the caller said, "this is Attorney General Travis Medlock calling . . . ."

Wanda closed her eyes as she listened. Placing her hand over her face, she hung up the phone and began to sob in relief. "It's over," she said a moment later. "It's over."

Epilogue

Wanda hurried up the ladder to the top of the racing trailer and stopped to look at Jimmy as he stood barking out instructions into his headset. She liked the way he looked with the single earpiece and microphone arched around his lucky cap. Jimmy glanced over at Wanda from his corner position where he was able to visually track the Charger car all the way around the five-eighths mile oval track and smiled. Wanda smiled back. The Main Event of the Nascar-sanctioned Saturday night race was about to begin. A win tonight for the #27 car, a white 1972 super-charged Chevrolet Camaro sponsored by Summers' Roofing, would be the sixth win in a row and a heck of a way to end the 1993 season.

● ❖ ●

A couple of years earlier, when Jimmy had the idea that sponsoring a race car would be exciting for his family and perhaps good for business, he contacted an already established team and arranged financial support. That first sponsorship, however, only allowed Jimmy and Wanda to sit in the stands during races, and that wasn't at all satisfactory for Jimmy, a hands-on kind of guy. So, when Olin Butler, a quiet, likable man with a wrecked race car came along, Jimmy saw an opportunity for more involvement, and he and Olin worked out an owner/sponsor partnership. The two men spent the winter of 1992 rebuilding Olin's car in the garage at the Summers' home, and by the 1993 season, the 350 horsepower, 350-cubic-inch engine Camaro was ready to race.

● ❖ ●

Wanda slipped up beside her husband, briefly touching his arm. Just behind Jimmy, facing the packed grandstand, Traci stood looking at a chart she had designed. Two stopwatches were permanently fixed to the top corners of the clipboard she balanced on her crooked arm. When she finished noting the starting positions of the cars, Traci walked over to the edge of the trailer and began descending the steps of the ladder.

"Here we go, baby-doll," Jimmy said, leaning toward Wanda. As the race cars settled into starting positions, the drivers revved the engines, prompting fans to yell louder to be heard over the noise.

"Yeah," Wanda said, continuing to smile. Wanda put her hands on her hips and looked down on the pit area where racers' families and friends had gathered during the day for pre-race activities. Each weekend from late March until early October, husbands, wives, children, and an assortment of in-laws and friends gathered at the Myrtle Beach Speedway for the running of the local weekend features of the Winston Racing Series.

A mechanic from the next pit looked in Wanda's direction and shook his head. Wanda turned and saw Jimmy nodding his head up and down in an exaggerated manner in response. "We're gonna' teach you something about racing again tonight, boys," Jimmy said loudly and laughed. The mechanic smiled and gestured dismissively with his hand.

Wanda didn't have room to pace on the top of the spotting trailer and glanced toward the ladder as if assuring herself that her path was clear. When a race began, she usually made it until lap three or so before she started her routine of climbing down to pace and then climbing back up again. She repeated this process a couple of times as a race progressed and several more times if the race was really close. The Main Event was a 25-lap race, and a fast lap time was 21 or 22 seconds. Caution flags signaling wrecks and flat tires, however, could slow the action down so that the entire race might take 30 minutes.

Wanda took a deep breath, looked down toward the pit area, and smiled at Traci.

Traci smiled back and continued to look at her mother for several moments after Wanda looked away. As Traci prepared to clock laps, she sat in her usual position in the chair that was specially mounted on top of Olin's toolbox, which had been positioned at pit wall for the race. If the race wasn't too close, Traci also clocked the speed of the car just behind the #27 car, which was, hopefully, the car in second place.

"OK, David," Jimmy said to the driver of the #27 car, as the pace car left the racing lanes. "Good luck. I'll count down the green." Jimmy carefully watched the arm of the flagman, looking for subtle movements indicating a sudden upward fanning motion of the flag.

"This looks like it," Jimmy said suddenly, " . . . three . . . two . . . one . . . "

Anticipating Jimmy's count, David hit the accelerator just as the flag came down and Jimmy yelled, "Go, go, go!"

The strain of the high-powered engines winding up stopped conversations as people in the stands covered their ears. David passed the flagman's stand just a couple of feet from the right of the pole car as the accelerating motors screamed down the straightaway into turn one. David eased off the pedal slightly and fell into a draft of car #54 as it settled in the groove, the fastest line around the track.

"It's a good start," Jimmy said calmly into his mouthpiece and then smiled when he saw Wanda hurrying down the ladder. She'd be back by the end of the race. She always was. "You got a car length behind you," he continued talking to the driver, "the 32 car, back right." Jimmy began stepping in place and slowly spinning as the cars went 'round and 'round.

Wanda and Traci screamed at the same moment and turned to face one another, their mouths still open in surprise and excitement. On top of the trailer, Jamie hugged his mother's waist, and then Jimmy wrapped his bear-like arms around both of them. The laughing huggers broke apart and

Jimmy suddenly turned, unable to wait any longer. "Y'all come on," he hollered over his shoulder. Down below, Traci, Olin, and the pit crew were shouting. Some of the men were swinging their caps wildly.

"Go on with your daddy, if you want," Wanda said to Jamie and the excited boy scampered after his father. Despite the cheering crowd and the thundering noise of the cars, Wanda heard Jamie's laughter as his father squeezed his shoulders, lifting him effortlessly off the ground.

Wanda climbed down from the trailer and skipped up to Traci. Mother and daughter embraced.

"You go ahead, honey," Wanda said to Traci.

"You're coming," Traci said, pulling her mother's arm. "I need you with me."

"I'm coming," Wanda said, looking into Traci's eyes. "Don't worry, honey, I'll be right there with you."

Family and friends of a winning car had only a few minutes to get to the Winner's Circle. Following earlier wins, Traci had noted with dismay that her camera-shy mother wasn't in any of the Winner's Circle photographs.

"Momma, I want you to come on with me, now," Traci said.

"I'm going to be there, honey," Wanda said reassuringly.

Traci's eyes moistened and she and Wanda again embraced. "Oh, Momma, I love you so much."

Wanda watched Traci run over to where Olin stood waiting. Following a quick hug, Traci and Olin ran holding hands to catch the other members of the race team who were trailing like ants down the pit wall to the spot where they would rush across pit road and into the back of the Winner's Circle. Wanda could see Jimmy and Jamie as they waited for a break in the rush of incoming race cars and then dashed across to greet the #27 car, which was just finishing a victory lap. After Traci and Olin had successfully crossed the busy lane, Wanda slowly turned and looked at the empty pit area where the race team had labored during the day and evening. Olin's toolbox, now carefully locked, sat next to jack stands that lift and provide support for the chassis of the car. Wanda smiled as she imagined legs poking out from beneath the raised car, a dirty hand groping for a tool lying on the black asphalt. *How many times have I laughed here?* she thought. Wanda imagined the sights and sounds of the racetrack each weekend. The sound of children, the smell of oil residue and gas fumes, the familiar tastes of chicken bog and steak sizzling on a grill. Wanda saw on the ground a cap someone had dropped as the cheering throng headed for the Winner's Circle. Smiling, she reflexively picked up the cap, brushed it with her hand and set it on the toolbox.

It's time, she thought and turned to follow her family.

Wanda loved the Winner's Circle. Their first win, five weeks earlier, had felt as nothing before. To have the opportunity to see her family, who had all worked so hard, gathered in their moment of victory was exciting. *And now,* she thought, *six wins in a row!*

Wanda crawled across the pit wall where the super stockcars were preparing for the final Main Event of the night and stepped among mechanics rushing around cars for that last moment of polishing to bring out the sheen of the layered-paint jobs. *No one deserves to be in the Winner's Circle more than Jimmy does,* Wanda thought and then hesitated. *No, wait, make that more than we do. I have to go.*

Wanda quickened her step when the voice booming over the loudspeaker announced that the winning car, the #27 Camaro, was sponsored by Summers' Roofing. As she weaved her way between cars, the image of Jimmy as a boy being asked to leave the Altman home after the evening Scrabble game brought a smile to her face. Wanda suddenly realized that Jimmy had never really left on those nights. *He had known from the first moment that he had found his home.* At a break in the traffic, Wanda vaulted with long strides across pit road. *It's our home, together.*

The crowd suddenly roared and Wanda knew the race trophy was being presented to David, the driver of the #27 car. The Winner's Circle was thick with people and Wanda looked for a spot where she could see the picture as it was being taken. The thought of Traci as a little girl so bravely sticking out her tongue at persons she thought were hurting her momma made Wanda's eyes mist. Traci was still very protective of her mother. *What a beautiful woman Traci has grown up to be.* Wanda began pushing through the crowd.

"Excuse me," she said, her heart beginning to pound. "Excuse me."

Wanda remembered that first moment when Jamie was born and she heard another life, felt another presence in the room where just moments before there hadn't been one. Jamie's birth had been another step in the long healing process for Wanda. Now he was growing so strong and complete. *Jimmy, Traci, and Jamie . . . Where would I be without them?*

"Excuse me," Wanda said again and stepped around a smiling man from another race team, on hand to watch the festivities.

"Well, get on in the picture, Wanda," the man said. "You belong in there."

Wanda's face flushed. *Even if I'm not in the picture,* she thought, *I'm here.* Before Wanda stood her family, her friends, her reason to live. Her chest rose as she took deep breaths.

Traci wrung her hands. Her eyes urgently searched the crowd.

Jimmy saw Wanda. "There she is," he called out.

"Is everybody ready?" the photographer asked loudly. Crowd noise in the background made it difficult to hear. Some weeks it seemed that the flash was the only signal that a picture had been taken.

Traci quickly looked at Jimmy and then followed his gaze to Wanda.

"C'mon, Momma," Traci yelled.

"I'm here with you, honey," Wanda said. "I told you I would be."

"What?" Tracy shouted, cupping her ear. "I can't hear you. Hurry, Momma."

Jimmy felt someone bend down behind him and grab his legs. He looked again at Wanda. Their eyes locked. Wanda saw Jimmy as he looked in the hospital when the bandages had first come off of her face and he had given her the assurance she needed to begin her long struggle to survive. Wanda saw in Jimmy's eyes the confidence with which he tackled all obstacles, the confidence from which she had derived the strength to stand on her own.

"OK, here we go," the photographer said loudly.

"I said I'm here," Wanda said softly.

Jimmy nodded his head and smiled. Though he didn't hear her words, he understood. Jimmy suddenly felt himself being lifted off of the ground.

"C'mon, Momma," Traci yelled.

Olin thrust the checkered flag skyward.

"I'm here," Wanda said smiling. "I am here."

"All right, everybody say, 'Cheese.'"

"I am here!" Wanda said again loudly. She then stepped forward, still looking at Jimmy, as the flash exploded.

Appendix

Jim Dunn retired after the Woomer case and moved to the Florida Keys to fish. He returned and reopened a practice in Conway two years later. He currently is again retired and lives quietly in Horry County.

When Captain Glen "Buddy" Causey retired in 1996 after over 37 years of "policing," *The Sun News* paid tribute to him with highlights of his impressive career described in the newspaper. In an interview for this book, Buddy recognized the unflagging support of his wife, Janice, throughout his career, and also the support of his good friends Enoch Smith and Jobe Blain, both of whom participated in Woomer's capture. The death of Smith at age 58 in 1983 saddened Buddy. When Jobe Blain, an African-American, was asked about Buddy, Blain remembered the old days when one of his jobs was to watch the office while white officers ate lunch. Blain remembered that Causey waited to eat lunch with him.

Buddy and Janice live in Conway.

Cleveland Stevens continued to serve the public and became Mayor of Atlantic Beach, S.C., in 1980. A caption below a picture in a local paper told the story. "The Honorable Cleveland Stevens was sworn in as the new mayor of Atlantic Beach by the Solicitor for the Fifteenth Judicial Circuit, Jim Dunn, during ceremonies New Year's day at the town community center."

Stevens' name was submitted in July, 1983, as a candidate for a South Carolina Appellate Court Judge position. The committee's decision not to award the position to Stevens was noted in a report that cited, among other reasons, that Stevens had been hospitalized for exhaustion. Stevens' health deteriorated in the late 1980s and he died of cancer on July 1, 1991. Irby Walker said that Stevens cried when a federal circuit court judge denied the last of Woomer's appeals.

Following the Woomer trial, Irby Walker left the public defender's office to fulfill a personal dream of earning a Master's Degree in tax law from Georgetown University. He earned his degree in May 1980 and currently maintains an active private law practice in Conway, S.C.

Don Sellers lives in Chesterfield, S.C. He never got over the death of his beloved Louise.

Dean and Rene Guyton continue to live and work in Horry County. In August of 1979, just after the first of Woomer's trials, Rene went to work for Jim Dunn in the solicitor's office. Her ten years of service with Dunn helped her process some of her own grief over the tragic loss of her parents, William and Myrtie Moon of Socastee.

Sgt. George Kisor, the officer fired upon by Eugene Skaar before Skaar and Woomer drove to South Carolina, still serves the public as a police officer in Cabell County, West Virginia. George vividly remembers the incident that catalyzed Skaar's and Woomer's escape from West Virgina. "It was snowing that night," Kisor said. "We had an APB out for the vehicle Skaar was driving. It was stolen. I tried to stop him in a housing development, but he gunned his motor and tried to outrun me. When he saw he couldn't, he pulled over. It was real late at night. Must have been two or three in the morning. No one was out but us. Since he tried to outrun me, I approached the car with my gun drawn. He got out, saw the gun, and reached over in his car. When he leaned back out, he had a rifle in his hands that had been laying on the seat. At that point, I put my gun in his face and he didn't raise the rifle. He suddenly began to run, the rifle still in his hands. Then he turned as he run and started shooting at me, but by then I was down beside the vehicle. His gun must have jammed because I later found a shell casing that is all mashed up on the side. I still have that casing. It happened so fast I was never in fear for my life. I called for help and we tracked him through the snow, but he got away." Kisor paused and ran his fingers through his gray hair.

"I had an opportunity to shoot him," he continued reflectively. "Had I done so it might have saved all those lives. 'Course that's something you can't know at the moment. But, when I think about it now, I sometimes think I should have killed that son-of-a-bitch the night I stopped him. It would have saved everyone in South Carolina a whole lot of trouble."

Jimmy and Wanda Summers continue to live in Pawley's Island where they work and tend to the everyday concerns of their growing family, which now numbers seven. The recently remodeled house in which they live is the Altman family home on the original land where Reggie and Betty raised Wanda and her brothers. Also living on the family's land are Traci and her husband, Olin, who have two little girls, Hallie and Mariah, the first of Jimmy's and Wanda's grandchildren. Rounding out the immediate family is Jamie, who is a busy teenager with a special aptitude for playing baseball, a game that Wanda loves.

The business the Summers have worked so hard to grow has, indeed, flourished. Summers' Roofing has benefited from the building boom along the Grand Strand over the last 15 years. Also, as Jimmy suspected, the high visibility of racing has been good for business. The OBR racing partnership between Jimmy and Olin now includes super-trucks, for the better prize money, and both men admit that although almost no one gets rich racing, breaking even is nice, too.

After finishing the 1993 racing season with six straight wins, OBR went on to win 13 of just over two dozen races the following year and was awarded the trophy for the highest point total in their class. At the awards banquet, where winners sit at the front tables, the Summers and the Butlers wore evening clothes and humbly enjoyed the admiration and envy of their friends.

The Summers' family enjoys a closeness and unity that is uncommon in this day and age. They work together, attend ball games and community functions together, and vacation together. Jimmy and Wanda see their grandchildren every day. The shared experience of the family tragedy and Wanda's subsequent recovery have shaped the Summers to rely primarily upon one another and upon a tight extended family of close, long-time friends and employees. Jimmy, in particular, when thinking about the relationships that really matter to him, remembers those who stood beside him during the hard times.

But, the Summers have drawn their circle inward because of the rapid growth of the Pawley's Island area and the resulting increase in the number of persons in the community who are unfamiliar with local history. Wanda frequently encounters persons who react to her appearance in a manner that makes her uncomfortable. Less than a year ago, a woman entering the animal clinic said in surprise, "My word, honey, what happened to your face?" On this occasion, Wanda wasn't able to be gracious, as she normally is, and retreated to a back room. The red-faced woman who apparently spoke without thinking left flustered after apologizing profusely to another employee of the clinic.

The accelerating frequency of such incidents has led Wanda and Jimmy to begin looking at land outside of town and has prompted thoughts of retirement, perhaps in a few years. A dream Jimmy and Wanda eventually intend to make happen is the two of them sitting on the front porch of their country home as the children, grandchildren and great-grandchildren come up the long drive for a visit.

Acknowledgments

Many persons contributed to this book and deserve to be recognized. As always, our fear is that when all is said and done, a contribution will have been overlooked. If this proves to be the case, and you are the person whom we neglected to recognize, please accept our apology.

First and foremost, we thank Wanda and Jimmy Summers for allowing us to be a part of their lives for the last two years. This book would not have been possible without their expressed permission and cooperation. From initial conversations to discuss the possibility of writing the story through dozens of hours of interviews and phone calls to check facts, the Summers were gracious hosts as we developed the manuscript. Special thanks also to Traci Butler for sharing important thoughts and ideas regarding private matters of her life.

In order to recognize the many persons who contributed to the story, we have provided the following list of name and county of origin for each person. From Horry and Georgetown Counties: Buddy Causey, Janice Causey, Irby Walker, Jim Dunn, Rene Guyton, Dean Guyton, Guy Osborne, Bob Riddle, Senator Luke Rankin, Ms. Cleveland Stevens, Arvella Moore, Ralph Wilson, Tommy Brittain, Billie Richardson, Raymond Finch, Jobe Blain, Billy Joe Weaver, Mary Anne Bishop, Cathy Floyd, Patty Fine, Karen Hampton, Jeannie Roberts, Kathy Patrick, and Freddie Hucks; from Colleton County: Ralph Putti, Jean Acosta, and Jina L. Pedigo; from Richland County: Michael Brown and Rita Schuller of SLED, Gaston Fairey, John Monk at *The State*, and Suzannah Cole of the Attorney General's Office for assistance in finding original transcripts. In addition, thanks to Sgt. George Kisor, of Cabell County, West Virginia, for his recollections, and to Jackie Griffith of Mountain State Investigations, Charlottesville, West Virginia, for her help in tracking down leads for the 20-year-old case. Also, thank you for the help to two additional persons who asked not to be identified.

Thanks to staff persons at Chapin, Horry County and Georgetown County Libraries for assistance with a thorough search of the archives for printed materials related to the case.

Thanks to the following persons for their professional reporting that helped us sort through details of the story. Please note that affiliations listed here were current for 1979-1990, the publication years of the original reports. From the *Georgetown Times*: Warren Johnston, Pat Newman, Ethlyn Missroon, Leigh Connor, and Jesse Tullos; *The Sun News*: Coyte White, Andy Zipser, Elaine Gaston, Ralph V. Ellis, Bob Bloodworth, Tom Burton, Mary Martin, Warren Cullen, Tom Strong, Bob Kudelka, Chrysti Edge, Andy Shain, Pierre Yves Glass (AP), Mary Brooks, and Bob Bestler; *The Post and Courier /The Charleston Evening and Post*: Leverne M. Prosser (Pee Dee Bureau), Bill Steiger, Schuyler Kropf, Sid Gaulden, and Ellen McGarrahan (Knight-Ridder Newspapers); *The State*: Jerry Dyer, Tim Goheen, Mike Livingston, Bhakti Larry Hough, Jeff Miller, Margaret N. O'Shea, Salley McInerney, Dawn Hinshaw, John Allard, Holly Gatling (Pee Dee Bureau), Steve Smith, and Diane Lore; the *Press & Standard* (Walterboro): Rob Novit and Dan Johnson; the *Horry Independent*: Kathy Ropp; *The Charlotte Observer*: John Monk and Rob Urban; *The Cheraw Chronicle*; *The Chesterfield Challenger*: Lynn Ingram; the *Field & Herald*. Special thanks to the *Coastal Observer* and the detailed stories of Zane Wilson (regarding Woomer's execution) and Kathy Kadane (for Wanda's trip to Washington, D.C.).

The historical description of the Horry County Courthouse in Conway was obtained from the authoritative work, *Horry County, South Carolina (1730-1993)*, by Catherine H. Lewis, and published by the University of South Carolina Press, 1998.

Readers of various portions and drafts of the manuscript include Wanda Summers, Peggy Bates, Carolyn Hills, Jim Hills, Buddy Causey, Faye Orr, Chrissy Bloome, Morgan Lewis, Ann Sullivan, Becky Hubbard, and Richard Causey. Thank you for your comments and suggestions.

Kudos to all our new friends at Sheriar Press in Myrtle Beach. Thanks to Damon Crespino, Tonya Parker and Cindy Ziegler for your enthusiasm and professional attention to our work. A special thanks goes to Tracy Floyd of Sheriar for his creative work on the jacket cover. Excellent job, Tracy.

The typesetting of the manuscript was expertly-handled by Kathy Bloodworth of Custom Typography, West Union, South Carolina. Thanks, Kathy, for your tireless devotion through the difficult process.

Photo credit for pictures goes to Gail Healey of Exposures Photography, Pawley's Island, South Carolina; Rita Schuller of SLED; Wanda Summers, for personal family photos; Bill Woodward, for the photograph of Jim Dunn; Buddy Causey; Ralph Wilson; and Dale Hudson.

Special thanks also go to our editor, Joan Piroch. The time spent around the table was time well spent and we appreciate every moment.

Lastly, we again wish to thank our families and friends for putting up with us through what can sometimes be a long and difficult process. None of this would be possible without your understanding. Thanks, y'all, from the bottom of our hearts!

Billy Hills and Dale Hudson
Horry County, South Carolina
February 2001